Discretion, Community, and Correctional Ethics

Discretion, Community, and Correctional Ethics

Edited by John Kleinig and Margaret Leland Smith

ROWMAN & LITTLEFIELD PUBLISHERS, INC.
Lanham • Boulder • New York • Oxford

ROWMAN & LITTLEFIELD PUBLISHERS, INC.

Published in the United States of America
by Rowman & Littlefield Publishers, Inc.
4720 Boston Way, Lanham, Maryland 20706
www.rowmanlittlefield.com

12 Hid's Copse Road, Cumnor Hill, Oxford OX2 9JJ, England

British Library Cataloguing in Publication Information Available

Library of Congress Cataloging-in-Publication Data

Discretion, community, and correctional ethics / edited by John Kleinig and Margaret Leland Smith.
    p. cm.
  Includes bibliographical references and index.
  ISBN 0-7425-0183-3 (alk. paper) — ISBN 0-7425-0184-1 (pbk. : alk. paper)
    1. Corrections—Moral and ethical aspects—United States—Congresses.
  2. Correctional personnel—Professional ethics—United States—Congresses.
  3. Prison administration—Moral and ethical aspects—United States—Congresses.
  4. Imprisonment—Moral and ethical aspects—United States—Congresses. I. Kleinig, John, 1942– II. Smith, Margaret Leland.

HV9469 .D57 2001
174'.9365—dc21

                                                    2001041700

Printed in the United States of America

♾™ The paper used in this publication meets the minimum requirements of American National Standard for Information Sciences—Permanence of Paper for Printed Library Materials, ANSI/NISO Z39.48-1992.

Contents

Foreword   vii

Preface   xiii

1   Professionalizing Incarceration   1
John Kleinig

Response:

The Shimmer of Reform: Prospects for a Correctional Ethic   17
Margaret Leland Smith

2   The Possibility of a Correctional Ethic   39
Derek R. Brookes

Response:

The Case for Abolition and the Reality of Race   69
John P. Pittman

3   Prison Abuse: Prisoner-Staff Relations   79
Audrey J. Bomse

Response:

Correctional Ethics and the Courts   105
William C. Heffernan

4   Health Care in the Corrections Setting: An Ethical Analysis   113
    Kenneth Kipnis

    Responses:

    First, Do No Harm   125
    Heather Barr

    Brokering Correctional Health Care   141
    John Kleinig

5   Ideology into Practice/Practice into Ideology:
    Staff-Offender Relationships in Institutional
    and Community Corrections in an Era
    of Retribution   149
    Joseph V. Williams

    Responses:

    Moral Reckoning and the Social Order of the Prison   179
    Polly Ashton Smith

    The Path of Least Resistance: Sexual Exploitation of Female
    Offenders as an Unethical Corollary to Retributive
    Ideology and Correctional Practice   193
    Zelma Weston Henriques

6   Management-Staff Relations: Issues in Leadership,
    Ethics, and Values   203
    Kevin N. Wright

    Response:

    The Ethical Dilemmas of Corrections Managers:
    Confronting Practical and Political Complexity   219
    Michael Jacobson

Additional Resources   235

Index of Names   237

Index of Subjects   243

About the Contributors   253

Foreword

There is a certain appeal to the idea that we might establish an ethic of correctional practice. Some of what goes on in correctional settings is troubling, and it is understandable that any mechanism of standards or principles that might constrain the worst of these practices might be seen as a good thing. After all, the correctional enterprise is intense with people, the confined and their captors, and it would seem that a mutually understood code of conduct would help soften what is too readily a hard circumstance for everyone involved.

There are, of course, ironies in this discussion of correctional ethics. For one thing, some of the most disturbing aspects of today's correctional effort stem from official policy. Among the many questionable routine practices in corrections are such everyday indignities as solitary confinement, censorship, stingy commissary routines, restrictions on movement or recreation, and many more of the institutional degradations that have been so frequently described in ethnographic works on prison life. Were there some principled way to ameliorate these habits of confinement, the quality of life for those who spend years behind bars, twenty-four hours a day or in eight-hour shifts, would surely be improved.

But it is odd to think of these matters as falling within a program of ethical prescriptions. Correctional authorities undertake these strategies, not as expressions of ethically defined relationships between keepers and kept, but as tangible manifestations of the moral standing of prisoners. These practices are not adopted heedless of their demeaning effects; they are chosen precisely because they demean. Thus, these extreme prison deprivations are intentional violations of the human spirit, undertaken to break that spirit.

To use the measuring stick of ethical relations as a mechanism to find them in violation of some objective standard of conduct is to judge a boxing match with the rules of badminton. Policies that have the express purpose of adding to the general suffering of captives are oddly dignified by a detached evaluation of their ethical value, as though some observer would need a massive, official blueprint to know for certain whether a particular structure is the Eiffel Tower. Some things are just obvious.

It is also important to stress that a meaningful correctional ethic has little to say about the common illegalities that occur in correctional environments. Most of the abuses described herein by Audrey J. Bomse, for example, cannot productively be the subject of a correctional ethic. The catalogue of mistreatments she lists is graphic and stunning. It reads like a grand jury indictment and raises basic challenges to our civilized social conventions. Likewise, the indignities and violations of women under prison authority, described by Zelma Weston Henriques, are in every way at odds with even a minimalist conception of the ethics of human relations, and actually may be, as she argues, an unintended consequence of the dominant ethic of retributive confinement. These kinds of human violation are, for the most part, more appropriately addressed through the criminal law than through ethical canons. The gratuitous harms inflicted through abuse and neglect of captives are so egregious that they need to be discussed in the context of human rights abuses, not ethical disputes. William C. Heffernan makes a similar point when he distinguishes hard ethical cases from easy ones, and urges us to build an ethic for the latter, as the former is not needed.

If it is true that an ethical structure is not needed to condemn pernicious prison practices that break the human spirit or unacceptable practices that break the law, then what does a useful correctional ethic describe? The chapters in this collection provide three strategic answers to the question. One is provided by Derek R. Brookes, who finds no chance that a correctional ethic can be logically excavated from the ruins of contemporary penal action. Today's penal activity is so unjust that it cannot serve as a home for ethical standards of conduct, no matter how carefully those standards might be developed. His is a persuasive argument, well developed, perceptively delivered. It calls for nothing less than the abolition of imprisonment. Yet even those who are sympathetic to the abolitionist perspective and are willing to work toward those ends might be troubled, in the meantime, by what happens to people who are confined and might wish to eradicate some of the most troubling ways in which they are treated in confinement. This concern is made all the more pressing by the large number of mentally ill, homeless, and otherwise socially damaged people who are in our prisons and jails, a point ably made by Heather Barr. Should we not develop an ethic that provides at least a modicum of protection for these, our fellow citizens in confinement?

A different idea, then, is that correctional ethics are helpful to consider the everyday decisions that fall within the legitimate discretion of authorities who regulate prison situations. Such an ethic might also help to show why the more oppressive practices of a given regime are wrong in virtue of either their consequences or their faulty premises. This is a perspective taken by coeditor John Kleinig, who urges that even within a disputable policy of incarceration, it is possible to imagine a coherent ethical yardstick that would govern the relations of people caught up in those institutions. An ethic of prison relations would seem to be useful in some of the more mundane considerations of confinement: How are correctional personnel trained to do their jobs? What priorities attach to the structuring of prisoner time? What ought to be the norms of mutual regard in the context of coercive confinement? As he lays out a case for ethics in correctional settings, we can see how a set of standards might help ameliorate some of the troubling aspects of prison life for those who work and live there. Confinement, from this view, can be seen as a special case of social relations, bearing useful similarities to hospitals, industrial workplaces, residential educational facilities, and other formal organizational settings.

This is the tack taken by two of the chapters in the collection. Both Kenneth Kipnis and Kevin N. Wright look to established ethical frameworks in noncorrectional professional contexts to find the skeleton of a correctional ethic. Kipnis, who considers ethical dilemmas that face today's correctional health care workers, argues that the ascendant values of health care trump the needs of correctional control. His three principles of correctional health care, assiduously followed, would remove health care workers from the authority of prison overseers and, if followed, might place them in frequent conflict with the everyday exercise of prison authority. Wright's elaborate explanation of the ethical standards for management-line staff relations in prison contexts borrows liberally from established understandings in industrial psychology and labor relations. In both cases, the importation of quasi-ethical structures from related free-world arrangements does not proceed willy-nilly to the prison setting. All social organizations face external constraints on their ability to formulate goals and develop strategies to achieve those goals, but as Polly Ashton Smith shows, the power of external forces in shaping prison practices often tends to eliminate some of the softer forms of correctional efforts from consideration. And so the perspective of Kipnis and Wright, to borrow ethically from other settings, is impaired by the degree to which corrections is guided not by its own intentions, but by other external forces.

Nonetheless, both Kipnis and Wright offer cogent arguments, made stronger by the existence of a well-established tradition outside the penal field. Taking this approach, we would build an ethical structure for correctional work by following the debates about ethics in these noncorrectional, but similar, settings and shifting the correctional version accordingly. Of course, the accepted ethics in these sister fields are sometimes in flux, and when this is true the same unsettled quality would presumably apply to the penal version. We could, by extension, build an ethic of correctional education, rehabilitation, vocational training, and so on by looking to the established traditions in those fields outside the corrections world.

Could this work? Assuming the point that a correctional ethic is itself a workable enterprise, there are considerable barriers to be overcome if such ethics are to play a role in molding correctional activity.

One obvious barrier is the overarching importance of the regimes of control, described by coeditor Margaret Leland Smith. Almost every other imported social activity, from libraries to telephones, exists in the prison setting in a form slightly (or more than slightly) distorted by account of the central value placed on control. Why would correctional ethics be different?

At least a partial answer is offered by Joseph V. Williams's political history of imprisonment. He would ask us to forge a correctional ethic that turns away from the contemporary emphasis on punitive practices, and embraces instead a community-based, offender-restorative model. Ironically, he offers a pessimistic review of prior efforts to do so. My own biases favor this kind of thinking. But the depth of public conversation about penal policy today is so shallow that it is hard to see how mere appeal to superior practical and ethical arrangements is likely to change the situation very much, no matter how well developed that appeal. And there is the very practical problem, described by Michael Jacobson (currently a college professor but who has administered prison systems in the past), that managerial prerogatives make it difficult to entertain basic ethical workplace rights for prison guards. What, then, for inmates?

The chapters contained in this volume can be seen as leading to a pessimistic conclusion about the possibility of a correctional ethic of confinement relations. Blunt objections to the possibility of such an ethic are countered either by a catalogue of ethical practices in alternative settings or by a listing of political and traditional forces that portray today's corrections in a distressingly negative light. A positive case for the urgency of a correctional ethic does not emerge.

There is a certain gravity to the question of penology in America, however, and it stems not from the prison itself but from the role the prison has come to play in society. Prison, at the outset of the twenty-first century, has changed from a socially rare experience, awesome in its meaning, to a skewed commonplace with politically charged but otherwise tedious meaning in society.

The prison experience is a skewed commonplace, in that it has become a social reality for some communities. Among African Americans, prison is not at all rare. Today, seven percent of all African American males are in prison or jail; but this pattern concentrates in some neighborhoods, where nearly one-third of the parent-age black male residents are incarcerated. Under present policies, more than one-fourth of African American males can expect to go to prison at some time during their lives. Again this pattern is spatially skewed: in some sections of Brooklyn, 12 percent of the black males of parenting age go to prison or jail *every year*.

Prison is politically charged, then, because it is, intentionally or not, a modern mechanism of race relations. This point, which seems obvious, is elaborately developed by John P. Pittman, who links today's American prison activity to past practices of slavery. Any hint that the contemporary prison aligns to historical patterns of bondage should alarm all of us. But you would never know this to listen to public discourse about punishment.

Racially, there are two viewpoints on crime policy. White Americans see crime as a problem, underestimate the severity of responses to crime, and (perhaps as a consequence) generally feel that criminal justice responses need to become more severe. It is fair to conclude that white Americans want more prisons. African Americans, on the other hand, feel crime is a problem, want the criminal justice system to be tougher on crime, but feel that the criminal justice system discriminates against people of color and that too many blacks are in prison. It is fair to see blacks as having an ambivalence about punishment. Most blacks personally know someone who has been to prison, and this knowledge seems to damage their confidence in systems of social control. Combine this with the way that prison differentially affects people of color, and it appears that incarceration distorts race relations in deeply ingrained ways.

Nevertheless, the reality of prison in American life has become tedious. You can count on the fingers of one toe the number of political candidates who publicly express concern about the fairness of the criminal justice system or the overrepresentation of African American men in confinement. Crime policy debates in contemporary political rhetoric are an empty vessel, mined for political capital but never exposed to the light of evidence.

Can we, should we, develop a correctional ethic? The question itself engages fundamental concerns about the whole enterprise of industrial penology. The chapters in this book provide a critical view of the depth of this question, a powerful critique of the status quo, and a fascinating contribution to the emerging debate on punishment through incarceration. I congratulate the writers for their thoughtful work and important effort.

Todd R. Clear
New York
November 2000

Preface

Most of the chapters included in this volume are revisions or expansions of papers that were originally prepared for a conference, "Discretion in a Closed Community: Issues in Correctional Ethics." It was held in May 1999 and sponsored by the Institute for Criminal Justice Ethics, John Jay College of Criminal Justice, City University of New York. In some respects, the conference was modeled on one that was held a few years earlier, in which the participants focused on discretion as a key factor in police professional ethics.[1] On that occasion, attention was focused on the nature of discretion, the extent to which police officers should be given discretion in enforcing the law, problems encountered in controlling discretion, and specific issues in discretionary decision making such as racial profiling and the handling of domestic incidents. Although the contributors differed in their ideas about the role of police in society, no one seriously queried the discussion of ethical problems in police decision making, or, more fundamentally, the legitimacy of a professional ethic for police. Of course, they might have, and some have done so; but full-scale challenges to police work generally belong on the margins of social criticism. Mostly we accept the legitimacy of the police role, arguing only about its details.

The conference on ethical decision making in correctional institutions—by administrators, officers, and health care (and other) workers—was designed to explore the general constraints under which correctional personnel must labor, and the challenges of discretionary decision making within the framework allowed to correctional administrators and officers, program directors, and health care providers. However, the dialogue about ethics in corrections or ethics in confinement developed very differently. Although a number of the participants were willing to accept the custodial environments of jail and prison as arenas for ethical decision making and also for the development of a professional correctional ethic, others were resolutely critical of incarcerative institutions as sites for a plausible professional ethic. Some highlighted what appeared to be the endemic nature of abuses that occurred in such environments or the social purposes other than punishment served by custodial institutions, whereas others claimed, more radically, that punishment in general and incarceration in particular constituted deeply flawed responses to social wrongdoing. With some two million Americans in jail or prison (as well as another three million under some form of correctional supervision), this represented a significant refocusing of the issue, and we have sought, therefore, to reflect and preserve this engagement in the published volume.

Incarceration is not just the flip side of policing—the criminal justice system's natural and appropriate response to good police work, its reasonable punishment of those whom the police have ushered into system as a consequence of their antisocial conduct. It is a very particular, historically conditioned, and controversial response to those convicted of violating social or ruling norms. Although there clearly is considerable popular support for custodial punishment in this—and other—countries, the continuing and growing controversies over the rationale for incarceration, its societal point, effects, and economic and social costs, make it clear that for an important and articulate minority incarceration may not express much more than a failure of nerve and imagination about what should be done with transgressors.

So, although the conference began with a discussion of incarceration as a "fact on the ground,"whose guardians needed, somehow, to be acknowledged and assisted in articulating the contours of their professional responsibility, conference participants were forced to confront the possibility that incarceration might not ever—and not merely always—be the most ethical response to criminal wrongdoing.

The failure to resolve this tension between abolitionists and reformists is mirrored in the present volume. Whereas Kenneth Kipnis, John Kleinig, Joseph Williams, and Kevin Wright write as though some renovation of custodial punishment is possible and the development of a professional correctional ethic can be advocated, Derek Brookes and Audrey Bomse see little hope for incarceration, albeit on different grounds. Respondents to these papers are also divided. Margaret Smith, John Pittman, Heather Barr, Polly Smith, and Zelma Henriques are sympathetic to radical solutions, whereas William Heffernan and Michael Jacobson are more accepting of some form of incarcerative response. We should not, however, draw the lines too sharply. As with so much of social life, we are caught between ideals and a deeply entrenched reality, and the participants in our discussion felt this tension as they grappled with the questions we had posed.

Like the gap between ideal and reality, the gap between idea and fruition is also fraught with challenges. We are particularly grateful to John Jay College, City University of New York, especially Provost Basil Wilson, for financial support and encouragement, to Margaret Leland Smith for the energy and administrative support that translated a proposal into a conference, to Dean Birkenkamp of Rowman & Littlefield, who waited patiently and supportively as we reworked a conference into a more permanent contribution, to Todd Clear, whose larger vision has enhanced this volume, and to Timothy Stephens, Chris Fisher, and Joanne Clendenen, who contributed their copyediting and indexing skills.

This addition to the correctional ethics literature may ultimately raise more questions than it answers, but even if it does it will have provided an agenda that is in great need of attention.

Note

1. Subsequently published as John Kleinig (ed.), *Handled with Discretion: Ethical Issues in Police Decision Making* (Lanham, Md.: Rowman & Littlefield, 1996).

Chapter 1

Professionalizing Incarceration

John Kleinig

No human institution, natural or artificial, perfectly exemplifies its raisons d'être. The plural is necessary because, even if institutions have some primary social purpose, they have generally come to serve other functions as well. The family might be seen as a major institution for ensuring the perpetuation of a peculiarly human society, a cocoon within which each new generation can be nurtured in the characteristics that give human existence its particular stamp. Yet the family may also have other functions, such as the determination of social status, the distribution of property rights, the primary sphere for personal privacy and secure intimacy, and so on. Schools, likewise, may have education as a central purpose, but they also distribute social and occupational opportunities and reproduce social ideology. Sometimes the varied functions served and acquired by particular institutions stand in some sort of tension, and this is one of the reasons why they do not perfectly exemplify their raisons d'être. The educative and certificatory functions of schools do not coexist easily, and where, in a city like New York, the public school system also provides a launching pad for the political careers of city officials, even its more manifest educative and certificatory functions may be jeopardized as resources and energy are siphoned off onto other projects.[1]

The criminal justice system and its so-called correctional expressions—jail, prison, probation, and parole—are no exception to these concerns.[2] Indeed, in some respects, they may seem to magnify the problems that beset institutional life, for part of their function is to accommodate powerful individual and social emotions—fear, outrage, vengefulness, indignation, resentment, and so on. When we conceptualize such institutions, we think immediately of punishment/retribution, rehabilitation, incapacitation, deterrence—concepts whose practical congruence in correctional institutions is as likely as not to be a matter of happenstance as of design. Add to this the fact that these correctional institutions may also be sites for administrative career paths, community employment opportunities, and party-political ambitions, and it is hardly to be wondered that they are frequently revealed as embarrassments to civilized sensibilities.[3]

The deeper question is whether these embarrassments are simply—or at least largely—contingent failures of custodial institutions or reflect a more fundamental failure—one, moreover, that is not tolerable as the lesser of two social evils. If the failings are only contingent or if they are tolerable as the lesser of two social evils (as the state itself might be), then we can focus on their rectification and on the construction of an ethic for those who work within them. This chapter is an attempt to explore the possibilities for a correctional ethic, given that the very institution is problematic.

Institutional Contingency

There is no special sacrosanctity about institutions, either broadly or narrowly conceived. Their mere existence does not establish their legitimacy, and even an institution that once possessed—or was thought to possess—legitimacy may lose whatever claim it had to public support. Slavery, once thought to be theologically, anthropologically, politically, and economically justified, has lost its allure (at least in Western society); the monarchy has been significantly transformed in most of those countries in which it still exists; capital punishment has been outlawed in as many "civilized" countries as it has been retained; capitalist economic structures must constantly answer for the burdensome inequalities that they engender; and though we have not devised a workable substitute for the state, governmental agencies are under continual and significant pressure to justify their scope and powers.

Even among those for whom punishment is a moral dictate of wrongdoing, there is no transcendental justification for incarceration. Although some form of incarceration appears to have existed for much of human history, the use of incarceration *as* punishment—especially on a wide scale—has a much more recent history. Ironically, given the challenges that it must currently face,[4] the modern prison was originally intended as a more humane and socially beneficial alternative to practices that had prevailed for some time.[5] Nevertheless, the fact that incarceration could at one time represent itself as a better way suggests that it, too, might need to confront the moral demands that led to its greater (even if somewhat more humane) utilization. Given the growth of incarceration in the United States over the past two decades, making the United States one of the most incarcerative countries in the world, the need for a moral interrogation of the status quo has become urgent.

Two broad questions might easily be conflated: Is there any moral place for incarceration as punishment? and, Are our current practices of incarceration broadly acceptable? A person might give an affirmative answer to the first and various kinds of negative answers to the second. Answers of the latter kind would be reformist; to answer the first question negatively, however, would be abolitionist.

Few who answer the second question affirmatively would deny that there is room for improvement. But they accept that incarceration as such is a relatively unproblematic penal option. In the United States, this would appear to be the dominant response. Were it not so, there would be less political support than there is for the current level of imprisonment and for the building of new jails and prisons. Even with lowered crime rates, "warring" against crime is politically popular. Such support may be largely unreflective, motivated by crass economic need, racial prejudice, and raw feelings of social vulnerability. Nevertheless, those who answer the second question affirmatively do not seem to be deeply troubled by any moral challenges to incarceration per se and are generally supportive of the social institutions that provide and administer it.

Broadly speaking, abolitionists are of two kinds. There are those who believe that the very act of incarcerating another human being is inhumane or degrading, and who therefore believe that criminal violations must be dealt with in some other way. Incarceration suffers from the same moral defects as slavery.[6] Then there are those who believe that even if an ideal world might have room for some form of incarcerative response to crime, the world of actual custodial institutions is almost uniformly degrading and destructive. When human beings are given the power over each other that incarceration entails, conditions are created that will almost inevitably lead to abuse. Once again, compare slavery: even though it might be possible to envisage a slave owner who treats his slaves with respect, the condition of ownership (even if not in itself problematic) creates a social situation that will inevitably tend to abusiveness.

The abolitionist challenges are strong ones, particularly if one looks at the actual history of incarceration. Moreover, carving out a reformist position that does not aid the excesses of those for whom incarceration is simply an efficient form of social sanitation is not easy. Nevertheless, what I propose in this chapter is the formation of a correctional ethic that presupposes and to some extent perpetuates a custodial regime whilst recognizing—and even arguing—that our current sentencing practices are desperately in need of overhaul. In other words, although I would answer the first question affirmatively, I am inclined to answer the second question negatively, though without the pessimism that would result in abolition.

. My basic position—here assumed rather than argued for in any detail— is that incarceration, though radical and intrusive, is a legitimate punishment option. By denying a person a significant degree of liberty, we express our societal disapproval of conduct in a manner that, unlike torture or enslavement, may still leave his or her essential humanity intact and may provide us with conditions under which social responsibility can be fostered or restored. However, I am also strongly of the opinion that we resort to incarceration far too readily and that we should be closing rather than building prisons. To a considerable extent, prisons are necessary only because (some of) those who offend are believed to pose an ongoing social danger, and acceptable punitive options cannot (yet) be developed that could leave them "at large."[7]

In a small, closely knit society, punitive options might be able to dispense with incarceration. A probable recidivist might be released to the oversight of others or deported or in other ways be disabled from reoffending. But I do not think that this is a realistic option for the social environments in which most of us live. Even though I believe we could safely diminish the prison population by two-thirds, using other punitive or reparative alternatives, there would still be a need for a custodial option.

One more clarification is necessary. Although I view incarceration as punishment, I believe that incarceration without other provisions that would foster the personal rehabilitation of the offender is almost certainly unacceptable. Punishment is justified by wrongdoing, but the state's authority to be an agent of punishment has a consequentialist aspect to it. If those who are punished emerge from punishment less suited to social life than they were before, its legitimacy as an agency of punishment is undermined.[8] Moreover, the old idea of a penitentiary, in which a person is forced into a solitary reflection on his or her situation, subsequently to emerge reformed and ready to rejoin society, is unrealistic for most of those who are imprisoned. Incarceration that does not take seriously the need to foster the broad elements of responsibility is no more acceptable than the nontherapeutic warehousing of the mentally disturbed. This is one reason why curbs on rehabilitative programs tend to delegitimate the state's involvement in punishment.

If this relatively modest case for incarceration is accepted, space is thereby created for the development of a professional ethic for incarcerative institutions. To the nature of such an ethic I now turn.

A Professional Ethic for Custodial Institutions?

All social life involves constraints. Because the paths of humans intersect, it is essential that rules or less formal understandings be developed that mediate such encounters. It is not, of course, simply a matter of crossing individual trajectories. From its very early stages, human life is communal as well as individual and social. Much of what engages us as humans involves the joint participation of others as coproducers or as the objects of our behavior. Orchestras and friendships are irreducibly communal. Ideally, the constraints that underpin our varied social and communal interactions will come to be self-imposed—they will reflect our capacity as deliberative beings to assess what situations require, given our ends and the equally legitimate expectations of others.

Realistically, a social world directed solely by informal and internalized understandings is impracticable. At very best it is an ideal, though, given our extremely varied conceptions of the good, a very remote ideal. Liberal democratic social theory tends to conceive of formal social institutions—and particularly of civil society—as a response to the diversity as well as inadequacy of sensibility, judgment, and motivation that characterize humans as we find them. To a certain extent, these formal institutional structures mirror or, perhaps better, comport with the more fundamental ethical constraints that govern human intercourse. John Locke, a principal architect of liberal democratic theory, encapsulates the general point. He notes that although the "law of Nature"—by which he understands fundamental ethical standards—can be rationally discerned, the bearers of rationality are frequently too partial, ignorant, or negligent to be guided by its dictates. It is therefore necessary to establish formal rules of conduct (that is, a legal system) "received and allowed by common consent to be the Standard of Right and Wrong, and the common measure to decide all Controversies between [people]."[9]

With this formation of a mediating institution, designed to secure, so far as reasonable, forms of human intercourse that are responsive to fundamental ethical norms (which Locke saw as human rights), the need is also generated for a second level of ethical norms designed to guide those who administer such institutional structures. Hence the beginnings of professional ethics, broadly speaking. Professional ethics is not ethics in general, but ethics constrained by the formal structures of institutions—ethics that has regard to the prerogatives, obligations, internal relations, means, and ends of the various formalized structures of social life. Sometimes these ethics have been given a formalized status in codes of ethics.

Locke argued that a state of nature—that is, social relations unencumbered by formal institutional structures—would be unable to sustain itself, the nature of human beings being as we encounter it. His solution—civil society—posited three essential institutional structures: a legislature, to promulgate societally acknowledged standards; a judiciary, to interpret and administer such standards; and an executive, to ensure that these legislatively determined and judicially applied standards are made effective. Included within this last category are those various social agencies vested with the authority to use coercive force—security, law enforcement, and correctional institutions.

Each of the foregoing structures provides an appropriate site for professional ethics. Political and legislative ethics focuses on the roles of those who possess political and regulatory power. Judicial ethics concerns itself primarily with the ethical constraints that must be observed by judges; their supporting cast of prosecutors and lawyers will also need to observe constraints appropriate to the roles they play. Police, security officers, and correctional personnel will in addition be subject to ethical constraints distinctive of their social roles. Police, security, and correctional ethics will attempt to provide a coherent articulation of those ethical constraints. In some cases, particularly as these institutions differentiate themselves into more specialized functions, a more specialized professional ethics will emerge.[10]

For reasons mentioned at the beginning of this chapter, the development of a distinctive and coherent professional ethic may be extremely difficult. Most formal institutions have become multipurpose entities, often with purposes in tension. These tensions will tend to reflect themselves in the ethical constraints deemed appropriate to their practitioners.

Shaping a Correctional Ethic

A fully fledged correctional ethic will take into account not only carceral relations, but a whole gamut of correctional activities—sentencing policies and practices, probation and parole, juvenile justice, victim services, and so on. Here I shall look only at the ways in which a professional ethic for prison and jail personnel might be developed.

Although custodial institutions have developed a multitude of social functions, a certain priority must be given to their role as instruments of punishment. Those about whom custodial institutions have developed have violated societal norms, and their incarceration is to be construed as punishment. There are of course large questions begged by such an account—questions concerning the status of the societal norms, the adequacy of the procedures by which people have been judged to have violated those norms, the fairness of the sentencing procedure, and the appropriateness of incarceration as a form of punishment. A fully developed correctional ethic will need to be open to such issues, in much the same way as a professorial ethic needs to be open to questions about school admissions, the social functions of schools, the compatibility of education with grading practices, and so on.

Here, however, I will sidestep these larger issues, legitimate though they are, in order to focus more carefully on the way in which a professional ethic might be developed for prison and jail personnel.

The central consideration, I have suggested, is that those about whom the institution revolves are incarcerated as punishment. This latter point is important. The incarceration *is* the punishment; the incarceration is not *for* punishment over and above the incarceration. It is true that with the deprivation of liberty there will also be other deprivations. But these need to bear some meaningful relation to the deprivation of social liberty rather than constituting some additional penalty. Broadly speaking, security measures will bear some relation to the deprivation of liberty, though not everything that is done in the name of security is ipso facto justified for security reasons. Thus, although some control over visitation may be justified by reference to the need for security (given limited resources), it may not thereby justify some existing practices regarding visitation, conjugal relations, and so on.[11] And though searches of prisoners may from time to time be justified, the prevailing practices of strip searching may include an element of punitive humiliation that cannot be justified in the name of security.[12]

Although inmates are appropriately subject to societal sanctions, they do not forfeit their essential humanity. They remain moral agents, capable of reflecting upon their situation, and able, within the constraints of their confinement, to make decisions about their conduct. They should not be subject to treatment that degrades or dehumanizes them; what is done to them is something for which they should be able to understand the reasons. Moreover, because they will, for the most part, reenter the life of the wider society at some point, what happens to them during incarceration should in some way assist them to do a better job of handling social responsibility than they previously managed.

There is obviously a great deal more that can and should be said on these issues. Elsewhere I have tried to address some of them at greater length.[13] There, however, I focused particularly on legislative, political, and judicial constraints on hard treatment and only indirectly on the professional conduct of prison and jail officers. The latter is, of course, affected by the former. If legislatively mandated conditions are inhumane, then prison officers will have to deal with the effects of that, and what they may feel compelled to do to contain discontent may serve only to exacerbate problems that already exist.

A viable correctional ethic must have regard to what is possible. It is not unprofessional if a corrections officer says: "I cannot in conscience do my job under these conditions." A similar dilemma may confront a physician required by an HMO to provide what is judged to be inadequate treatment, or a professor required by an administration to discriminate against students who adhere to a particular religious tradition. For the most part, though, practitioners are not forced to take dramatic and heroic stands, though they may often need to take difficult stands. Like taxpayers who continue to pay their taxes even though they disapprove of some of the uses to which their taxes are put, they judge that the existing institution has enough going for it to work for change from within rather than to opt out or engage in civil disobedience, with all the consequences that those options may involve.[14]

Central to a professional correctional ethic for incarcerative institutions, then, will be an understanding of those about whom the institutions revolve: wrongdoers denied liberty and some of its privileges, but not their humanity.

Making the incarcerated the central focus of a professional correctional ethic should raise no eyebrows. It is the same with other professional ethics. Medical ethics takes as its central concern the status of the patient who is the object of medical treatment; business ethics focuses first of all on the legitimate expectations of consumers/customers; and legal ethics is particularly concerned to secure the rights of clients. There are, of course, larger societal considerations as well, and there are ethical concerns about the internal relations that exist among service providers and between these service providers and others with whom they interact. But the object of a professional ethic is first and foremost the "client." The reason is a fairly simple one. Occupations that have generated the need for an articulated professional ethic must deal with a vulnerable clientele, one whose trust can be easily lost (if it ever existed), and we therefore need to be assured that in providing the service that professionals do, certain ethical minima will be observed. It is no accident that medical ethics is of such long standing. Patients are particularly vulnerable, and physicians may and do exercise enormous control over them.

It is only a matter of prejudice that we have not until relatively recently begun to articulate a comprehensive correctional ethic. Like the mentally ill, violators of social norms have usually been treated as social outcasts, as people worthy of only minimal respect, or, even worse, as those who have forfeited their claim to humane treatment. The fact that in some societies (for example the United States) they have been and are disproportionately drawn from historically disadvantaged minorities or discrimination-prone immigrant groups has only perpetuated this lack of concern. Additional social facts have contributed to such tardiness: the greater likelihood that middle class and white collar offenders will receive fines or probation rather than incarceration; the likelihood that, if incarcerated, they will be assigned to the comparatively better conditions of a minimum security institution; the relatively secretive operations of jails and prisons; the historical reluctance of the Supreme Court to involve itself in the details of prison conditions; the low educational expectations of prison officers (and hence the relatively small or selective interest in prison dynamics shown by researchers in higher education); and so on. But probably none of these factors has counted for as much as the social opprobrium felt toward criminal violators. Death row has attracted a great deal of public scrutiny, but much of the societal response has been only to reaffirm whatever barbarities it has involved. It is only with the very recent recognition that a significant number of those sentenced to death may actually be innocent of the crimes for which they were convicted that there has been an expanded willingness to look more carefully at the operations of the criminal justice system. Put simply, for the vast majority of citizens, the incarcerated do not constitute a sympathetic constituency. Quakers, historically involved in prison reform, have not succeeded in producing large-scale public conscientization.

Even so, along with the development of professional ethics generally, there has also been some interest in developing a professional ethic for correctional personnel. From Bob Barrington's Correctional Officers' Creed (1979) to the Code of Ethics developed by the American Correctional Association (1975, but subsequently revised), to more specialized codes such as those developed by the American Correctional Health Services Association (initially, 1990) and American Correctional Chaplain's Association (1992),[15] there has at last been a formal acknowledgment of the inadequacy of the status quo by those who provide or monitor correctional services. Of course, that is still a long way from changing the status quo.[16] To some extent, significant change will be as dependent on external factors (court decisions, legislative enactments, and financial allocations) as on internal restructuring.

Although inmate treatment represents the core of a professional correctional ethic, it does not exhaust it. Wherever humans stand in some individual or collective relationship, ethical considerations are involved and a professional ethic must therefore take account of the various role relationships in which correctional officers stand with regard to others. They will, for example, interact with each other, and there will be expectations of respect, backup, and support flowing out of that connection. Their security role will also need to be coordinated with the work of other practitioners—health care providers, psychiatrists, social workers, psychologists, chaplains, program officers, lawyers, and so on.[17] Officers will also be part of a hierarchical administrative structure, and that will create its own network of reciprocal obligations. More remotely, but maybe no less importantly, the institution and its officers will stand in some ethical relationship to outside bodies (such as a legislature) and the larger society. For the authority of correctional personnel is ultimately vested in the society that is served even if responsiveness to that larger society is most appropriately undertaken representatively via a legislature and its institutional structures.

A comprehensive professional ethic for personnel in incarcerative institutions would need to review the role expectations associated with each of the aforementioned categories of persons. Particular attention would need to be given to relations in which there are strong power differentials, to interactions in which conflicts of interest are likely to be involved, and to decision making in conditions involving uncertainty and/or inadequate resources. Where there are strong power differentials, exploitation is likely to occur; where there are conflicts of interest, partiality is a strong temptation; where there are conditions of uncertainty or inadequate resources, perceptions of danger are likely to be exaggerated.

When correctional personnel are accorded special moral privileges, there needs to be a justificatory structure in place that connects the privileged conduct to the general moral standards under which we expect human beings to operate. David Luban has spoken of a "fourfold root of sufficient reasoning" whereby the apparently privileged conduct of the practitioner is to be deemed acceptable only if:

1. the conduct is essential to the fulfillment of the role obligation;
2. the role obligation is essential to the role;
3. the role is essential to the institution; and
4. the institution is justified.[18]

In other words, the conduct in which custodial personnel engage, and especially conduct that would otherwise be morally questionable, needs to have its credentials established via a set of considerations that place the conduct within a broader framework of ordinary morality. That all four steps are followed through is important lest plausible-sounding appeals are made that cannot ultimately be sustained. Even so, it is necessary to ensure that the structure does not become routinized so that, for example, appeals to public security come to be used as unexplicated moral carry-alls whose substance is political rather than practical.

Fostering Professionalism

In her 1985 study of Massachusetts's prisons, Kelsey Kauffman paints a picture of correctional institutions that, though somewhat depressing, is relatively benign.[19] It is certainly not as grim as the picture one gets from time to time when prison conditions make it into the courts. Nevertheless, the picture that Kauffman paints is one of a system under considerable stress, in which officers and inmates develop informal codes that allow them to cope and, for the most part, to coexist. It is fairly clear, however, even from Kauffman's inside study, that jails and prisons easily foster a culture in which the humanity of inmates is essentially denied and that of prison officers is corrupted. The problems are probably worst in maximum security prisons. But that is little comfort, given that prison officers may be required to serve their "apprenticeships" in a maximum-security institution before being eligible for employment in an easier establishment.[20]

There is some reason to think that the problems of developing a professional ethic begin in correctional training academies. In a recent book detailing the year he spent as a New York State corrections officer, Ted Conover indicates how staff-recruit relations in the corrections academy might have prepared the way for meting out similarly degrading treatment on the job.[21] In eleven weeks,[22] new recruits were conditioned to humiliation and emotional detachment as part of the job and then "broken in" by assignment to Sing Sing, a maximum-security prison: "Everybody's got to do their time at the bottom of the barrel." Needless to say, the experience conditions novice officers to develop crude defenses for themselves and to see those in their "care, custody, and control" in a certain light.

There appears to have been no focus on ethical issues in Conover's training.[23] At best, recruits were taught managerial skills for which the constraints were more pragmatic than ethical. An academy training that fails to focus explicitly and pervasively on the ethical dimensions of correctional work undermines any claim it may have to professionalism, and a correctional institution that fails to cast its concerns, both explicitly and implicitly, in morally sustainable ways, will substitute power for authority.[24]

As is the case with law enforcement, incarcerative institutions are hierarchically organized. Hierarchicalism, with its exertion of and deferral to authority, is not particularly conducive to the development of professionalism because it saps initiative, discourages the development of discretionary professionalism and independence, and refocuses attention on status rather than service. Prison officers find themselves caught between seasoned officers who do not want trouble and have definite ideas on how things are done and prisoners who have learned from their own experience or that of other inmates how best to work the system. Nevertheless, given that the paramilitary structure of incarcerative institutions is not likely to vanish, we might at least consider how the existing system can be made to work most conformably with the development of a professional ethic. Two internal factors are likely to be crucial.

First, as with all hierarchically structured institutions, how well a jail or prison is run will depend significantly on its leadership. If a leader has a vision for the institution that looks beyond "care, custody, and control" to the ultimate reintegration of inmates into open society, or at least to their restoration to some form of dignified and even productive activity, *and* has the ability to impart that vision effectively to others, this will almost certainly engender a more professional commitment on the part of many of those who have daily contact with inmates. Because the leadership in a hierarchical organization ordinarily has considerable control over work assignments, work conditions, advancement within the organization, and so forth, a particular leadership style is likely to permeate the way in which the institution does its business.

Second, the ability of institutional leadership to effectuate a vision will often depend significantly on rank-and-file support, especially as it is expressed in the officers' union(s). In almost all hierarchical organizations, unions have become necessary as foils to managerial exploitation. Yet union power, like managerial power, can be abused and come to serve interests that are at variance with the primary purposes of the institution. The industrial concerns that tend to dominate union affairs are frequently in tension with professional concerns. Unless both officer unions and management share some sort of professional vision, reformist energies are likely to be dissipated by institutional politics.

But these conditions alone are not sufficient to secure the professionalism of correctional officers. Unless there is outside support—judicial, political, and economic—for fostering professionalism, internal efforts are likely to be frustrated. If incarceration becomes an easy social option in dealing with rule violators, if custodial institutions are allowed to be overcrowded, understaffed, and underfunded, if reintegrative programs are treated as easily dispensable options, and so on, then the development of a workable professional ethic is made extremely difficult.

This development is made even more difficult by historical considerations. It is hard enough to coordinate training reform, progressive leadership, professionally oriented staff associations, and enlightened community support. But there is an entrenched history of training styles with hidden and not so hidden curricula, of politically motivated and conservative institutional leadership, of tunnel-visioned union power structures, and of community prejudice, each feeding off the other's failures, and no element is willing to trust itself to reformative change. The result is an institutional environment that seems almost incapable of significant self-initiated change. Short of a crisis in institutional life, galvanizing incentives for significant change do not appear to exist. That, perhaps, is not so unusual as we contemplate the sweep of public life. Nevertheless, it is not encouraging.

Notes

1. See, for example, Lydia Segal, "The Pitfalls of Political Decentralization and Proposals for Reform: The Case of the New York City Schools," *Public Administration Review* 57 (Spring 1997): 141–49.

2. Although a comprehensive treatment of correctional ethics would need to take account of probation, parole, and various other community correctional alternatives, the present chapter will focus almost exclusively on issues raised by incarceration.

3. It might be argued that prisons and jails are embarrassments to civilized sensibilities in a way that schools and/or families (to use my previous examples) are not. I am not altogether convinced that this is so, or, if so, think it may be

explained in a way that does not weaken the analogy I have drawn. First, it is not too difficult to find critics of schools and (nuclear) families who are as critical of the way in which they affect those whom they are primarily intended to serve. Second, it is just as easy to find supporters of the status quo, who explain the horror stories recounted by critics as aberrations. And third, it is possible that the peculiar horror that attaches to stories of rampant prison abuse is associated peculiarly with its physicality—coercion, beatings, etc. In the same way we are more deeply horrified by stories of physical than of psychological child abuse and of street crime than of white collar crime. These may not be morally justified differentiations.

4. Admirably explored in a number of chapters in this volume.

5. For a provocative account, see Michel Foucault, *Discipline and Punish: The Birth of the Prison* (New York: Vintage, 1977).

6. This position is powerfully represented in Derek Brookes's chapter, "The Possibility of a Correctional Ethic," in this volume, 39–68.

7. To a certain extent, I think of punitive incarceration in the same way as I think of compulsory schooling, military service, and even state obedience. They are social responses to the failure of humans to develop more flexible, responsive, and informal means of relating to each other. Yet each is deeply flawed and in need of constant reform.

8. For a more extended discussion, see John Kleinig, *Punishment and Desert* (The Hague: Martinus Nijhoff, 1973), chapter 4: "Getting What One Deserves."

9. John Locke, *Second Treatise: Of Civil Government* (1690; London: J.M. Dent, 1924), chapter 9: "Of the Ends of Political Society and Government."

10. There are, for example, codes of ethics for the handling of computerized data, codes of ethics directed specifically to chiefs of police, codes of ethics for fire and military police, and so on. See John Kleinig with Yurong Zhang (comp. and ed.), *Professional Law Enforcement Codes: A Documentary Collection* (Westport, Conn.: Greenwood Press, 1993); see also <www.lib.jjay.cuny.edu/cje/html/policeethics. html#codes> (August 8, 2000).

11. In his essay, Derek Brookes sees "liberty, heterosexual relationships, autonomy, material goods and services" (42–43) as being forcibly denied by incarceration—and with this denial the denial of the dignity and worth possessed by each human being. I, on the other hand, see these goods as being *forcibly limited* rather than *denied* by incarceration—though I accept that in a good many cases the limitations, especially given the manner in which they come about, cross a threshold that constitutes such limitations degrading and inhumane. Being keep-locked or placed in solitary confinement are much more serious deprivations of liberty than being kept in a regular cell or being remanded to a minimum-security prison. And, of course, because these limitations may be for longer or shorter periods, depending on the offense, the impact may be very different.

Brookes makes a good deal of the forcible nature of these limitations. It is true that forcibly depriving people of some of their liberty, etc., may impact more profoundly on personality than voluntary deprivations (as drafting people into military service may also do). But the forcible nature of imprisonment differs from slavery in an important respect. Whereas slaves are forcibly deprived of their liberty willy nilly, criminals have—at least in theory—voluntarily chosen to act in ways that are understood to incur such deprivations.

12. See Tracy McMath, "Do Prison Inmates Retain Any Fourth Amendment

Protection from Body Cavity Searches?" *University of Cincinnati Law Review* 56 (1987): 739–55; see also *Jordan v. Gardner*, 986 F. 2d 1521 (9th Cir. 1993).

13. John Kleinig, "The Hardness of Hard Treatment," in *Fundamentals of Sentencing Theory*, ed. Anthony Ashworth and Martin Wasik (Oxford, U.K.: Oxford University Press, 1998), 273–98.

14. What Albert O. Hirschman memorably spoke of as "giving voice" rather than "exiting" in *Exit, Voice, and Loyalty: Responses to Decline in Firms, Organizations, and States* (Cambridge, Mass.: Harvard University Press, 1970).

15. Other codes include those of the American Probation and Parole Association, the United Nations Standard Minimum Rules for the Treatment of Prisoners, and the International Council of Nurses Statement on the Role of the Nurse in the Care of Detainees and Prisoners, as well as, of course, various other state and national codes. See <www.lib.jjay.cuny.edu/cje/html/correctional.html#codes> (August 7, 2000).

16. Indeed, the development of codes of professional ethics is often more closely linked with a social struggle for *professionalization* rather than with the fostering of *professionalism*. Professionalization, as I have stated elsewhere, "is a social process in which some purveyors of a service organize themselves to be the primary or recognized providers of that service, establishing that title through such means as certification, continuing education, and the promulgation of a code of ethics," whereas professionalism is "a dedication to doing what one does out of a commitment to it, with a determination to do it to the best of one's ability." *The Ethics of Policing* (Cambridge, U.K.: Cambridge University Press, 1996), 44–45. Correctional personnel should seek professionalism before professionalization.

17. These "civilian" personnel will have their own professional ethics, which in turn will need to be attuned to the constraints of a custodial institution. For a useful indication of some of the challenges, see Michael Puisis (ed.), *Clinical Practice in Correctional Medicine* (St. Louis, Miss.: Mosby, 1998); Michael Decaire, "Ethical Concerns within the Practice of Correctional Psychology," <www.uplink.com.au/lawlibrary/Documents/Docs/Doc93.html> (July 25, 2000); and Kenneth Kipnis's chapter, "Health Care in the Corrections Setting: An Ethical Analysis," in this volume, 113–24.

18. David Luban, *Lawyers and Justice: An Ethical Study* (Princeton, N.J.: Princeton University Press, 1988), chapter 7: "The Structure of Role Morality."

19. Kelsey Kauffman, *Prison Officers and Their World* (Cambridge, Mass.: Harvard University Press, 1988).

20. In his chapter for this volume, Joseph Williams refers to the problems created when officers transfer from maximum- to minimum- security institutions and bring with them attitudes fostered by the former. See "Ideology into Practice/Practice into Ideology: Staff-Offender Relationships in Institutional and Community Corrections in an Era of Retribution," in this volume, 149–78.

21. Ted Conover, *Newjack: Guarding Sing Sing* (New York: Random House, 2000), chapters 2–3. Conover describes the ways in which recruits are broken down and then rebuilt, the development of an us-them mentality, the fostering of informal codes and the "gray wall of silence," the reconceptualizing of prisoners as subhuman, the substitution of power relations for those of justice, and so on.

22. Seven weeks in the academy followed by four weeks on-the-job training.

23. "[T]he Academy seemed to embrace an institutional denial that what we

were being taught to do had a moral aspect." Conover, *Newjack*, 42.

24. For a description of one attempt to integrate ethics into the curriculum and life of a correctional system, see Gary Barrier, Mary K. Stohr, Craig Hemmens, and Robert Marsh, "Idaho's Method for Implementing Ethical Behavior in a Correctional Setting," *Corrections Compendium* 24, no. 4 (April 1999): 1–3, 14–15.

Response to Chapter 1

The Shimmer of Reform: Prospects for a Correctional Ethics

Margaret Leland Smith

Introduction

The punishment of wrongdoers has long been a central problem for defenders of liberty and aspirants to justice. For hundreds of years the debate has been vigorous, but only in the last thirty years has imprisonment become a prominent feature of social life in the United States. At year 2000, the enterprise of punishment, or corrections, approaches parity with education among social institutions.[1] The homology extends to the number of persons enrolled, the yearly budget,[2] the capital costs, and the pervasiveness of the cultural impact. John Kleinig has written widely in ethics, with work on punishment, paternalism, and professional ethics. He has now provided an argument for the plausibility of a professional ethic for those who work in closed correctional institutions, in prisons and jails.[3] The importance of considering the applicability of professional ethics to these institutions of punishment is clear: we are concerned with the health of those who work and live in them, and we may continue to support the use of imprisonment or we may withdraw that support.

Kleinig adjusts the conditions for his argument in an important way by requiring that incarcerative institutions provide prisoners with avenues for personal rehabilitation. He recognizes that, "[i]f those who are punished emerge from punishment less suited to social life than they were before, [the] legitimacy [of an] agency of punishment is undermined."[4] Since most experts who study prisoners would agree that a term of imprisonment now leaves a person disadvantaged and, in many cases, deeply harmed,[5] Kleinig's insistence on the prospect and materiality of rehabilitation in prison is most welcome. It does, however, lift the discussion of a correctional ethics from the dank corridors and relentless noise of jail and prison to another level of generality. I will try to pull away from the pain and barbarity of prison life as I know it to raise some general questions about what may, or may not, be possible.

Three significant claims anchor Kleinig's prospect of a correctional ethics: (1) punishment by imprisonment may be justified; (2) with rehabilitation built in to the incarcerative regimen, the prisoner retains dignity and moral agency; and (3) with principled recognition of the essential humanity of the prisoner, adept leadership, and support of the rank and file, a system of correctional ethics can guide the practice of imprisonment. I question the second and third claims, and thus hope to call into question the first. I argue here that the inequalities embedded in the project of incarceration, and the security requirements they set up, make moral action an extremely hazardous path for a prisoner, and very difficult for a corrections officer. Can a person's dignity survive forced silence in the face of injustice? Second, I ask how well the moral subject he envisions matches up to those who are now living in prison.

If one is satisfied that a professional ethics for corrections is a plausible moral project, the recent history of attempts to apply a set of standards to the practices of imprisonment raises further questions. In the 1970s and 1980s, federal courts in almost all U.S. jurisdictions imposed some degree of oversight on prison practices in an effort to bring about compliance with constitutional standards. More recently, advocates for human rights have lobbied for adherence to the mandates of international human rights treaties. And now the proponents of privatization argue that the principles of the free market will bring improvement to corrections. I review here the trajectory of each of these efforts and conclude that these histories present a significant challenge to the notion of principled leadership for correctional ethics.

Prison and the Dignity of the Person

Those who argue that imprisonment may be morally justified do not typically ground that justification in the experience of the person being punished, but in some greater good for a society. This greater social good is not seen to be at the expense of the prisoner, but includes her. Kleinig takes the unusual step of placing the prisoner at the center of his conceptualization of correctional ethics.

Prisons are run like police forces: they are modeled on the vertical organization of the military, with a handful of administrators, a small number of managers, and a large group of line officers. Although some contributors to this volume see an opportunity here for enlightened leadership, I worry more about the lack of opportunity for problem solving. If a prisoner or an officer observes an officer-prisoner interaction that she feels is unjust, what may she do? The primacy of the security mandate—to ensure the "safety and security of the institution"—coupled with the authorization to use force and the disciplinary sanction, will yield conflict, not negotiation.

An officer may be expected to be bound by ties of loyalty and demands of security. She is likely to be seen as undermining the other officer and the control of the area if she objects on the spot to the action being taken by the other officer. Events that result in discipline of a prisoner may receive some limited review by way of a hearing on the sanction, but events such as the denial of a pass for sick call or a refusal to move a prisoner from a cell shared with a violent individual are unlikely to receive review. Conflict among officers about racist behavior is one type of conflict that has been reported and, to a limited extent, studied.[6]

Even if one can imagine avenues for officers to express criticism about the behavior of other officers, what can be instituted for prisoners? If a self-respecting subject, a prisoner, sees the suffering or abuse of another prisoner, what does her dignity require of her? A moral response will involve recognition of the wrongfulness and some expression of that recognition. But this response will bring her into immediate conflict with the coercive project of prison, may increase the suffering of others around her,[7] and will very likely increase the pain and harms she bears. The experience of witnessing injustice and of being unable to give voice or aid without further penalty is a daily event for a person who is incarcerated. To ask a person to choke back the words that would challenge a beating, or get help for an injured person, or explain the act of someone in despair, because her actions will mean that all in the tier will be locked in their cells for days, or that she will lose her ability to receive visits from her family, is no condition of dignity or self-respect. Protest is among the most severely sanctioned actions in prison.[8] Perhaps smothering the expression of one's recognition of injustice can be managed for some period without dulling self-respect, but can this be sustained for years?

Kleinig contends that prison regimes may not inflict cruelty on prisoners, or be characterized by inhumaneness or degradingness. He insists that the condition of imprisonment permits the retention of dignity, the external sign of self-respect, and the basic human rights of prisoners. But prison today is a totalitarian regime, whose centrifugal force is coercion. A professional ethic must involve dialogue: Can these values be reconciled?

Prisoners as Moral Subjects

Kleinig has argued elsewhere that the good of retribution, the value of the imposition of legal punishment proportional to a crime, is a sufficient moral mandate for the institution of punishment. Censure is not sufficient; he writes: "Where others have been harmed, endangered, or otherwise set back by the moral derelictions of another, some significant deprivation is signaled as appropriate."[9] The moral weight of retribution rests on respect for persons — the person of the wrongdoer and the person of the victim. The Kantian idea that punishment is required in recognition of the free will, or capacity for freedom, of the wrongdoer places the decision-making subject at the center. In other words we honor the accused's capacity for freedom by holding her responsible for her wrongdoing. A society that values fairness and freedom will not withhold punishment from the wrongdoer.

John Kleinig recognizes that prisons are filled with the least advantaged—most prisoners are poor, and fifty percent are descendants of colonized or enslaved peoples. That nonwhites are at most 20 percent of the general population in the United States but roughly half of its prison population has persuaded many observers that the primary activity of prison is to sustain postsegregation inequality.[10] Although it is not necessary to adopt this position, it is certainly necessary to grant the social and historical framework in which it is argued. It is the experience of many individuals of American Indian, African American, or Latin American descent that they are not afforded respect or the necessary tools for a dignified life in our society, much less in the prisons.

It is difficult to reconcile Kleinig's focus on the rehabilitative potential of prison with what we know about who is behind bars in the United States and what happens to them when they are there. In the United States today, prisoners are serving longer sentences[11] and more of them are sentenced to death or to life in prison.[12] The deprivations associated with poverty and lack of social esteem—emotional and physical abuse, poor interpersonal and reasoning skills, limited work experience, and poor health—scar many prisoners. As more men and women are sentenced to life terms, the maximum security institutions become filled with those who will grow old and die in prison.[13] At some point in the next few years, some prisons in New York and New Jersey will be completely filled with prisoners serving terms of twenty-five years to life.[14]

Although Kleinig would limit the use of prison to perhaps a third of those now confined, it may be that the mentally ill would represent a greater fraction in his reconfiguration.[15] The problem of disentangling or distinguishing mental and emotional illness from criminal behavior for which a person may be said to have responsibility is a subject of active debate. In many cases, the illness is recognized along with the responsibility for the crime. What would it mean to treat mentally ill prisoners with dignity and offer them the prospect of rehabilitation? The wider social question about the provision of mental health services is not settled, and there is substantial disagreement about what adequate treatment entails. The Americans with Disabilities Act (ADA) was passed in 1990, but the extent of its implementation is far from clear.[16] Surveys show that between twenty and forty percent of adults suffer from a disabling condition.[17] In June 1998, the Supreme Court decided that the ADA covers state prisons and prisoners.[18] If mental illness is a disabling condition, as most agree that it is, and the ADA applies to prisons, then many changes are in order. And rehabilitation is not yet a part of the picture.

Another challenge to Kleinig's view of what is possible in corrections is the growing reliance on isolation as a source of control. Solitary confinement is used in many ways in prison systems: to house those who are sentenced to death; to punish those who break prison rules; to limit the risk of harm to vulnerable prisoners; to limit the influence of individual prisoners; and to manage prison systems.[19] In the last decade, most jurisdictions have built one or more special super-maximum security institutions.[20] These new facilities magnify every painful aspect of imprisonment: coercion, humiliation, idleness, and sensory deprivation.[21]

And do we understand how to think about the dignity of those prisoners who are living out their lives in prison, in prisons where almost all are serving life sentences, where many are infirm or mentally ill, and where it is common to spend extended periods of isolation out of contact with others?

Can Prison Practices Be Guided by Principled Leadership?

The history of prisons is a story of the exchange of scandal and commitment to reform. The nineteenth-century prison reformers—the Quakers in the United States and John Howard in Britain—were clear in their demand for the humane treatment of prisoners. It is not a simple task to understand why now, 150 years and many reform movements later, we are still faced with dehumanizing prison practices in a field that has expanded with each round of outcry and revision.

The administration of prison has been influenced by three reform movements that overlap in time over last thirty years: the prisoners' rights movement, the human rights movement, and the movement for the privatization of prisons. Each of these efforts is an attempt to implement a set of principles that would guide the activities of imprisonment, and in each effort representations about the dignity of prisoners is featured. As the short-lived interest in the prospect of rehabilitating those in prison faded in the 1970s, both critics and supporters searched for a rationale that would frame the practices of imprisonment. The maintenance of control over those being punished has come to be acknowledged as the primary task of corrections. I will argue that this commitment to control has successfully undermined the impact of these reform movements and dims any prospect of the recognition of the dignity of the incarcerated.

The Movement for the Civil Rights of Prisoners

The federal civil rights statute allows individuals to bring complaints of constitutional violation directly to court, and provides for class action complaints (complaints that include all persons who are in a similar situation).[22] The use of class action litigation to assert the civil rights of prisoners and bring prison practices into compliance with constitutional mandates came in the wake of the success of federal litigation to end segregation in the southern states.[23] The thrust of the civil rights movement generally (and the prisoners' rights movement specifically) was to extend constitutional protections for individual and collective rights, and thus the dignity of citizenship, to individuals from groups that had been traditionally excluded. Thirty years later, the efficacy of these examples of what has been called "institutional reform litigation" is in question.[24]

The prisoners' rights movement had multiple sources. The events of the civil rights and antiwar movements sent many activists to jail and prison to feel firsthand the indignities of incarceration; heightened consciousness of the civil rights struggle ignited the hopes of prisoners, inspiring protest about First Amendment freedoms; public interest lawyers and activists had seen the effect of federal civil rights injunctions against segregation in the South. Building on the decisions of the United States Supreme Court led by Chief Justice Earl Warren, prisoner plaintiffs, activists, and lawyers pushed for structural reform of prisons and jails. In 1968, less than two years after the federal rule governing the use of class action litigation was revised,[25] the first prisoners' rights class action was decided in Alabama and found the racial separation of prisoners to be unconstitutional, a decision that affected all persons held in confinement in the state.[26] Prisoner plaintiffs and their attorneys would typically ask the federal court to make a judicial finding that one or more prison policies or practices was unconstitutional (declaratory relief) and to issue an order that the policy or practice may not be continued (injunctive relief). Claims for damages have often been resolved through negotiation, leading to a settlement agreement between the parties, to be overseen by the federal court or its appointed representative.

Class action claims by prisoner plaintiffs began with the assertion of First Amendment freedom of religion[27] and freedom from racial segregation under the Equal Protection Clause,[28] but were soon extended to include many aspects of the conditions of confinement, contact with families and with the courts, and the use of excessive force by guards.[29] These successful claims, and the language of the decisions and the judicial orders that accompanied them, affirmed prisoners as "rightsholders," exciting prisoners and provoking prison staff.[30] Resistance to judicial oversight from corrections professionals was widespread but not universal. Many prison and jail administrators saw the federal court attention to imprisonment practices in a positive light, as support for efforts to increase resources and gain recognition for unsolved problems.[31]

In 1970, a federal district court judge placed all of the prisoners in Arkansas under federal jurisdiction, and the judicial oversight was not lifted until 1982.[32] By 1983, 15 percent of U.S. jails, in forty-four of the forty-six jurisdictions that have jails, were under court order.[33] In 1984, the first year for which summary data is available, 24 percent of U.S. prisons were under federal court supervision, at least one facility in each of forty-three states and the District of Columbia.[34] Many of the larger facilities and systems were involved in litigation, so that the court orders affected more than 40 percent of U.S. prisoners and detainees in the mid-1980s. Ten years later, in 1995, 20 percent of facilities were still under court orders or consent decrees.[35] The large prison systems in Texas, Florida, and Georgia were thoroughly reorganized through civil rights litigation. Malcolm Feeley wrote in 1998 that forty-eight of the fifty-three U. S. jurisdictions[36] had had at least one facility declared unconstitutional by the federal courts.[37]

Yet despite the wide scope of this effort to change the daily experience of oppression that accompanies imprisonment, new developments in penal practice across the country challenge any appearance of progress. The expansion of the use of imprisonment has been dramatic—a 400 percent increase in the incarceration rate between 1975 and 1995.[38] Criminal sanctions now include more time in prison[39] and often an extended period of post-release supervision. Failure to comply with the conditions of supervision can return an individual to prison and can bring additional charges that extend the period of imprisonment. The architecture of confinement has been toughened with the elimination of large open spaces (yards) and an increase in the use of razor wire and concrete. Educational programs have been largely eliminated and solitary confinement has become the primary legal tool for the enforcement of prison regulations.[40] Most prison systems now include one or more super-maximum-security institutions, with conditions of confinement unimagined when prison rights litigators began their work.[41] And, finally, on July 1, 2000, the United States had 3,682 prisoners waiting for execution; as of October 1, 2000, 668 people have been executed since the ban on execution was lifted by the U.S. Supreme Court in 1976.[42]

Even those who support the premise that well-developed and well-executed prison litigation can cure serious harms in particular facilities agree that the history of recent prison litigation has not led to more humane prisons. Former federal civil rights prosecutor Margo Schlanger reflects that she would

> second Feeley and Rubin's worry that by promoting the comforting idea of the "lawful prison," the litigation movement may have smoothed the way for ever-harsher sentences and criminal policies and contributed to the current situation, in which our prisons and jails confine over 1.8 million people at last count.[43]

It is not the 1960s: No prison administrator openly refuses to comply with federal court orders. But evasion of the thrust of much of the reform litigation is precisely a refusal to acknowledge the personhood, the dignity, of those who are incarcerated. The practice of strip searches, the visual inspection of body cavities,[44] is, at once, a regular and painful humiliation for prisoners, and a central feature of prison security. Federal court decisions regulating strip searches have been ignored by professionals and when acknowledged have inspired new provisions to nullify the impact of the judicial orders. In New York City, a 1995 Second Circuit Court of Appeals decision barring Department of Corrections employees from strip searching those arrested for misdemeanor charges was flouted for many months, and it is expected to cost the city millions of dollars.[45] In New Jersey, prison administrators responded to judicial orders requiring regulations to specify the conditions for a strip search by writing a second regulation that all prior regulations were subject to discretionary abrogation in the name of security.[46] Similar paperwork evasions have been created to comply with due process requirements for solitary confinement,[47] for prison discipline, and for the parole process.

In Texas,[48] twenty-seven years after the initial claims about unconstitutional prison conditions were filed by David Ruiz and others,[49] supervision by the federal court has not been able to bring about sufficient change to meet legal standards. In a remarkable eighty-five-page decision, William Wayne Justice, the federal judge in the case, rebuffed a March 1999 effort by the defendants, the Texas Department of Criminal Justice, to terminate the consent decree and the court's supervision. He set out a summary of continuing substandard practices and abuse in four broad areas: medical and psychiatric services, segregation of prisoners, the safety of prisoners, and the use of excessive force by officers. The opinion concludes with the following sad statement:

> The measure of a prison system's constitutionality, as always, is not its production of policies, but its treatment of inmates. Texas prison inmates continue to live in fear—a fear that is incomprehensible to

most of the state's free world citizens. More vulnerable inmates are raped, beaten, owned, and sold by more powerful ones. Despite their pleas to prison officials, they are often refused protection. Instead, they pay for protection, in money, services, or sex. Correctional officers continue to rely on the physical control of excessive force to enforce order. Those inmates locked away in administrative segregation, especially those with mental illnesses, are subjected to extreme deprivations and daily psychological harm. Such practices and conditions cannot stand in our society, under our Constitution.[50]

International Human Rights and U.S. Prisoners

Since the end of World War II, U.S. government representatives have taken an active role in the drafting of international human rights documents.[51] International human rights documents include both United Nations (UN) standards, agreements that depend on moral force, and treaties, or instruments with legal force. The United Nations standards codify many of the same principles as the United States Constitution and Bill of Rights, and require states to respect the personhood and autonomy of their residents and citizens. Although the primary focus of U.S. interest has been political rights, or, more specifically, freedoms of expression, the right to multiparty democratic government, and a commitment to what is known as the rule of law, imprisonment practices have received consistent attention. UN standards provide specifically for the protection of adults and juveniles in detention and in prison, for those facing the death penalty, for refugees, and for those who work in the criminal justice system (judges, prosecutors, and lawyers).[52] The UN documents are inspiring texts that call on states and their representatives to take affirmative steps to construct a more humane society and an equitable future for all. Despite extensive participation in the development of these documents, and the apparent commitment to the ideals therein, the United States has been slow to sign the treaties,[53] slow to comply with the reporting requirements,[54] and reluctant to recognize the oversight of the United Nations bodies.[55]

The opportunities for progress in the treatment of accused persons promised by the UN standards have not found organized support at any level of government in the United States. U.S. participation in the United Nations, and the obligations consequent to the treaties, have become problematic for conservatives and their representatives in the last twenty years.[56] During the Cold War, the United Nations was a valued forum to counter socialist and communist ideas; more recently, as the U.S. economic position has brought increasing dues and greater criticism of its policies, doubts have swelled to resistance. At a time when deference to states' rights has persuaded a majority of United States Supreme Court justices to regard any federal oversight with skepticism,[57] and to inveigh against coercion of states,[58] it is not surprising that the Supreme Court rejected the effort of Paraguay to stop the execution of one of its nationals.

In violation of the Vienna Convention on Consular Relations, police officials in Virginia had failed to inform Angel Francisco Breard of his right to contact Paraguayan consular officials at the time of his arrest.[59] The Supreme Court ignored the pending hearing before the International Court of Justice and rejected the request for a stay of execution on procedural grounds: Mr. Breard was executed on April 13, 1998.[60] If federal oversight is suspect, international oversight by way of the treaty power of the executive branch is considered completely unacceptable. If, as Justices Thomas and Scalia hold, the Eighth Amendment to the Constitution forbids only discrete punishments that are cruel and unusual, and does not, therefore, apply to imprisonment at all,[61] it is difficult to see that the UN standards will be morally suasive.

Each year, Amnesty International (AI) names a country as the target of international scrutiny for violations of human rights. In 1998 the United States was the campaign subject; the report by AI researchers focused on the uneven application of rights protections for residents of the United States. The country report, *Rights for All,* identifies widespread patterns of police brutality and abuse of prisoners, detainees, and asylum seekers. It further condemns the United States for its use of the death penalty, its armaments industry, and its avoidance of the responsibilities entailed by the UN agreements and treaties.[62]

The International Covenant on Civil and Political Rights was ratified in June 1992, and the Convention against Torture and Other Cruel, Unusual, or Degrading Treatment and the International Convention on the Elimination of All Forms of Racial Discrimination was ratified in October 1994. The treaties have periodic reporting requirements, and the United States submitted an Initial Report to the Committee against Torture in October 2000. The overdue U.S. report did acknowledge problems with mentally ill prisoners and conditions in super-maximum-security facilities, but other nongovernmental organizations argued that the convergence of these problems constitutes torture for a group of prisoners.[63] After the Committee's consideration of all submissions to its May 1–19, 2000, hearing on the United States, it expressed concern about many aspects of imprisonment and issued recommendations that the United States enact a federal crime of torture, ensure that Convention violators are punished, abolish stun belts and restraint chairs, and ensure that minors are not confined with adult prisoners.[64] Finally, the Committee required the United States to submit another periodic report by November 19, 2001. In principle, the next United States report should include changes undertaken to comply with the Committee's conclusions and recommendations.

On September 21, 2000, the State Department submitted the Initial Report of the United States of America to the UN Committee on the Elimination of All Forms of Racial Discrimination.[65] The Report discusses the legal protections for minorities in the United States and includes pages of Clinton administration initiatives. On the subject of overrepresentation of racial and ethnic minorities in U.S. prisons and jails, it is brief—including only a paragraph that begins with the acknowledgment, "The majority of all federal, state and local prison and jail inmates in the United States today are members of minority racial or ethnic groups."[66] Responses to this Report from the active nongovernmental organizations will argue that imprisonment as practiced by the United States extends and sustains the legacy of Atlantic slavery.[67]

The belated ratification of the treaties, even with the anti–United Nations thunder coming from Congress,[68] has sparked new interest among advocates for prisoners.[69] The language of the human rights documents is well suited to an analysis of the totality of conditions facing an individual prisoner or detainee. As Audrey Bomse explains, arguments that prison conditions constitute "cruel and unusual punishment" in violation of the Eighth Amendment have been clipped back by the Prison Litigation Reform Act of 1996.[70] The federal courts now rely on a "core conditions" standard, rather than using an assessment of the overall impact of the conditions of confinement on a person or designating specific circumstances as per se definitive of an Eighth Amendment violation.[71] The American Correctional Association fought for minimum standards in floor space, heat and light, sanitation, clothing, and food in correctional institutions:[72] the courts now use those core conditions (along with medical care and personal safety) to measure the cruelty of imprisonment. The more generous human rights standards offer a chance to return the *experiences* of imprisonment—the pain and suffering of isolation, the humiliation of the total absence of privacy brought about by overcrowding, the anxiety and tension of complete idleness, and constant fear—to the discussion of cruelty and torture.[73] Despite widespread popular acceptance of the principles framed by the human rights documents, it seems to be easier for Americans to recognize the violation of human rights in other countries' prisons than to be responsive to violations in this country.

Private Prisons and the Discipline of Capitalism

It is not surprising that proposals for the privatization of prisons would find a receptive audience in the 1970s and 1980s. Correctional populations were rising faster than anyone anticipated, cutting back on "big government" was a popular idea, and many municipalities already used private profit or nonprofit contractors for a wide range of tasks. A 1982 survey found that, on average, twenty-nine percent of a list of fifty-nine municipal services were performed by private-sector contractors.[74] In corrections, privatization may apply to the provision of selected services, to the construction and operation of entire facilities, and to the operation of statewide systems. Medical and psychiatric services are widely contracted using fee-for-service or comprehensive contracts; private operators build prisons, and then fold the capital costs into the per diem charge per prisoner.

Those who argue for the privatization of entire prison facilities, or entire state systems, argue that private sector entrepreneurs will bring innovation, efficiency, and cost-effective management to the task of incarceration. The corporations who seek contracts for prison construction and management are expected to apply the most up-to-date business models: in contrast to public employees, the argument goes, private managers are rewarded for success, efficiency, and innovation. While public servants struggle with government red tape and the needs of politicians, private operators can reward the best practices. Supporters of privatization reject as simplistic the presumption that prisoners will be further deprived in order to produce profits, and instead suggest that market incentives and performance-based evaluation will enhance quality. Notably, most comparisons weigh private and public services, such as hospitals, that compete for clients who are free to choose a service provider. Quality assurance, it is said, will be a product of a competitive contracting environment and the performance-based measures used for selection.[75]

At the beginning of 2000, forty-three states had contracted with private correctional health service providers for about a quarter of all medical and psychiatric services.[76] Correctional Medical Services (CMS) is the leading provider of prison- and jail-based healthcare, reporting that it serves 260,000 prisoners and detainees in 300 facilities in twenty-seven states.[77] The CMS vision statement on their web site spells out their commitment to respect for individual dignity, to quality health care, to innovation, and to leadership.[78] Despite the promise of care and the enthusiasm of prison administrators, oversight, or contract monitoring, has been difficult to come by. There has been no comprehensive evaluation of private versus public correctional health care, but news stories and court filings provide some unsettling information. In New Jersey, the Department of Corrections and co-defendants CMS and Correctional Behavioral Services (CBS) settled a class action lawsuit on behalf of the state's mentally ill prisoners by providing $16 million in additional funds for facilities and treatment.[79] The plaintiffs' expert had found the treatment of mentally ill prisoners by the private providers to be "among the worst I . . . have ever seen in 15 years of inspecting correctional systems nationwide."[80] In New York, the suicide of a young schizophrenic woman in the Westchester County Correctional Facility led the county leaders to cancel the contract with the private provider.[81]

The number of prisoners in privately run facilities has ballooned from a little more than 10,000 to more than 150,000 in a decade. In a census of private prison beds done in December of 1999 (not including those in immigration facilities and jails), privatization supporter Charles Thomas lists 113,000 in thirty-two states.[82] In 1995, although a government review of five studies comparing private and public correctional facilities found little difference in terms of cost savings or quality of service,[83] supporters of privatization could tell Congress confidently that there had been no major problems and only one cancellation of a contract. Not so in 2000: the industry leaders, Wackenhut Corrections Corporation (Wackenhut), with a 27 percent market share, and Corrections Corporation of America (CCA), with 49 percent, have been marked by scandal, lost contracts, and lowered profit expectations. Prisoner civil rights and personal injury litigation is the primary reason for reduced earnings: not only must companies put aside funds to settle prisoner claims, but premiums for liability insurance have risen.[84]

Wackenhut surrendered control of a Louisiana juvenile prison in April 2000 rather than face a Department of Justice lawsuit; lost a $12 million annual contract for a Texas jail; earned a highly critical review in New Mexico following a prison riot, several deaths, and use of excessive force by prison staff; and faces litigation in Florida and Texas for failure to protect women prisoners from sexual assault by staff and other prisoners, and also in New Mexico for poor medical care and substandard conditions of confinement.[85]

CCA has recently agreed to pay $1.65 million in damages to settle a complex case involving stabbing deaths, escapes, and medically related deaths at a facility in Ohio. The settlement was prompted by a 1998 Department of Justice report that noted lack of training, excessive use of force, and failure by CCA to recognize its responsibilities to provide constitutionally adequate conditions of confinement. CCA reported a net loss of $203 million for 1999 and has had to reorganize to avoid bankruptcy. The same issues surface in facility after facility: (1) inexperienced staff, with minimal training and low salaries, react to the environment of incarceration with abuse and violence, and (2) more experienced staff members, who might have been expected to recognize and correct staff misbehavior, are caught between the balance sheet and good management.

The Supreme Court justices may have anticipated this conflict: in 1998, they denied private prison staff the presumption of qualified immunity. Qualified immunity shields public employees from liability while they are on the job, unless they are found to have knowingly violated the constitutional rights of another person. Justice Breyer, writing for the majority, reasoned that employees of private prisons function differently in their jobs as a consequence of profit-based management:

> Competitive pressures mean not only that a firm whose guards are too aggressive will face damages that raise costs, thereby threatening its replacement, but also that a firm whose guards are too timid will face threats of replacement by other firms with records that demon-

strate their ability to do both a safe and a more effective job. . . .

[T]he most important special government immunity-producing concern—unwarranted timidity—is less likely present, or at least is not special, when a private company subject to competitive market pressures operates a prison. Market place pressures provide the private firm with strong incentives to avoid overly timid, insufficiently vigorous, unduly fearful, or "non-arduous" employee performance . . . . To this extent, the employees before us resemble those of other private firms and differ from government employees.[86]

The most recent comparative evaluations of privately and publicly operated prisons have failed to show significant differences in cost[87] or effective management.[88] It is far from clear whether this result indicates that the incentivized framework of the private sector simply reduces to a search for the bottom line, as opponents of this trend have argued, or that the task of incarceration is more complex than the private contractors anticipated. But when the evidence of abuse, as spelled out in the litigation, is joined to an absence of overall success, the promises of privatization's possibilities fade. Despite the different principles they invoke, private and public prisons are doing pretty much the same job at failing those they confine.

It is not that I do not accept the good faith of those who have worked to reform prison: they have simply not understood the intractable brutalities that inhere in the practice of imprisonment. It may be that a commitment to the moral value, or overall importance, of punishment obscures for the free person the impact of the practice on a whole human being. The mandate to punish with imprisonment accepts coercion: it is the products of that coercion that are so difficult to accept. If John Kleinig is to persuade us that a humane prison is possible through the implementation of a correctional ethic, he must first provide an explanation for the persistence of failure on the route to reform.

Notes

1. For the purposes of this chapter, punishment includes detention, imprisonment, parole, probation, and the various other forms of community supervision.

2. Robert Gangi, Vincent Schiraldi, and Jason Ziedenberg, *New York State of Mind?: Higher Education vs. Prison Funding in the Empire State, 1988–1998* (San Francisco: Justice Policy Institute, 1998); Dan Macallair, Khaled Taqi-Eddin, and Vincent Schiraldi, *Class Dismissed: Higher Education vs. Corrections During the Wilson Years* (Washington, D.C.: Justice Policy Institute, 1998). These two studies, part of a series of research reports by the Justice Policy Institute (a private nonprofit organization) that are critical of the costs of incarceration, have been widely reported in newspapers across the country. These researchers have found that spending for correc-

tions outpaced spending for higher education in New York State in 1998 (leaving capital costs out of consideration); that, in 1995, states spent more in the aggregate on corrections than on universities; and that many states have reduced spending on education at the same time that they have sharply increased spending on prison construction and overhead.

3. John Kleinig, "Professionalizing Incarceration," in this volume, 1–15.

4. Kleinig, "Professionalizing Incarceration," 4.

5. See generally, Todd Clear, *Harm in American Penology* (Albany, N.Y.: SUNY Press, 1994); for a recent summary of the collateral consequences of imprisonment, see Nora V. Demleitner, "Preventing Internal Exile: The Need for Restrictions on Collateral Sentencing Consequences," *Stanford Law & Policy Review* 11 (Winter 1999): 153.

6. See Kelsey Kauffman, "The Brotherhood: Racism and Intimidation among Prison Staff at Indiana Correctional Facility—Putnamville," <http://www.prisonjustice.org> (November 2000).

7. In order to increase peer pressure on outspoken prisoners, jail and prison administrators use group punishments. All individuals in a tier or housing unit may be locked in their cells and denied calls, visits, showers, and/or recreation as a calculated response to an act of protest.

8. Robert Buchanan, Cindie A. Unger, and Karen Whitelow, *Disruptive Maximum Security Inmate Management Guide* (Washington, D.C.: National Institute of Corrections, 1988), 37 and Appendix A,19. Organizing group demonstrations is at the top of the list of corrections administrators' list of dangerous acts, placed above assault on a officer or escape, but behind murder and hostage taking.

9. John Kleinig, "The Hardness of Hard Treatment," in *Fundamentals of Sentencing Theory*, ed. Andrew Ashworth and Martin Wasik (Oxford, U.K.: Oxford University Press, 1998), 276.

10. Angela Davis, "The Prison Industrial Complex," CD-ROM (January 2000); Orlando Patterson, *Rituals of Blood: Consequences of Slavery in Two American Centuries* (Boulder, Colo.: Counterpoint Press, 1999).

11. Paula M. Ditton and Doris James Wilson, *Truth in Sentencing in State Prisons* (Washington, D.C.: Bureau of Justice Statistics, 1999). Forty states have passed truth-in-sentencing laws that do not allow certain categories of offenders to be released before they serve a fixed percentage of the term of imprisonment. The most common fixed term is 85 percent of the sentence. In 1997, 91 percent of those persons charged with Part One offenses under the Uniform Crime Reports scheme were sentenced to serve 85 percent of their prison terms.

12. The Bureau of the Census conducts a survey of a representative, weighted sample of prisoners in state correctional facilities approximately every five years for the Bureau of Justice Statistics of the Justice Department. This survey is the single best indicator of the characteristics of the nation's prisoners in state institutions. The *1991 Survey of Inmates in State Correctional Facilities: United States* found that 5.6 percent of those surveyed were serving sentences of life in prison or death. <http://www.icpsr.umich.edu/cgi/SDA11/hsda?nacjd+siscf91> (December 2000). Given the substantial increase in sentence length and the growing use of the death penalty between 1991 and 1997, it is likely that the *1997 Survey of Inmates* results, when they are publicly reported, will find that nearly 10 percent of prisoners are serving sentences of life or death.

13. Nadine Curran, "Blue Hairs in the Bighouse: The Rise in the Elderly Inmate Population, Its Effects on the Overcrowding Dilemma and Solutions to Correct It," *New England Journal on Criminal and Civil Confinement* 27 (Summer 2000): 225.

14. Informal conversations with corrections staff and regular prison program volunteers suggest that more than 75 percent of prisoners in New Jersey State Prison in New Jersey and Greenhaven in New York State are serving sentences of twenty-five years to life at present.

15. Paula Ditton, *Mental Health Treatment of Inmates and Probationers* (Washington, D.C.: Bureau of Justice Statistics, 1999), 1. Statistician Ditton estimates that 16 percent of prisoners in state facilities suffer from mental illness. Using data from the *1997 Survey of Inmates in State and Federal Facilities*, she finds that 53 percent of mentally ill prisoners were convicted of a violent offense, compared to 46 percent for all state prisoners.

16. 42 U.S.C. §12132.

17. "State-Specific Prevalence of Disability Among Adults—Eleven States and the District of Columbia, 1998," *Morbidity & Mortality Weekly Report* 49, no. 31 (2000): 711–14.

18. *Pennsylvania Department of Corrections v. Yeskey*, 524 U.S. 206 (1998). Senator Strom Thurmond has introduced legislation to reverse the *Yeskey* decision and to exempt state and local corrections facilities from the provisions of the ADA, but this bill has not yet been passed

19. National Institute of Corrections, *Supermax Housing: A Survey of Current Practice* (Longmont, Colo.: NIC Information Center, 1997). This survey of state and federal jurisdictions reports that the percentage of systemwide capacity, or prison beds, set aside for segregation of prisoners ranges from 3 percent to 25 percent, with the average at 10 percent (Table 1, pp. 4–6).

20. National Institute of Corrections, *Supermax Housing*, Table 1, pp. 4–6. The survey reports current or expected use of supermax facilities in thirty-six states and the Federal Bureau of Prisons. When the survey was done in December 1996, 13,000 prisoners were housed in these facilities.

21. Human Rights Watch reports:

> There are currently more than twenty thousand prisoners in the United States, nearly two percent of the prison population, housed in special super-maximum security facilities or units. Prisoners in these facilities generally spend their waking and sleeping hours locked in small, sometimes windowless, cells sealed with solid steel doors. A few times a week they are let out for showers and solitary exercise in a small windowless space. Supermax prisoners have almost no access to educational or recreational activities or other sources of mental stimulation and are usually handcuffed, shackled, and escorted by two or three correctional officers every time they leave their cells. Assignment to supermax housing is usually for an indefinite period that may continue for years. Although supermax facilities are ostensibly designed to house incorrigibly violent or dangerous inmates, many of the inmates confined in them do not meet those criteria.

Human Rights Watch, *Out of Sight: Super-Maximum Security Confinement in the United States* (New York: Human Rights Watch, 2000), 2.

22. 42 U.S.C. §1983.

23. Jack Greenberg, "Civil Rights Class Actions: Procedural Means of Obtaining Substance," *Arizona Law Review* 39 (Summer 1997): 578.

24. Malcolm Feeley and Edward L. Rubin, *Judicial Policy Making and the Modern State: How the Courts Reformed America's Prisons* (Cambridge, U.K.: Cambridge University Press, 1998), 376–77.

25. In 1966, Rule 23(b)(2) of the Federal Rules of Civil Procedure was amended to permit class action litigation "where a party is charged with discriminating unlawfully against a class, usually one whose members are incapable of specific enumeration."

26. *Lee v. Washington*, 390 U.S. 333 (1968).

27. *Cooper v. Patz*, 378 U.S. 546 (1964).

28. *Wilson v. Kelley*, 294 F. Supp. 1005 (N.D. Ga. 1968); *Mason v. Peyton*, Civ. No. 5611-R (E.D. Va. 1969); and many more.

29. Audrey Bomse reviews the scope and history of prison rights litigation in detail in "Prison Abuse: Prisoner-Staff Relations," in this volume, 79–104.

30. Jim Thomas, *Prisoner Litigation: The Paradox of the Jailhouse Lawyer* (Totowa, N.J.: Rowman & Littlefield, 1988), 85–90.

31. Elizabeth Alexander, "The New Prison Administrators and the Court: New Directions in Prison Law," *Texas Law Review* 56 (1978): 967–71; Mark Kellar, "Responsible Jail Programming," *American Jails* (January–February 1999): 78, 79. (But over the next twenty years Alexander would revise her view of the prospects for reform.)

32. The initial federal court decision is *Holt v. Sarver*, 309 F. Supp. 362 (E.D. Ark. 1970), and the final decision finding compliance and granting dismissal of the litigation is *Finney v. Marbry*, 546 F. Supp. 628 (E.D. Ark. 1982). There are more than ten intervening decisions over the course of the litigation.

33. Bureau of Justice Statistics, *National Jail Census, 1983* (ICPSR 8203). <http://www.icpsr.umich.edu/NACJD/archive.html> (November 2000).

34. Bureau of Justice Statistics, *Census of State and Federal Adult Correctional Facilities, 1984* (ICPSR 8444). <http://www.icpsr.umich.edu/NACJD/archive.html> (November 2000).

35. Bureau of Justice Statistics, *Census of State and Federal Adult Correctional Facilities, 1995* (ICPSR). <http://www.icpsr.umich.edu/NACJD/archive.html> (November 2000).

36. The fifty states, the District of Columbia, Puerto Rico, and the Virgin Islands.

37. Feeley and Rubin, *Judicial Policy Making*, 40.

38. Franklin Zimring and Gordon Hawkins, *Incapacitation: Penal Confinement and the Restraint of Crime* (Oxford, U.K: Oxford University Press, 1997).

39. The Violent Crime Control and Law Enforcement Act of 1994 provided funding to states that have laws requiring violent offenders to serve at least 85 percent of their sentences.

40. National Institute of Corrections, *Supermax Housing*, Table 1, pp. 4–6. State departments of correction report the allocation of between 1 percent and 20 percent of all prison beds for disciplinary isolation. The average allocation for a state system is 4.3 percent.

41. See generally, National Institute of Corrections, *Supermax Housing*, 14. Administrators in thirteen jurisdictions do not allow interpersonal contact between prisoners and corrections officers. Officers "suit up" in body armor and plexiglass if an encounter with a prisoner is necessary.

42. Death Penalty Information Center. <http://www.deathpenaltyinfo.org/facts.html#execution> (November 2000).

43. Margo Schlanger, "Beyond the Hero Judge: Institutional Reform Litigation as Litigation," *Michigan Law Review* 97 (1994): 1998, fn. 19. See also Feeley and Rubin, *Judicial Policy Making*, 375: "Judicial reform has, on balance, enhanced the ability of officials to pursue this mission [safety and security by means of a tight system of control]; they are now more, not less, effective and efficient. As such, the courts may have contributed to an increased willingness to rely on prisons and even to the increasing oppressiveness that results from the development of super-maximum facilities."

44. A strip search is typically an order to disrobe fully and to present the naked body to view, from the front and back, and then to make body openings visible for inspection. Mouths and ears are pulled open, and the prisoner is instructed to turn away from the officer, bend over, and pull open the vagina or anus using her fingers, and then to cough energetically.

45. Benjamin Weiser, "Strip Search Case Leaves City Facing a Bigger Liability," *New York Times*, May 12, 1999, A1; John T. McQuiston, "Nassau Jail Ends Strip Search Policy for Minor Offenses," *New York Times*, June 8, 1999, B1.

46. On November 31, 1993, before Judge Anne Thompson and a jury in the federal district court in Trenton, New Jersey, Clifford "Dhoruba" Roberts, Taharka Senghor, and Bomani Kubweza, pro se, argued the position that the mandatory strip searches to which they were subjected whenever they left their cells in the administrative isolation unit at New Jersey State Prison violated their First, Fourth, Eighth, and Fourteenth Amendment rights. The searches were governed by regulations reflecting federal court decisions as to the circumstances in which they were appropriate. The routine use of such searches seemed to be a prima facie violation of the regulations. Deputy Attorney General Diane Moretti called her only witness, the Chief of Security Operations at New Jersey State Prison, William Stanley Nunn, who testified that the regulations governing prisons, Section 10A of the Administrative Code of New Jersey, had been retroactively amended to permit the Commissioner of Corrections to exempt an institution from compliance with any regulation on the basis of security interests of the institution. Commissioner William Fauver had written the order lifting any requirement to comply with regulations governing strip searches.

47. When a prisoner is disciplined for a rule infraction, and the sanction is a specified period of isolation from other prisoners and a reduction of privileges, the due process requirements are limited to the hearing and appeal process. But when conditions of isolation and limited program participation are imposed administratively, regular review of the prisoner's status is required. See *Wolff v. McDonnell*, 418 U.S. 539 (1974). But the courts of appeal have been reluctant to specify the substance of this due process review, and consequently, the process is often an empty one.

48. Texas is the third-largest state prison system with 132,273 sentenced prisoners on October 4, 2000. <http://tdcj.state.tx.us/statistics/stats-idoffenders.htm> (November 2000).

49. *Ruiz v. Estelle*, 503 F. Supp. 1265 (S.D. Tex. 1980).

50. *Ruiz v. Johnson*, 37 F. Supp. 2d 855, 940 (S.D. Tex. 1999).

51. The Universal Declaration of Human Rights was signed in 1948.

52. The UN *Body of Principles for the Protection of All Persons under Any Form of*

Detention or Imprisonment; the UN *Standard Minimum Rules for the Treatment of Prisoners*; the UN *Safeguards Guaranteeing Protection of the Rights of Those Facing the Death Penalty*; the *United Nations Rules for the Protection of Juveniles Deprived of Their Liberty*; the *Code of Conduct for Law Enforcement Officials*; *Guidelines on the Role of Prosecutors*; *Basic Principles on the Role of Lawyers*; and *Basic Principles on the Independence of the Judiciary*.

53. The United States and Somalia are the only two UN members who have not ratified the Convention on the Rights of the Child; the Convention on the Prevention and Punishment of the Crime of Genocide was ratified in 1988, forty years after it was signed; the International Convention on the Elimination of All Forms of Racial Discrimination was ratified twenty-eight years after it was signed.

54. The Initial Report of the United States to the Committee against Torture on the implementation of the Convention against Torture was due in 1995 and was submitted October 15, 2000. <http://www.state.gov/www/global/human_rights/torture_index.html> (November 2000).

55. Amnesty International, "Double Standards: The USA and International Human Rights Protection," in *United States of America: Rights for All* (London: Amnesty International Publications, 1998), 121–34.

56. A discussion of the conflict between the executive treaty power and the Tenth Amendment's protection of the powers of states, with a defense of the nationalist position, may be found in David M. Golove, "Treaty-making and the Nation: The Historical Foundations of the Nationalist Conception of the Treaty Power," *Michigan Law Review* 98 (2000): 1075.

57. Richard H. Fallon, Jr., "The Supreme Court, 1996 Term: Foreword: Implementing the Constitution," *Harvard Law Review* 111 (1997): 151.

58. *Printz v. United States*, 521 U.S. 898, 925, 935 (1997). The decision built on the Court's earlier decision in *New York v. United States*, 505 U.S. 144 (1992), prohibiting Congress to "commandeer" a state legislature by directing it to enact legislation for the implementation of a federal regulatory program.

59. 21 UST 77 (TIAS 6820).

60. *Breard v. Greene*, 523 U.S. 371 (1998).

61. "Surely prison was not a more congenial place in the early years of the Republic than it is today; nor were our judges and commentators so naive as to be unaware of the often harsh conditions of prison life. Rather, they simply did not conceive of the Eighth Amendment as protecting inmates from harsh treatment."

"Today's expansion of the Cruel and Unusual Punishment Clause beyond all bounds of history and precedent is, I suspect, yet another manifestation of the pervasive view that the Federal Constitution must address all ills in our society. Abusive behavior by prison guards is deplorable conduct that properly evokes outrage and contempt. But that does not mean that it is invariably unconstitutional. The Eighth Amendment is not, and should not be turned into, a National Code of Prison Regulation." *Hudson v. McMillian*, 503 U.S. 19, 28 (1992), Justice Thomas, joined by Justice Scalia, dissenting.

62. Amnesty International, *United States of America, Rights for All* (London: Amnesty International Publications, 1998).

63. Jean Maclean Snyder, *Response Concerning the Housing of the Mentally Ill in Super Maximum Prisons* (MacArthur Justice Center, University of Chicago Law School, May 1, 2000).

64. Committee against Torture, "Conclusions and Recommendations of the Committee against Torture—United States of America" (24th Session, May 1–19, 2000).

65. *Initial Report of the United States of America to the United Nations Committee on the Elimination of Racial Discrimination.* <http://www.state.gov/www/global/human_rights/cerd_report/cerd_index.html> (November 2000).

66. The full text of the statement on overrepresentation in the criminal justice system is as follows:

> The majority of all federal, state and local prison and jail inmates in the United States today are members of minority racial or ethnic groups.
>
> The incarceration rate for Blacks is 7.66 times that for Whites and approximately four times their proportion in society at large. While Blacks make up approximately 12.5 percent of the U.S. population, in 1997 approximately 47 percent of state prison inmates were non-Hispanic Blacks. While approximately 11.5 percent of the U.S. population is Hispanic, 16 percent of the state prison population is Hispanic. As of December 31, 1998, 57.8 percent of the total Federal inmate population was White (including White Hispanics), 38.9 percent Black, 1.7 percent Asian/Pacific Islander, and 1/6 percent Native American. Additionally, 30.3 percent of federal prisoners were identified as Hispanic (who can be of any race, though the overwhelming majority of Hispanics in the U.S. are classified as White for racial purposes). The reasons for these disparities are complex and disputed.

Report, Part II. <http://www.state.gov/www/global/human_rights/cerd_report/cerd_index.html> (November 2000).

67. Ann Fagan Ginger, the Executive Director of the Meiklejohn Civil Liberties Institute in Berkeley, California, is actively circulating the questionnaire from the UN High Commissioner for Human Rights and collecting data for presentation at the UN Conference against Racism to be held in South Africa in August 2001.

68. Senator Jesse Helms, Chairman of the Senate Foreign Relations Committee, is a consistent critic of UN initiatives and, with Republican assistance, regularly obstructs U.S. participation.

69. With respect to abuses of women prisoners, see Martin A. Geer, "Human Rights and Wrongs in Our Own Backyard: Incorporating International Human Rights Protections under Domestic Civil Rights Law—A Case Study of Women in United States Prisons," *Harvard Human Rights Journal* 13 (2000): 71; with respect to the overcrowding of detained immigrants, see Susanna Y. Chung, Note, "Prison Overcrowding: Standards in Determining Eighth Amendment Violations," *Fordham Law Review* 68 (May 2000): 2351.

70. Bomse, "Prison Abuse: Prisoner-Staff Relations," 79–82.

71. *Cody v. Hillard*, 830 F. 2d 912, 914 (8th Cir. 1987), *Hoptowit v. Ray*, 682 F. 2d 1237, 1245–47 (9th Cir. 1982); see also *Kitt v. Ferguson*, 750 F. Supp. 1014, 1020 (D. Neb. 1990).

72. The paperback version of *Standards for Adult Correctional Facilities* is published annually by the American Correctional Association.

73. The Convention against Torture and Other Cruel, Inhuman or Degrading Treatment or Punishment reads in relevant part:

> For the purposes of this Convention, the term "torture" means any act by which severe pain or suffering, whether physical or mental, is intentionally

inflicted on a person for such purposes as obtaining from him or a third person information or a confession, punishing him for an act he or a third person has committed or is suspected of having committed, or intimidating or coercing him or a third person, or for any reason based on discrimination of any kind, when such pain or suffering is inflicted by or at the instigation of or with the consent or acquiescence of a public official or other person acting in an official capacity. It does not include pain or suffering arising only from, inherent in or incidental to lawful sanctions.

74. E. S. Savas, "Privatization and Prisons," in Symposium: Privatization of Prisons, *Vanderbilt Law Review* 40 (May 1987): 892–93.

75. Bruce L. Benson, *To Serve and Protect: Privatization and Community in Criminal Justice* (Oakland: The Independent Institute, 1998), 35–36.

76. Rachel Maddow, "Big Business: Private HMOs Tap a New Niche: Prisons," *HIVPLUS Special Report*, no. 6 (January 2000). <http://www.aidsinfonyc.org/hivplus/issue6/report/privat.html> (November 2000).

77. <http://www.spectrum-healthcare.com> (November 2000).

78. <http://www.cmsstl.om/news.htm> (November 2000).

79. *D.M. v. Terhune*, 67 F. Supp. 2d 401 (D. N. J. 1999).

80. New Jersey Prison System Report of Dr. Dennis F. Koson, *D.M. v. Terhune*, Civil Action No. 96-1840 (AET), 4.

81. Elsa Brenner, "Lawsuit over Jail Suicide," *The New York Times*, August 27, 2000, Sect. 14WC, 2 col. 5.

82. Charles Thomas, a Professor Emeritus at Florida State University, has been a vocal supporter of prison privatization. He was fined $20,000 in 1999 by a university ethics committee for failing to disclose ties to private prison companies. <http://web.crim.ufl.edu/pcp/census/1999/Chart1.html> (November 2000).

83. Government Accounting Office, *Private and Public Prisons: Studies Comparing Operational Costs and/or Quality of Service*, Letter Report, 8-16-96, GAO/GGD-96-158.

84. "WHC's Third and Fourth Quarter Earnings to Be Below Previous Expectations," Press Release, Palm Beach Gardens, Fla., September 19, 2000 (available at <http://www.sec.gov/Archives/edgar/> [November, 2000]).

85. James McNair, a staff writer for the *Miami Herald*, has published a series of articles about the problems of Wackenhut, a Florida-based corporation. See "Allegations Plague Wackenhut" (April 7, 2000); "Wackenhut Corrections: A Prisoner of Its Own Problems" (April 15, 2000); and "Wackenhut Corporation: Prisons, Profits, and Problems" (April 16, 2000).

86. *Richardson v. McKnight*, 521 U.S. 409–410 (1997).

87. Travis C. Pratt and Jeff Maahs, "Are Private Prisons More Cost-effective than Public Prisons? A Meta-Analysis of Evaluation Studies," *Crime and Delinquency*, 45, no. 3 (July 1999): 359.

88. Douglas McDonald, *Private Prisons in the United States: An Assessment of Current Practice* (Cambridge, Mass.: ABT Associates, 1998); Judith Greene, "Comparing Private and Public Prison Services and Programs in Minnesota: Findings from Prisoner Interviews," *Current Issues in Criminal Justice* 11, no. 2 (November 1999): 204–06.

Chapter 2

The Possibility of a Correctional Ethic

Derek R. Brookes

> Imprisonment as it exists today is a worse crime than any of those committed by its victims; for no single criminal can be as powerful for evil, or as unrestrained in its exercise, as an organized nation. Therefore, if any person is addressing himself to the perusal of this dreadful subject in the spirit of a philanthropist bent on reforming a necessary and beneficent public institution, I beg him to put it down and go about some other business. It is just such reformers who have in the past made the neglect, oppression, corruption, and physical torture of the old common gaol the pretext for transforming it into that diabolical den of torment, mischief, and damnation, the modern model prison.
>
> —G. B. Shaw, *The Crime of Imprisonment*[1]

Introduction

At a seminar I recently attended, an eminent criminologist was defending the privatization of prisons. When questioned about the moral justification of privatization, one of the arguments he produced ran as follows: We accept that there is nothing morally wrong about the privatization of schools and hospitals; so why should we think any different about prisons?[2]

One objection to this kind of argument is that it is unethical to profit from human suffering; and—unlike schools and hospitals—one of the principal objectives of the prison is to inflict human suffering.[3]

The criminologist might, of course, have replied by arguing that not all human pain or suffering is inherently evil or malicious. Causing others to suffer or depriving them of various goods may be morally obligatory or even praiseworthy, namely, where it serves as a necessary means to a greater good, such as medical care, education, character development, moral rehabilitation, deterrence, public safety, or a combination of these ends. Or it may constitute a greater good in itself where it is conceived of as justly deserved punishment.[4] According to this line of thought, the criminologist's defense of the morality of privatization would seem to depend upon the following key assumption: The prison, as a public institution, is similar to the school or hospital inasmuch as any deprivation or suffering imposed upon its principal subjects[5]—as an integral part of its central function—is designed to constitute or bring about a greater good and, as such, is morally justified.

Fortunately, the issue of privatization is not my concern here, but the truth of this assumption certainly is. The central function of the prison is, in a purely administrative sense, to provide the kind of regime or social system that is required to hold and control a collection of human beings in forced captivity for extended periods of time.[6] But this objective cannot be carried out without depriving prisoners of some of the most highly valued of human goods: liberty, heterosexual relationships, autonomy, material goods and services, and security.[7] Naturally, the forced removal of such goods will, in turn, give rise to considerable suffering or pain, albeit experienced in different ways and to different degrees by each prisoner.[8] It is crucial to note that the pains of imprisonment are not an accidental or unintended by-product of the institution, but are an essential component of what the prison is designed to do, what it is for. One cannot have a prison without depriving the goods listed above, and one cannot deprive human beings of such goods without inducing significant pain and suffering. The question is this: Can the imposition of this kind of suffering by an institution be morally justified? If not, then—as I hope to show—the prison would not be the kind of institution for which an ethic is logically possible. To propose or construct a correctional ethic would be an oxymoron, rather like presenting oneself as a married bachelor or a violent pacifist; or, closer still, like constructing an ethic for slave-masters.

Setting out the criteria for logical possibility is only half the story, however. I shall also attempt to show that the prison does in fact fail to meet these criteria; and, therefore, that anything posing as a correctional ethic is a nonsense—a dangerous nonsense. An ethic for slave-masters may well be a contradiction in terms, but it is the kind of contradiction that, left unnoticed, would function as a Trojan horse—presenting itself as a gift to the oppressed, but, in reality, serving only to legitimize and thereby entrench the institution most responsible for their oppression.

Thus, if I hope to achieve anything in this chapter, it is to persuade philanthropic readers to abandon the false hope of a correctional ethic and turn their attention instead to (a) ways of meliorating the institutional harm inflicted upon prisoners and their families, (b) restorative justice alternatives to crime prevention and response,[9] and (c) political strategies for penal abolition.

The Argument

Put formally, the core argument of my chapter is this:

> *Premise 1:* If there can be no moral justification for the suffering imposed by the prison upon its principal subjects as an integral element of its central function, then a correctional ethic would be logically impossible.
> *Premise 2:* There can be no such moral justification.
> *Conclusion:* A correctional ethic is logically impossible.

The argument is logically valid, so the strategy of this chapter will be to defend each premise in turn. My argument for *Premise 1*, put formally, will be this:

1a. It is logically possible to use a rational decision-making procedure to adjudicate between two or more options only if it can permit at least one of the options on relevant grounds (that is, if, given the grounds available to the procedure, it can only prohibit every one of the options under consideration, then it cannot, logically, function as a means of adjudication for that set of options).

1b. An "institutional ethic" is, minimally, a rational decision-making procedure by which institutional decisions[10] are adjudicated on moral grounds.

It follows that:

1c. It is logically possible to use an "institutional ethic" to adjudicate between institutional decisions only if it can permit at least one of the options available on moral grounds.

Now:

1d. If an integral element of the central function of an institution is to impose the kind of suffering upon its principal subjects for which there can be no moral grounds or justification, then, by definition, no institutional decision could be permitted on moral grounds.

It follows from *1c* and *1d* that:

1e. If an integral element of the central function of an institution is to impose the kind of suffering upon its principal subjects for which there can be no moral grounds or justification, then no ethic could be used to adjudicate between its institutional decisions—in other words, an ethic designed for that institution would be logically impossible.

We can apply the general premise *1e* straightforwardly to the specific case of the prison and so infer *Premise 1* of the core argument:

1. If there can be no moral justification for the suffering imposed by the prison upon its principal subjects as an integral element of its central function, then a correctional ethic would be logically impossible.

In Section 1 of this chapter, I will defend premises *1a* to *1e* in some detail. My argument in support of *Premise 2* of the core argument, again put formally, will be this:

2a. The suffering imposed by an institution upon its principal subjects as an integral element of its central function can be morally justified only if it constitutes or brings about a greater good to those subjects—that is, a good that (i) is for the principal subjects; that (ii) redeems the kind of suffering imposed on them; and that (iii) gives the institution its moral purpose and direction.
2b. The only kind of greater good that is available to the prison is justice.

It follows from *2a* and *2b* that:

2c. If the suffering imposed by the prison upon its principal subjects[11] constitutes or brings about injustice for them, then it cannot be morally justified.
2d. The suffering imposed by an institution upon its principal subjects constitutes or brings about an injustice for them if it (i) disregards their uniqueness and (ii) fails to meet their basic human needs—both of which are owed to them by virtue of their intrinsic dignity and worth as human beings.
2e. The suffering imposed by the prison upon its principal subjects is caused by the manner in which it forcibly deprives them of liberty, heterosexual relationships, autonomy, material goods and services, and security.

2f. The manner in which the prison forcibly deprives its principal subjects of liberty, heterosexual relationships, autonomy, material goods and services, and security (i) disregards their uniqueness and (ii) fails to meet their basic needs—as owed to them by virtue of their intrinsic dignity and worth as human beings.

It follows from *2d* to *2f* that:

2g. The suffering imposed by the prison upon its principal subjects constitutes or brings about injustice for them.

And from *2c* and *2g*, we can infer *Premise 2* of the core argument:

2. The suffering imposed by the prison upon its principal subjects as an integral element of its central function cannot be morally justified.

In Section 2, I will defend premises *2a* – *2g* in some detail. For the purposes of this chapter, this should complete my defense of the conclusion that a correctional ethic is logically impossible.

Section 1

1a. It is logically possible to use a rational decision-making procedure to adjudicate between two or more options only if it can permit at least one of the options on relevant grounds.

There are various ways in which we adjudicate between decisions. Some will be selected on economic grounds, others will be based on aesthetic, pragmatic, political, ethical, or other types of grounds. Let the term "rational decision-making procedure" be defined as a way of adjudicating between decisions by an appeal to relevant kinds of grounds or justifications. So, for instance, we might have an economic decision-making procedure, so called because it adjudicates by appeal to economic grounds.[12]

The interesting point here is that the possibility of using a particular decision-making procedure depends on the kind of choice at hand. For example, a decision between two colors, where the cost of the paint is the same, will not be something an economic decision-making procedure can settle. It might give us reason to refrain from choosing both colors; but if we need to find a reason for choosing one over the other, it would make no sense to use an economic procedure—put another way, it would be logically impossible.

In general terms, this is the point of premise *1a*.

1b. An institutional ethic is, minimally, a rational decision-making procedure by which institutional decisions are adjudicated on moral grounds.

There are any number of decisions taken within an institution, some of which are sanctioned or required by formal policy procedures and others of which, within set parameters, are left to the discretion of the individual. Let the term "institutional decision" be defined as (a) any formal or discretionary decision taken by an employee or employer of the institution and (b) any decision that is consistent with or contributes to the central function or ultimate goal of that institution. Now, whatever else an institutional ethic is supposed to do, it must at least provide a rational way of sifting out the ethical wheat from the chaff when it comes to institutional decision making. In other words, it is a kind of decision-making procedure that is distinguished by its appeal to moral grounds—which typically will include principles or values such as fairness, honesty, impartiality, the dignity and worth of human beings, and so on.[13]

For example, suppose a shop manager needs to pay off his debts and realizes he can do so either by making it store policy to overcharge his customers or by opening on weekends. There are a number of considerations that might justify the decision to overcharge—a deeper attachment to his weekends than to his customers, for instance. But none of these reasons for overcharging could possibly involve a rational appeal to moral grounds.[14] Thus we have premise *1b*.

1c. It is logically possible to use an institutional ethic to adjudicate between institutional decisions only if it can permit at least one of the options available on moral grounds. (From 1a, 1b)

Suppose the shop manager's decision was between two evils, for instance, between overcharging customers or underpaying his employees. There might be a rational basis for choosing one rather than the other—one might be more likely to succeed, for instance. But he could not decide between the two on moral grounds. If he could, it would not be a decision between two evils.

The situation is very like using economic grounds to choose between two colors. What the shop manager wants is to find some rational way of determining which of the two decisions to make. But an ethical decision-making procedure could tell him only to refrain from making either decision: for both options involve an evil, and evil cannot be justified on any moral grounds. If the manager is truly bent on finding a rational justification for stealing, it would make no sense for him to turn to this kind of decision-making procedure. Put another way, it would not be logically possible for an ethical decision-making procedure to adjudicate between these two choices. So, from 1a and 1b, we arrive at the conclusion 1c.

1d. If an integral element of the central function of an institution is to impose the kind of suffering upon its principal subjects for which there can be no moral grounds or justification, then, by definition, no institutional decision could be permitted on moral grounds.

The examples we have used up to now have been straightforward institutional decisions for good or evil. But our concept of an institutional decision allows—as it should—for a good deal more complexity. Suppose that we have a group of people intent on stealing a large sum of money from the city bank. They are very organized, having set up an administrative framework and a hierarchy of roles and functions. In other words, they create a kind of institution. Not all of these roles will be directly involved in the act of stealing, but the tasks of each role are consistent with and contribute to the ultimate goal of stealing from the bank. Again, not every decision made in the context of this organization will appear to be unethical; there might be evidence of honesty, loyalty, and even compassion in the day-to-day preparations of the organization. However, if any of these decisions is consistent with or contributes to the ultimate goal of theft, then it cannot be justified on moral grounds. For any such decision will be a decision between various ways in which to realize an evil end. Thus we have premise 1d.

1e. If an integral element of the central function of an institution is to impose the kind of suffering upon its principal subjects for which there can be no moral grounds or justification, then no "ethic" could be used to adjudicate between its institutional decisions—in other words, an ethic designed for that institution would be logically impossible. (From 1c, 1d)

It follows that this organization cannot, logically, make use of a decision-making procedure that provides rational justification for distinguishing between ethical and unethical decisions. For such a procedure would rule out—on rational grounds—every decision that might be consistent with or contribute to the organization's ultimate goal of theft. An ethic for this kind of organization would, in other words, make no sense: it would be logically impossible.

Take another example: suppose an employee of a government that has the ultimate goal of ethnic cleansing decides to do what he can to thwart this evil, for instance, by destroying communication systems to which he has access. In so doing, the employee is clearly making a decision that can be justified on moral grounds. The problem is that the decision is patently inconsistent with the goals of the institution he serves: it is not, as such, an institutional decision. We do not have here grounds for an ethic of genocide.

Suppose this same employee decides to transfer to a position that does not involve any direct act of ethnic cleansing, for instance, a secretarial post. The employee, in this case, has not decided to act against the institutional goals, and yet we might want to say that the decision to transfer could be justified on moral grounds. Nevertheless, even a secretarial post must, in some small way, contribute to the ultimate goal of such a regime. The machinery of any government would soon grind to a halt were it not oiled by the "clean hands" of a thousand grey-suited bureaucrats.

We can also learn from this example that institutional decision making cannot be morally evaluated merely by reference to the goals of a specific department or substructure of that institution. Devising an efficient reference system may, in itself, be of no moral significance. But if the system is to be used for an exhaustive registration of a racial group so as to ensure its extermination, we would not hesitate in issuing the strongest form of condemnation. Institutional decision making must also be evaluated by reference to the central function or the ultimate goal of the institution that it serves.

This completes my defense of the premises supporting *Premise 1* of the core argument, namely:

1.   *If there can be no moral justification for the suffering imposed by the prison upon its principal subjects as a integral element of its central function, then a correctional ethic would be logically impossible.*

The Interim-Ethic Objection

There are many institutionally imposed forms of suffering that (most of us feel) cannot be morally justified—for example, those imposed by slavery, ethnic cleansing, child pornography, and the like. The point of the discussion thus far has been to show that, if imposing such unjustified suffering upon others is an integral element of the central function of an institution, then an ethic for that institution would be logically impossible.

There is an important objection to this claim, however, a discussion of which will do much to clarify my argument.

> It is not clear why an interim ethic [for the prison] cannot be developed. A pacifist may argue for certain rules of combat (*jus in bello*), even if not thinking there can be a just war (*jus ad bellum*); animal rights activists might argue for improvements in research protocols

even if they want ultimately to eliminate animals from scientific experiments; I can even think that Paul was recommending some rules of slavery to Philemon in his dealings with Onesimus (the issue may not be one of redeeming slavery, but of meliorating it: in a nonideal world, may not that be a valuable project?).[15]

Few would doubt that the melioration of the suffering caused by an institution, such as slavery, would be a valuable project. But how we conceive of such a project is crucial. In arguing for certain rules of combat, pacifists would utterly betray their commitment if they did so on the grounds that a war in which both sides strictly adhered to such rules would produce a morally acceptable outcome. Likewise, it makes perfect sense for us to think that working toward more humane conditions for slaves is morally praiseworthy, even obligatory. But it makes no sense to suppose that, at some point, our efforts will render the situation morally acceptable—that is, unless and until we have managed to set the slaves free.

The reason for this, of course, is that the central function of slavery—the forced captivity of and trade in human beings—is fundamentally immoral. More precisely, the forced deprivation of human goods that this central function entails gives rise to the kinds of suffering for which no moral justification is possible. There are various moral considerations to which we can appeal in our decision to improve the plight of slaves. But we cannot sensibly construe this decision as being consistent with or contributing to the central function of slavery. Put another way, in our efforts to meliorate the harm done to slaves, we would certainly use an ethical decision-making procedure; but no such procedure could, logically, be enlisted to adjudicate between any of the institutional decisions that might be made by slave-masters, drivers, or overseers. For these decisions are simply a matter of selecting between various ways of realizing an evil end.

The issue, then, appears to turn on what is meant by the term "interim ethic" in this context. On the one hand, it could mean the following:

A. *A rational decision-making procedure for adjudicating, on moral grounds, between decisions that are consistent with or contribute to the goal of preventing an evil institution—in lieu of its abolition—from realizing its central function of imposing unjustified suffering upon others.*

If this is what is meant, then I have no complaints whatsoever with the notion of an interim ethic—and, so far as I can tell, this is precisely the kind of decision-making procedure used by pacifists, animal rights activists, and St. Paul in the examples given above. But as the foregoing discussion should make clear, this kind of ethic is a long way from what I mean by an institutional ethic. And it is certainly not what would ordinarily be understood by correctional ethics: that is, the kind of thing that is likely to be studied by prison officers, administrators, and support staff, written up into official codes of ethics for correctional departments, promoted by correctional officials as another important step toward professionalization, and touted by government ministers on the defensive as one of the mechanisms available for protecting the rights of prisoners. Given the official commitment of these individuals to the prison as an institution, it is highly implausible to suppose that a correctional ethic might be conceived of by its chief users as a means of preventing an evil institution from realizing its goals.[16]

One alternative sense of an interim ethic might be this:

B. *An ethic designed for a specific institution that, by virtue of its prohibition of unethical decisions, would ultimately serve to contribute to the eventual reform of an evil institution.*

The basic idea here is that, far from serving the goals of an evil institution, the application of a specific ethic for that institution would have an extremely important role in undermining its operations. For example, suppose the evil goals of an institution were consistently thwarted or ameliorated by individuals and groups opposed to those goals. Some of them work within the institution, surreptitiously undermining its activities. Some manage to prevent the institution from inflicting certain kinds and degrees of suffering by legal reform, public protest, or even armed intervention. The arduous task of keeping the institution in check may even spawn a host of caregivers, social workers, and humanitarian agencies, along with opportunities for altruism, courage, compassion, and so forth. Why could we not develop an interim ethic for this institution that aims to work alongside these forces for good and promote its reform? Cannot evil institutions be transformed? Would an ethic even be necessary if an institution did not require such reform?

There is some plausibility to this line of thought. However, it fails to come to terms with the structural boundaries of an institution. There is only so much reform that an institution can take before it collapses into a quite different institution, with altogether different goals. What kind of reforms, for instance, would so transform the institution of slavery that it still managed to achieve its ultimate goal, but in such a way as to be morally acceptable? Can we even imagine a code of ethics for slave-masters? Would slavery be morally permissible were it strictly regulated by a United Nations Minimum Standards for the Treatment of Slaves? What moral values could possibly be at work here?

In short, an ethic that is specifically designed for an institution must seek to regulate those decisions that are consistent with or contribute to its central function or ultimate goal. If the ultimate goal is evil, then such an ethic will collapse into incoherence. For there can be no moral grounds for distinguishing between decisions that, in one way or another, all lead to an evil end. The role of an "institutional ethic" is not to regulate evil institutions so that they are rendered harmless in practice. Such an ethic would not merely be incoherent, but would also constitute, indeed encourage, straightforward moral compromise and hypocrisy. The function of an "institutional ethic" is to enable a good institution to realize its worthy goals, not to ensure that an evil institution's goals are thwarted.

To put the point slightly differently: There is nothing incoherent or morally untoward about devising an ethical decision-making procedure that will have a broad applicability to various public service professions. But important questions must be raised if this procedure is to be tailored to suit the various roles in a particular institution with particular goals. There is all the difference in the world between a broadly-based "public service ethic" and an "ethic" that is designed for specific institutions, such as "police ethics," "nursing ethics," or "correctional ethics." A general "public service ethic" can be adapted to serve institutions with perfectly respectable goals. But it can just as easily be co-opted to legitimize an institution with evil goals.[17]

Herein lies the practical importance of our investigation. If it turns out that the suffering imposed by the prison as part of its central function *can* be morally justified, there would be every reason to try to bring it back into accord with its foundational values, for instance, by eradicating any excessive, nonessential (and hence) unjustified suffering. And if a "correctional ethic" can contribute to this reform, then, given the state of prisons today, such an "ethic" could not be more urgently needed. But if the suffering imposed by the prison as an integral part of what it does cannot be morally justified, then a "correctional ethic" will not only be incoherent, it will also—as Shaw might say—transform the prison into even more of a "diabolical den of torment, mischief, and damnation" than it already is. This brings us to my defense of *Premise 2* of the core argument.

Section 2

2a. The suffering imposed by an institution upon its principal subjects as an integral element of its central function can be morally justified only if it constitutes or brings about a greater good—that is, a good that (i) is for the principal subjects; that (ii) redeems the kind of suffering imposed on them; and that (iii) gives the institution its moral purpose and direction.

(i) A greater good for the principal subjects

History reveals to us that some institutions—such as slavery—were, during certain periods, thought to be perfectly respectable. But, at some later stage, these same institutions came to be regarded as morally abhorrent. The point here is that evil institutions are not always obviously evil.

There is an important reason for this lack of clarity. The survival of an evil institution depends, to a considerable extent, upon its ability to redirect our attention from what an institution does with its principal subjects to the benefits that will thereby accrue to the rest of us. Put another way, an evil institution is typically perpetuated by ensuring that only its benefits are examined, deftly ignoring any barbarity that has been imposed upon the principal subjects to produce those benefits. For example, slavery might be regarded as a useful, even beneficent public institution were it evaluated solely by reference to the following list of outcomes:

1. the provision of cheap and efficient labor;
2. a relatively effortless means to financial success; and
3. the attendant goods of social status, power, authority, and so on.

The problem with this list, of course, is that it gives us only the benefits of the institution, which, as it happens, accrue entirely to the slave-owner and his or her class. The list does not divulge what it is about the institution of slavery that brings about these so-called benefits, namely, the forced captivity of and trade in human beings. And it is surely this reality—not merely the supposed benefits—that we must evaluate if we are to determine whether the institution's treatment of its principal subjects might constitute or bring about a greater good. Put another way, the suffering that slaves undergo can be morally justified only if it constitutes or brings about a greater good for the slaves themselves—not (or not merely) for those who might benefit from their suffering.

Likewise, if we are to evaluate the suffering imposed by the prison, we must ensure that our attention does not focus merely on the so-called benefits it might bring. For example, the prison might be defended as constituting or bringing about a greater good on the grounds that it will:

1. enable the immediate victims and the wider community to experience the moral satisfaction of retribution;
2. protect the public, first, by equipping the offender better for civil life, and, second, by deterring potential offenders;
3. affirm and legitimize the power and authority of the judiciary, the police force, the current political regime, and, more generally, the norms and values of our civil life;

4. ground the considerable economy of the correctional system, its employees, and the private firms who supply and purchase goods; and
5. serve as a politically expedient substitute for providing adequate social welfare, education, and public health to marginalized groups, such as the homeless, the mentally ill, drug-users, the illiterate, immigrants, racial minorities, and the like.

The problem with this list is that it gives us only the so-called external benefits of the prison—which, as it happens, accrue in the main to all but its principal subjects, the prisoners. Such a list serves only to hide from the public conscience the reality and the seriousness of the human suffering that imprisonment entails.

Of course, it might be argued that—in our present political climate— imprisonment is necessary to produce the alleged benefits listed above and, moreover, that these benefits are, in themselves, morally permissible or even obligatory. Our task here is not to dispute these views, as contentious as they are. For, as I have argued, we cannot determine whether the suffering imposed by an institution upon its principal subjects constitutes or brings about a greater good solely by examining the benefits that it might produce for the rest of us. Such a procedure has legitimized the most barbaric institutions in our history. We must also determine whether such suffering might constitute or bring about a greater good to those upon whom it is imposed.

(ii) A greater good that redeems the suffering imposed on the principal subjects

A government bent on ethnic cleansing might have rational grounds for deciding between various means of realizing its goal: a gas chamber may be less expensive than bullets, for instance. My argument thus far has claimed that it would make no sense to employ an ethic to adjudicate between the bullets or the gas chamber. For there are no moral grounds to which one could possibly appeal in deciding between these two evils.

But there is an important objection to this. We might think that, were we forced to make such a decision, we would choose the bullet on compassionate grounds. Compassion is a moral virtue; hence, it looks as though it is possible, after all, to choose between two evils on moral grounds.

We can best respond to this by looking at an example of decision making in the hospital. Suppose we have to decide between spending scarce funds on the vaccination of a large number of children for measles, or on providing a lung transplant that may rescue the life of one premature infant. Whatever our decision, an evil will result: either the infant will die or the children will not be protected against measles. It will be the right decision, we think, only if it results in the lesser of these two evils. In this sense, our decision will be based on compassionate grounds. But there is more to the story here. Whatever our decision, a good will result: either the infant will live or the children will be protected. And we tend to think that it will be the right decision only if it results in the greater of these two goods.

Now this kind of story is not available for a decision between methods of genocide: a bullet is, perhaps, a lesser evil than the gas chamber, but this hardly implies that the bullet would be the morally right option. Why? Because neither option will result in a good. A lesser evil is morally permissible only if it is redeemed, that is, only if it is, at the same time, a greater good. To cause less suffering than you could have caused is still to cause suffering. You might be less evil than others, but you are still evil. To murder someone with a bullet simply because of that person's racial difference, and then to justify your action as compassionate because you could have herded him or her into a gas chamber, is beneath contempt. This is so, because—for any such decision—there is always the option (typically requiring the sacrifice of one's own interests) of deciding against either option.[18]

Likewise, the modern prison may well be an improvement on the beatings, hangings, guttings, decapitations, and so forth of penal history.[19] But this, in itself, can hardly provide moral justification for the suffering experienced by modern prisoners. No imposition of suffering can be justified merely because it is a lesser evil; it must also be a greater good: it must be, in this sense, a redeemed evil.

(iii) A greater good that gives the institution its moral purpose and direction

Thus far, I have argued that a greater good must accrue to the principal subjects and must also redeem their suffering. But one further criterion is necessary. Suppose we are trying to determine a greater good that might result from the sufferings imposed by medical staff upon their patients in carrying out their official duties in a hospital. One greater good might be the financial interests of shareholders. Suppose it is a private hospital in which only shareholders are admitted as patients. Thus we have a greater good that accrues to the principal subjects and that (the patients might think) redeems their sufferings. But is this the kind of good that might provide a moral justification for their suffering? Surely, it could offer only some kind of prudential or pecuniary justification. Moreover, it is hardly a good for which one would need to undergo the kind of suffering experienced within a medical context. There must be a far stronger connection between the suffering and the goals of the institution. For the hospital, the most natural candidate for this kind of greater good would appear to be healing or adequate medical care, in other words, the kind of good that gives the hospital its specific moral direction and purpose. And so we have our third criterion for what might count as a greater good.

2b. The only kind of greater good that is available to the prison is justice.

There are various goods that imprisonment might bring about, such as food, shelter, and education. But these goods are not specific to the prison and could well be delivered without the kind of suffering entailed by forced captivity; hence, they cannot provide the prison, as a unique institution, with its moral purpose or direction. Nor can we adduce the kind of goods we have identified as external benefits of the institution, since they do not accrue to the prisoners themselves. Punishment is, of course, one possibility, but it is not at all easy to conceptualize punishment as a good, perhaps because the term typically refers to the actual deprivations or suffering imposed, rather than the good they supposedly constitute or bring about. A far more likely candidate is justice. If the pain of imprisonment constituted or brought about this good, then it would, indeed, satisfy all three criteria. First, it would be a greater good for the prisoners insofar as they understood and experienced their suffering as justice (or just deserts), and this would be so whatever the benefits for others might be. Second, it would be more than sufficient to redeem their suffering, for it would not merely be a lesser evil; it would also instantiate one of the supreme human goods. Finally, it would give the prison—as an instrument of the criminal justice system—its specific moral purpose and direction.

2c. If the suffering imposed by the prison upon its principal subjects constitutes or brings about injustice for them, then it cannot be morally justified. (By 2a, 2b)

We thus have the following consequence. The kind of suffering imposed by the prison as an integral element of its central function must be such as to bring about the greater good of justice for its principal subjects. So, if we can show that the kind of sufferings thereby imposed exclude the possibility of justice—if, in doing what it was designed to do, the prison turned out to inflict injustice upon its prisoners—then we must conclude that the prison does not constitute or bring about the greater good that would otherwise accrue to its principal subjects, redeem the suffering it causes, or give it moral purpose or direction. In that case, the kind of suffering it imposes cannot be morally justified—and so we would have our conclusion as regards the logical impossibility of a correctional ethic. But we have much work to do yet.

2d. The suffering imposed by an institution upon its principal subjects constitutes or brings about an injustice for them if it (i) disregards their uniqueness and (ii) fails to meet their basic human needs—both of which are owed to them by virtue of their intrinsic dignity and worth as human beings.

To get a handle on the nature of injustice, we need to be clear about what is meant by intrinsic dignity and worth.[20] First, intrinsic dignity and worth are essential to what it is to be human: there are a myriad of qualities that make each person distinct and unique. There are some qualities that many of us have in common, such as intelligence, wealth, or social status. But no such quality can constitute the borderline between a person and a nonperson. Second, these attributes are not quantifiable: no one has more intrinsic dignity or worth than another. Nor do they come in a variety of grades or standards: no one has a higher-quality or a more-refined share of intrinsic dignity or worth. Third, these qualities are inviolable: just as no one can create intrinsic dignity and worth so also no one can destroy them.[21] Finally, while we can have cognitive and emotional access to the intrinsic dignity and worth of ourselves and of others, this access is typically not as clear-sighted or as responsive as it ought to be.

Herein lies the connection between our nature and our morality. Intrinsic dignity and worth are not metaphysical abstractions, having no point of contact with our day-to-day lives. They lie at the core of our social relations. Were our cognitive and emotional facilities perfectly attuned to the intrinsic dignity and worth in ourselves and in others, and were this reflected in our behavior and attitudes, then ethics or morality would be superfluous. It is only our failure to see and to respond to these qualities as we ought that gives our talk about morality and ethics a purpose and a point of reference.

So how should we respond? How do we see as we ought? These are not easy questions, but we can perhaps make some headway by an imaginative focus on the two qualities in question, that is, in isolation from the ordinary, complex array of human attributes.

To begin, dignity and worth do not seem to be the kind of qualities before which we can comfortably remain neutral or indifferent. Ushered into their presence—uncluttered and uncloaked—we should probably feel a kind of awe or reverence. Their possessor, we feel, might be aptly described as magnificent, noble, most excellent, worthy of honor, exquisite, even sacred. To ascribe these attributes to human nature is to have the highest view of humankind imaginable. Whatever variables we might use to rank ourselves as better or worse, superior or inferior—all are overridden by this default perspective on the supreme value of a human person. We might be utterly useless, powerless, friendless, and even morally hideous. But there is a core to each human being that remains untouched, a core that demands nothing less than our most profound respect and highest esteem.[22]

What is interesting is that we spend most of our lives trying to earn respect and to be valued for what we have achieved. On one view, this might be seen as a bewildering and tragic miscalculation: we are owed respect and esteem just by virtue of being human. These are not attitudes we can sensibly earn. A more plausible view, I think, is this: the human sciences frequently point out that we are, in essence, social creatures. We would wilt or self-destruct in isolation. One reason for this, I suggest, is that we are dependent on others for maintaining an adequate cognitive and emotional grasp of our own intrinsic dignity and worth. How others treat us—the respect we are afforded and the degree to which we are valued—affects our sense of humanity. We feel more human, more at home with our nature, when we receive that basic respect and esteem from others that is, somehow, our birthright. Our attempts to earn respect and esteem are not misguided or superfluous. Given our social nature, they are the only means we have to shore up a subjective grasp of our own dignity and worth.[23]

In a perfect world, of course, there would be none of the competition or frenzied grasping for respect and value that we find in our society. Not because we would be self-sufficient, but because there would be no failure on the part of others to bestow the respect and value we are, by nature, owed. In such a world, there would be no market value in the reciprocation of respect and value—"I will respect or value you if you are or do X, Y, or Z." And since there would be no failure to bestow the respect and value owed, there would be no talk of duties, obligations, rights, or justice.[24] In this world, however, such language makes perfect sense. We are perfectly familiar with what it is to engage in immoral behavior, to violate a person's rights, to abstain from our duty, or to commit an injustice. For we are all perfectly familiar with what it is to withhold the value and respect that is owed to fellow human beings by virtue of their intrinsic dignity and worth.[25]

There are two basic kinds of withholding that can occur in an institutional context. One involves disregarding the uniqueness of principal subjects, that is, their particular character, abilities, actions, or whatever makes them the individuals they are; the other involves failing to meet their basic human needs. Both, I will argue, are ways in which an institution might inflict an injustice upon its principal subjects. But we need first to examine the nature of these two forms of injustice in more detail.

(i) Injustice as disregarding a person's uniqueness

The fact that human beings are equal—by virtue of sharing an intrinsic dignity and worth—does not imply that we should treat everyone in the same way. Suppose an illiterate person applied for a job as an English teacher. There is an array of social graces that would enable us to turn down the applicant in such a way as to demonstrate our continued respect and esteem for that person as a human being. But would it be possible to show a genuine respect for the applicant were we to award the position to him or her? Would we not instead demonstrate a blatant disregard, and thus contempt, for the applicant and his or her capabilities?

In other words, it is by virtue of what we have in common—our intrinsic dignity and worth—that we owe each other the highest respect and esteem. But we do not show this respect and esteem by ignoring what makes us distinct and unique. Our character, our abilities, our achievements, our relationships, all of these make up what we are. They do not make us fundamentally better or superior human beings: we do not, on account of them, have more or less worth or dignity as human beings. Nevertheless, were someone to treat us in a way that showed an utter disregard for our unique qualities— for who we are and what we have made of ourselves—we would interpret and feel this as a sign of disrespect and contempt: it would be an insult to our sense of dignity and worth.

Suppose that our character, our abilities, and our achievements are less than spectacular. In such a case, we might not want to be treated in a way that accurately reflects who we are. We might want others to disregard our failures and transgressions. But this is not a counterexample. It is simply a matter of our wanting to avoid the pain of shame and rejection. For were it certain that we should be exposed and called to account, we would still want to be treated fairly; that is, we would want to be held accountable only for who we are or what we have done, and not for the faults or wrongs of others. To do otherwise would, again, show an utter disregard and contempt for who we are: it would be an insult to the dignity and worth that we are owed as human beings. This desire, I suggest, is nothing more than a desire for justice. But we need a little more background here.

In some contexts, we might say that an injustice occurs in just those cases in which we are discriminated against on grounds that have nothing to do with the matter in question: being denied employment on the grounds of race, being passed over for promotion on account of a family connection, and so on. These cases are unjust because they are unfair. To strive for justice is to insist that all persons be treated in the same way in cases in which there are no relevant grounds for treating them otherwise. This principle is founded on the bedrock assumption that all persons—stripped of their unique character, abilities, actions, and so forth—share in common an intrinsic dignity and worth.

Suppose two persons are being evaluated for their possession of some specific collection of attributes, for instance, their physical strength, intellectual achievements, or whatever. Now if these two are identical insofar as they each have these traits to the same degree, then there could be no grounds for special treatment. For, if their character and abilities do not distinguish them, and so must be taken out of the equation, there is nothing left but their basic equality as human beings. To treat them differently would be to deny this equality. Put another way, it would be to acknowledge the intrinsic dignity and worth of one, but not the other. Put yet another way, it would be to deny them justice.

(ii) Injustice as failing to meet basic human needs

There is a range of basic human needs: physical, emotional, and social. Each of these is basic in the sense that, if it goes unsatisfied, we feel that our very humanity is at stake. This is not because its absence threatens our existence—which it may well do—but because it threatens our status as human beings. When we see an ethnic group being forcibly deprived of food, water, and shelter, for instance, we are outraged because we feel that its human dignity has been violated and its fundamental worth called into question. We use the term "injustice" because we feel that there could be no possible grounds for such treatment. No matter what its members might have done to provoke their oppressors, no one deserves to be treated in a such a way. To deprive people of such basic needs is to treat them as less than human beings. It is to deny our fundamental equality with them. It is to deny them justice.

One important qualification must be raised here. A number of institutions deny basic human needs, but not all of these warrant condemnation. A religious order, for instance, might deprive its initiates of personal property, sexual intercourse, freedom of association, and so on. How does this kind of institutional deprivation differ from that involved in, say, slavery?

My suggestion is this: the deprivations of a religious order would be designed to deliver a certain kind of good to its primary subjects, such as a heightened experience of God. But there is no such design to the deprivations in slavery: there is no good that will thereby accrue to the primary subjects. This distinction makes all the difference in the world. In either case, the deprivations may be much the same. But the mere fact that the principal subjects are not forced, but voluntarily submit themselves to such deprivations in order to obtain a certain kind of good so transforms the manner in which these deprivations are imposed and how they are experienced, that the principal subjects are unlikely to feel that their humanity has been in any way violated or called into question.

First, even in cases in which the deprivations are regarded as a matter of duty or obedience, there would be no point at which the principal subject's basic autonomy was undermined. They would freely choose to undergo the deprivations, without coercion, manipulation, or duress. And they would possess the ultimate freedom of opting out of the exercise at any point. None of this would be true of an institution such as slavery.

Second, those who would be involved in depriving the principal subjects of their basic needs would be doing so not merely for their own benefit, but for the good of the principal subjects. For this reason, they would continue to show the respect and esteem the subjects would be owed as human beings, as exhibited in a variety of social graces, such as politeness, listening, empathy, concern, honesty, admiration, helpfulness, and so on. It is no coincidence that those who impose or enforce deprivations upon principal subjects merely for the benefit of themselves or others inevitably do so in a manner that strips the subjects of their human dignity and denies their intrinsic worth.

2e. The suffering imposed by the prison upon its principal subjects is caused by the manner in which it forcibly deprives them of liberty, heterosexual relationships, autonomy, material goods and services, and security.

The pains of imprisonment have been well documented by psychologists and sociologists. The particular list that premise *2e* proposes is drawn from Gresham Sykes's *The Society of Captives*, and—since I lack the space here—it is to this work I would refer readers for a detailed elaboration of each kind of deprivation.[26] My task, here, is to show how the manner in which the prison imposes these deprivations might constitute an injustice to the prisoners, and this brings us to premise *2f*.

2f. The manner in which the prison forcibly deprives its principal subjects of liberty, heterosexual relationships, autonomy, material goods and services, and security (i) disregards their uniqueness and (ii) fails to meet their basic needs—as owed to them by virtue of their intrinsic dignity and worth as human beings.

(i) The prison disregards the uniqueness of its principal subjects

The source of the problem with imprisonment is twofold: first, people are imprisoned for different kinds of crimes, some being more serious than others; second, each prisoner is culpable for his or her crime to a different degree. This, of course, presents severe difficulties for legal sentencing. Seriousness and culpability come in degrees that are typically so subtle or complex that it is extraordinarily difficult for the legal system to take this variability into account—that is, without making the kind of rough assessment that may be satisfactory (because workable) to all but those who must suffer under its blinkered judgments.[27]

But this problem is not (primarily) my concern here. For even if we allow that legal judgments of seriousness and culpability are as fair as can be expected, the likelihood of a prison sentence amounting to no more and no less than what is justly deserved (in view of the degree of seriousness and culpability as determined by the court) is surely minuscule. Imprisonment is simply too blunt and too sweeping an instrument for responding appropriately to the uniqueness of each individual case—even where much of this uniqueness has already been eroded by the roughness of sentencing guidelines.

Suppose we could fine-tune the experience of imprisonment so as to provide various benefits or goods and services for prisoners who are less deserving of justice, and these could be graded according to their value to the prisoners or by the degree to which they alleviated certain kinds of suffering, and so on. The problem with this proposal is not merely that the kind of calculations here are no more likely to find precision. It is rather that it fails to recognize the distinction between what is essential to the experience of imprisonment and what is not.

For example, whether or not a prisoner has a TV set will, no doubt, make a considerable difference to his or her experience while a prisoner; but it is not, in itself, relevant to his or her experience as a prisoner. Nonprisoners have TV sets, and many prisoners do not. Having a TV set is accidental to captivity. But what all prisoners experience is, to take one example, the loss of liberty. No amount of fine-tuning or supplementary goods and services can compensate for this deprivation. Each prisoner may feel this loss in different ways and to different degrees, but—at some level—it is a deprivation that causes a kind of suffering that does not discriminate between prisoners. It is imposed in utter disregard for the uniqueness of each individual; it takes no account of whether a fine default is more or less deserving of this kind of deprivation than child molestation. Sykes states that "what makes this pain of imprisonment bite most deeply is the fact that the confinement of the criminal represents a deliberate, moral rejection of the criminal by the free community."[28] But can it really be the case that a fine defaulter is equally deserving of such rejection as the child molester? We can modify the conditions of imprisonment as much as we like (minimum, maximum, single cell, shared, dorm, TVs, computers, whatever),[29] but it is the simple fact of confinement that inflicts the pain of this kind of rejection.[30] In sum, prisoners guilty of widely differing offenses and degrees of responsibility will experience the blanket pains of captivity in the same way, and thereby will experience a kind of suffering that disregards what they uniquely deserve.

Again, suppose we managed to limit a prison to holding only those offenders who had committed one type of crime and who shared exactly the same degree of responsibility for their respective crimes. And in case anyone supposes that we can determine proportionality with fairness by the measure of time spent in prison, let us suppose that each prisoner is given the same length of sentence. The key problem with this proposal is that there would be "as many prisons as there are prisoners."[31] As I have argued, there are certainly common elements to the pains of imprisonment. But each prisoner will experience this pain in different ways and to different degrees. Even the length of time is experienced in different ways by different individuals: a one-year sentence would, for one person, feel like an eternity; for another, it would be a blip on his or her life-screen. It is also experienced in different ways by the same person in different contexts: one month in an isolation cell, in one context, would be unbearably painful for a person; in another context, removal of visitation rights for the same length of time would be equally painful for the same person. As Mathiesen points out:

> The severity of punishment is bound up with and relative to the vantage-point, especially proximity. The meaning of prison time, the meaning of two months, two years, twenty years of imprisonment, is therefore morally relative and relative in terms of perspective. This fact is reflected in the great international differences which exist concerning the evaluation of the importance of prison time. If prison time were objective, various nations should converge towards the same punishment times. We know that they certainly do not converge, but show dramatic differences.[32]

In sum, even though every prisoner in our hypothetical prison would—according to the demands of justice—deserve the same kind and degree of suffering, the nature of imprisonment is such that it could never deliver, again, because it cannot take account of the unique deserts of each prisoner.

(ii) *The prison fails to meet the basic human needs of the principal subjects*

I have argued that the prison forcibly deprives its principal subjects of five types of human goods. It would not be difficult to make a case for the view that either possessing or having access to each of these goods constitutes a basic human need, and so—due to lack of space—I shall simply assume this here. The point I do want to make, however, is that the prison's failure to meet these needs is not the issue. As I suggested earlier, a religious order might also deprive each of the five goods (to varying degrees), and yet the initiates of that order would not regard this as an injustice. The problem is the manner in which the prison deprives its principal subjects of these basic needs. The chief difference between the religious order and the prison is that the principal subjects of the former voluntarily submit themselves to such deprivations in order to obtain a certain kind of good—a heightened experience of God, for instance. Prisoners, on the other hand, are forcibly deprived; and this, I suggest, so transforms the manner in which these deprivations are imposed and how they are experienced, that prisoners are likely to feel that their humanity has thereby been violated or called into question. And this is, indeed, the consensus of empirical research on the psychology of imprisonment.[33] As Sykes puts it, "the deprivations and frustrations pose profound threats to the inmate's personality or sense of personal worth."[34]

Now this should be a source of deep perplexity and discomfort for prison advocates. For retributive punishment is typically defended as a humanitarian response to crime. Unlike the medical or utilitarian responses, it takes seriously the freedom and responsibility of the individual, and, thereby, is intended to uphold his or her dignity and worth as a human being.[35] As C. S. Lewis argues:

> To be "cured" against one's will and cured of states which we may not regard as disease is to be put on a level with those who have not yet reached the age of reason or those who never will: to be classed with infants, imbeciles, and domestic animals. But to be punished, however severely, because we have deserved it, because we "ought to have known better," is to be treated as a human person made in God's image. [36]

But if the pains of imprisonment are conceived of and morally justified as punishment (or just deserts), why do prisoners feel their deprivations as such a bitter attack on their sense of dignity and self-worth? Why do they feel that their punishment is designed to bring about precisely the opposite of C. S. Lewis' noble intentions, namely, to treat them as little more than "infants, imbeciles, and domestic animals"?

Let me put the point slightly differently: Suppose we have wronged another person. What would we expect the experience of justice being done, in this context, to feel like?[37] It might, of course, involve substantial pain, but would we not also expect to feel a kind of dignity or pride in having done what it took to ensure that justice was done, that the harm had been repaired, the wrong righted? Perhaps we might feel a sense of moral relief or the burden of guilt lifted? And would not those around us respect and value our achievement, welcoming us back as a moral equal?[38] But does it not then follow that, were we to experience the pain of being a prisoner (and then of being an ex-prisoner), it would be highly unlikely that we would sense justice was being done to us in these circumstances?

It might be argued that many prisoners feel no sense of guilt or shame over their crime; many fail to recognize or care about the harm they might have caused their victim; they have no desire to right the wrong or repair the harm; and so, with no sense of what they might deserve or owe, their experience of imprisonment—even were it justice being done—would, naturally, be felt as an injustice to them. I have no doubt that this is frequently the case, but it is not at all clear how this fact might be used to show that the pains of imprisonment are morally justified.

As I have argued, the suffering imposed by an institution upon its principal subjects must constitute a greater good for those subjects. One sense in which this might occur, in the context of the prison, is that the prisoners understand and experience their suffering as justice (or just deserts). We have already seen the obstacles for this approach. But another possibility is that the suffering induces in them the kind of moral transformation that

enables them to appreciate the seriousness of their wrongdoing and so come
to understand and experience their suffering as justice. The problem here,
however, is that the lessons learned within a prison are highly unlikely to
effect a change of heart.[39] As Feinberg puts it:

> [Many] criminals are not predisposed to repentance, being either
> dedicated zealots or revolutionaries, calculating amoral risk-takers
> paying the price, without regret, for their losing gamble, sullen pris-
> oners of the class war (in their own eyes), or sociopathic personalities.
> Inflicting pain on these individuals by depriving them of their liberty
> may be socially necessary to protect others, but its most likely effects
> on the prisoners themselves will be to confirm their cynicism and
> hatred, or convince them to take greater precautions against discov-
> ery next time around—hardly "moral messages."[40]

In sum, those prisoners who would embrace justice, if given the chance,
will, it seems, experience quite the opposite of what one should expect justice
to involve. It would also appear that those prisoners for whom the experience of justice is irrelevant will be even further removed from the recognition
of what justice demands of them. In either case, whether or not others might
think that the prison is where justice is done, the pains of imprisonment do
not constitute or bring about justice so far as the prisoners are concerned.

Finally, what of those prisoners who appear to submit to the pains of
imprisonment, in the sense of accepting that they deserve their suffering—
that having done the crime, they must do the time? In one view, this may be
nothing more than a coping mechanism: "The phenomenon of men identifying themselves with their oppressors—of publicly proclaiming the virtues
of rulers, expressing their values, or, still worse in the eyes of the inmates,
obeying them all too gladly—may represent a deliberate Machiavellian attempt to flatter those who have power in order to gain favors."[41]

Another explanation might be that they actually do believe that their
suffering is justly deserved—not because it really is, but because, as Freire
puts it, "[t]he very structure of their thought has been conditioned by the
contradictions of the concrete existential situation by which they were
shaped."[42] With no other options for what counts as justice, individuals
who long for redemption will tend to embrace the only form of justice offered
to them.

It might, of course, be said that these two explanations beg the question
against suffering as a form of justice. There will be individuals who are
consumed with guilt for causing others to suffer, and such persons may feel
that their own suffering in prison would at least achieve some kind of justice
insofar as it serves to counterbalance the suffering experienced by the victim(s)
of their crime.[43] The problem is that the prison, as we have seen, is too blunt

and indiscriminate an instrument to address the imbalance of suffering in a way that might be remotely proportionate. The pains of imprisonment would either be too much or too little or of the wrong kind. As Mathiesen puts it:

> [T]he pains [of the victim and the prisoner] are so *different* that they cannot be compared, at least not in so precise a way as to provide a basis for punishment values, punishment scales, and proportionality or balance of punishment. How much deprivation of liberty, medical services, self-esteem and personal autonomy is necessary to balance the breaking and entering of a home or the vandalism of a summer house? The two "versions" of pain, in this hypothetical example, contain so many complex factors, and such a strong element of subjective experience, that proportionate justice, the balancing-of-scales justice breaks down.[44]

Conclusion

I have argued, in Section 2, that the suffering imposed by prison upon its principal subjects both disregards their uniqueness and fails to meet their basic needs in a manner that violates their dignity and worth as human beings. For this reason, it follows that:

2g. The suffering imposed by the prison upon its principal subjects constitutes or brings about injustice for them. (From 2d, 2e, 2f)

And since the suffering of prisoners fails to constitute or bring about for them the greater good of justice, we must therefore infer *Premise 2* of the core argument:

2. The suffering imposed by the prison upon its principal subjects as an integral element of its central function cannot be morally justified. (From 2c, 2g)

It remains only to conclude that, if the foregoing defense of *Premises 1* and *2* is sound, then it must follow that a correctional ethic is, indeed, logically impossible.

Notes

1. George Bernard Shaw, *The Crime of Imprisonment* (New York: Philosophical Library, 1946), 13.

2. An invitation brochure for a conference on privatizing prisons held in Dallas, Texas, in 1996 began: "Dear Executive, Can you afford to bypass a tremendous opportunity to invest in stock showing great performance and high returns? Privatization of correctional facilities is the newest trend in the area of privatizing previously government run programs that can offer such optimal rewards. . . . While arrests and convictions are steadily on the rise, profits are to be made—profits from crime. Get in on the ground floor of this booming industry now!" Quoted in Vivien Stern, *A Sin against the Future: Imprisonment in the World* (Boston: Northeastern University Press, 1998), 290.

3. "[I]mposing punishment within the institution of law means the inflicting of pain, intended as pain." Nils Christie, *Limits to Pain* (Oxford, U.K.: Martin Robertson, 1981), 5.

4. "The offender may justly be subjected to certain deprivations because he deserves it; and he deserves it because he has engaged in wrongful conduct—conduct that does or threatens injury and that is prohibited by law." Andrew von Hirsch, *Doing Justice: The Choice of Punishments* (New York: Hill and Wang, 1976), 51.

5. That is, where a principal subject stands to an institution as a student stands to a school, a patient to a hospital, a slave to slavery, or a prisoner to a prison.

6. As Sykes suggests, the kind of social system required to carry out this function is "what we would usually call a totalitarian regime: . . . The detailed regulations extending into every area of the individual's life, the constant surveillance, the concentration of power into the hands of the ruling few, the wide gulf between the rulers and the ruled . . . [t]he threat of force [lying] close beneath the surface." Gresham Sykes, *The Society of Captives* (Princeton, N.J.: Princeton University Press, 1958), xiv.

7. This list is drawn from Sykes, *The Society of Captives*, chapter 4: "The Pains of Imprisonment."

8. "[E]ach man brings to the custodial institution his own needs and his own background and each man takes away from the prison his own interpretation of life within the walls. . . . Yet when we examine the way the inmates of the New Jersey State Prison perceive the social environment created by the custodians, the dominant fact is the hard core of consensus expressed by the members of the captive population with regard to the nature of their confinement. The inmates are agreed that life in the maximum security prison is depriving or frustrating in the extreme." Sykes, *The Society of Captives*, 63.

9. For a good introduction to restorative justice, see J. Braithwaite and H. Strang (eds.), *Restorative Justice and Civil Society* (Cambridge, U.K.: Cambridge University Press, 2001).

10. That is, formal or discretionary decisions that are consistent with or contribute to the central function of the institution in question. See pp. 60–62 infra for more detail.

11. In this and the remaining premises, please qualify this suffering as only that which forms an integral element of the institution's central function.

12. One decision may, of course, be made on the basis of a variety of different kinds of grounds, but for our purposes, it will be useful nevertheless to distinguish decision-making procedures according to the kinds of grounds that may be adduced.

13. See, for example: "The *Code of Conduct and Ethics* sets a framework for

ethical decision making and defines the standards of behaviour expected of all of us who work in the Department of Corrective Services." And again, "The *Code of Conduct and Ethics* covers all employees of the Department. It provides an ethical framework to guide your decisions, actions and behaviour, so that they will, at all times, be rational and fair. It advocates values that require integrity, efficiency, economy, honesty and impartiality." *Code of Conduct and Ethics* (New South Wales [NSW] Department of Corrections, April 1998), Commissioner Leo Keliher's "Fore-word" and 1.

14. The use of overcharging (or stealing) as an example of a moral evil is, of course, not as straightforward as I imply here, particularly since "property . . . is not an unproblematic moral idea" (John Kleinig, personal communication, October 16, 2000). To simplify matters, I would ask the reader who doubts the wrongfulness of the acts of stealing portrayed in the following examples—or even more gener-ally—nevertheless to regard them, for the sake of argument, as actions that, in certain circumstances, would be morally wrong for the agent in question to per-form.

15. John Kleinig, personal communication, October 16, 2000.

16. See, for example: "The vast majority of you act responsibly and have nothing to fear. It is, therefore, in your interests to report suspected corrupt con-duct or unethical practices, so that public confidence in the Department and your standing in the community is enhanced. Each of us is entitled to be proud to be an employee of this Department and to feel valued, respected and supported by the Department." Keliher, "Foreword," in *Code of Conduct and Ethics*.

17. The "Code of Conduct and Ethics" used by the NSW Department of Cor-rections in Australia was "developed from the *Model Code of Conduct for NSW Public Agencies* [among other sources]." Keliher, "Foreword," in *Code of Conduct and Eth-ics*.

18. For an alternative view, see Gertrude Schneider, *Muted Voices: Jewish Sur-vivors of Latvia Remember* (New York: Philosophical Library, 1987), 137.

19. That things have thus improved is not uncontroversial: "the modern pains of imprisonment are often defined by society as a humane alternative to the physi-cal brutality and the neglect which constituted the major meaning of imprisonment in the past. . . . [But the] deprivations or frustrations of the modern prison . . . can be just as painful as the physical maltreatment which they have replaced." Sykes, *The Society of Captives*, 64.

20. This view is known as the (Kantian) egalitarian theory of human worth. See Jean Hampton, "The Wisdom of the Egoist: The Moral and Political Implications of Valuing the Self," *Social Philosophy & Policy* 14, no. 1 (Winter 1997): 21–51, 27 et seq.

21. "[Egalitarian] theories of worth (e.g., of the sort held by Kant) . . . insist that [human worth] does not and cannot diminish no matter what we do (so that even a wrongdoer is held to be valuable, and deserving of our respect)." Hampton, "The Wisdom of the Egoist," 28.

22. This point—that human worth is independent of moral status—should be clearly distinguished from the view that human worth is determined by moral status: "on a moral-inegalitarian view, moral evaluation actually determines where a person falls on the scale of human worth: the higher the moral evaluation, the higher the worth, and vice versa." Hampton, "The Wisdom of the Egoist," 29–30.

23. "Most of us tend to care about what others (at least *some* others, some

significant group whose good opinion we value) think about us—how much they think we matter. Our self-respect is *social* in at least this sense, and it is simply part of the human condition that we are weak and vulnerable in these ways. And thus when we are treated with contempt by others it attacks us in profound and deeply threatening ways." Jeffrie Murphy, "Forgiveness and Resentment," in Jeffrie G. Murphy and Jean Hampton, *Forgiveness and Mercy* (Cambridge, U.K.: Cambridge University Press, 1988), 25. Compare the following report of burglary victims: "'It's like we were raped. The stuff they took was all given to us for our wedding presents . . . they went through our clothes.' . . . It wasn't just a house they invaded, it was people's property and real live human beings that they offended." Mark Umbreit, "The Meaning of Fairness to Burglary Victims," in *Criminal Justice, Restitution, and Reconciliation*, ed. Burt Galaway and Joe Hudson (Monsey, N.Y.: Criminal Justice Press, 1990), 49.

24. "I come more and more to think that morality, while a fact, is a twisted and distorted fact. Or perhaps better, that it is a barely recognizable version of another fact, a version adapted to a twisted and distorted world. . . . I think it may be that the related notions of sacrifice and gift represent (or come close to representing) [this] fact. . . . Imagine a situation, an 'economy' if you will, in which no one ever buys or trades for or seizes any good thing. But whatever good he enjoys it is either one that he himself has created or else one that he receives as a free and unconditional gift. And as soon as he has tasted it and seen that it is good he stands ready to give it away in his turn as soon as the opportunity arises. In such a place, if one were to speak either of his rights or his duties, his remark might be met with puzzled laughter as his hearers struggled to recall an ancient world in which those terms referred to something important." George Mavrodes, "The Queerness of Morality," in *Rationality, Religious Belief, and Moral Commitment: New Essays in the Philosophy of Religion*, ed. Robert Audi and William J. Wainwright (Ithaca, N.Y.: Cornell University Press, 1986), 225–26.

25. "In many societies, some kind of egalitarian theory of human worth is standardly advocated. . . . However, such official endorsement often betrays the reality of a variety of views of worth in those societies that are inegalitarian, and that place people of certain sorts (e.g., those in a certain racial, gender, or ethnic group) higher than people of other sorts (e.g., those belonging to other racial, gender, or ethnic groups)." Hampton, "The Wisdom of the Egoist," 29.

26. See Sykes, *The Society of Captives*, chapter 4.

27. "I think a rulemaking body can take a number of practical steps that will enable it to formulate a workable, if not perfect, seriousness scale for use in its guidelines. At least so far as typical crimes of theft, force, and fraud are concerned, one can develop a rough assessment of their consequences using the legal definition of the crime and available common knowledge of its probable effects. One can also make commonsense moral judgments about the relative importance of the rights and interests that different crimes invade. One can grade culpability at least according to whether intentional, reckless, or negligent conduct is involved." Andrew von Hirsch, *Past or Future Crimes: Deservedness and Dangerousness in the Sentencing of Criminals* (Manchester, U.K.: Manchester University Press, 1986), 74; quoted in Thomas Mathiesen, *Prison on Trial: A Critical Assessment* (London: Sage Publications, 1990), 120.

28. Sykes, *The Society of Captives*, 65. Compare also: "Formal criminal punish-

ment is . . . a degradation ceremony with maximum prospects for stigmatization"; "Prisons are warehouses for outcasts; they put problem people at a distance . . . from those who might help reintegrate them." John Braithwaite, *Crime, Shame and Reintegration* (Cambridge, U.K.: Cambridge University Press, 1989), 14, 179.

29. I am not intending here to minimize the significance and value that various goods and services will have to prisoners. "From the outside one might think that the benefits and burdens controlled by the prison are not so important. From the outside, the difference between an isolation cell and a regular cell may appear small. So may the difference between six and eight crowns per day as allowance. In any case, the cell is cramped and the allowance small. Seen from within, however, much of this appears differently. Seen from the inside, differences which appear small from the outside are often magnified or enlarged and in part receive vital significance." Mathiesen, *Prison on Trial*, 130.

30. Sykes does acknowledge that a "small number of prisoners" will not be touched by this moral stigma (being psychopathic or immersed in the criminal subculture). *The Society of Captives*, 66. Consider as well: "[W]hen we become outcasts we can reject our rejectors and the shame no longer matters to us." Braithwaite, *Crime, Shame and Reintegration*, 55.

31. Sykes, *The Society of Captives*, 63.

32. Mathiesen, *Prison on Trial*, 134.

33. See Stern, *A Sin against the Future*, chapter 6: "People and Imprisonment," and Hans Toch, *Living in Prison: The Ecology of Survival*, rev. ed. (Washington, D.C.: American Psychological Association, 1993).

34. Sykes, *The Society of Captives*, 64.

35. "Retributivism is the only theory of punishment which takes the notion of human responsibility seriously because it justifies punishment solely on the basis of acts and situations which were under the control of the perpetrator concerned. Only those facts which are believed to be free human acts are relevant in assessing guilt and deciding about punishment; all circumstances independent of the offender are considered as irrelevant." Wojciech Sadurski, *Giving Desert Its Due* (Dordrecht, Neth.: Reidel, 1985), 241.

36. C. S. Lewis, "The Humanitarian Theory of Punishment," *Res Judicatae: The Journal of the Law Students' Society, Victoria* (Australia) 6 (1953): 2.

37. "Although Kantian beings who could know morality without relying upon their emotions are perhaps conceivable—just barely—that surely is not us. We need our emotions to know about the injustice of racial discrimination, the unfairness of depriving another of a favorite possession, the immorality of punishing the innocent. Our emotions are our main heuristic guide to finding out what is morally right." Michael Moore, "The Moral Worth of Retribution," in *Responsibility, Character and the Emotions*, ed. F. Schoeman (Cambridge, U.K.: Cambridge University Press, 1987), 189.

38. It is worth noting that this experience of justice has been frequently documented in the context of victim-offender mediation or family group conferencing schemes, that is, where the processes of victim-offender reconciliation and reparation are initiated: "[T]he forgiver is able to respond to the wrongdoer as someone other than 'the one who hurt me,' and the wrongdoer himself is able, thanks to this new perspective, to regard himself as liberated from his burden of moral debt.

Such liberation puts the two parties on an equal footing once more, and makes possible renewed relationships." Jean Hampton, "Forgiveness, Resentment and Hatred," in Murphy and Hampton, *Forgiveness and Mercy,* 49. "The major parties attend the [family group] conference in the roles of victim or offender. The labels of 'victim' and 'offender' may gradually be removed, and the conference process may begin that longer process of restoring the moral equality between them." David B. Moore, "Transforming Juvenile Justice, Transforming Policing: The Introduction of Family Conferencing in Australia," in *Comparative Criminal Justice: Traditional and Nontraditional Systems of Law and Control,* ed. Charles B. Fields and Richter H. Moore (Prospect Heights, Ill.: Waveland Press, 1996), 595.

39. Victim-offender mediation is one of the few ways in which this kind of inner transformation might be facilitated: "The experience of being caught for an offense and being charged will be sufficient to incite a degree of regret in most offenders (if only out of self-pity). The task of the mediation scheme is then to build on this spark of remorse to encourage even more insightful realization of the harm caused and thereby to make that remorse deeper, more genuine, and less self-centered." Tony F. Marshall and Sally Merry, *Crime and Accountability—Victim/Offender Mediation in Practice* (London: HMSO, 1990), 97.

40. Joel Feinberg, *Harmless Wrongdoing: The Moral Limits of the Criminal Law* (New York: Oxford University Press, 1988), vol. 4: 304–05.

41. Sykes, *The Society of Captives,* 90.

42. Paulo Freire, *Pedagogy of the Oppressed,* rev. ed., trans. Myra B. Ramos (New York: Continuum Publishing Company, 1994), 27.

43. "When someone infringes another's rights, he gains an unfair advantage over all others in the society—since he has failed to constrain his own behavior while benefiting from other persons' forbearance from interfering with his rights. The punishment—by imposing a counterbalancing disadvantage on the violator— restores the equilibrium: after having undergone the punishment, the violator ceases to be at an advantage over his non-violating fellows." von Hirsch, *Doing Justice,* 47. Compare Herbert Morris, "Persons and Punishment," *The Monist* 52 (1968): 475, 478.

44. Mathiesen, *Prison on Trial,* 132. Victim-offender mediation is, perhaps, the most promising way available for addressing the psychological needs of the victim. "Meeting the offender and being able to express one's feelings to the culpable party, to witness them as human beings rather than vague impersonal threats, to receive their apologies and exercise the privilege of forgiveness may help victims restore their social and personal equilibrium in a more direct and immediate way than would otherwise be possible." Marshall and Merry, *Crime and Accountability,* 182.

Response to Chapter 2

The Case for Abolition and the Reality of Race

John P. Pittman

Derek Brookes's chapter offers some arguments aimed at rattling our assumptions and fostering our suspicions concerning the enterprise of a correctional ethic.[1] Proceeding in the somewhat abstract style of conceptual clarification, Brookes begins with the principle that it makes sense to embark on the enterprise of an ethic of/for an institution only if that institution is a beneficent one. He goes on to suggest minimal conditions for regarding an institution as beneficent: these are that it provides for some basic human needs and that it respects the dignity, moral worth, and uniqueness of human individuals. Although he does not draw the expected connections fully in this chapter, Brookes takes the force of the considerations to militate against the coherence of the enterprise of correctional ethics.

I am quite sympathetic to Brookes's critical stance toward the enterprise of correctional ethics. His argument that prisons are inherently and irredeemably unjust institutions and that, consequently, the enterprise of correctional ethics is a nonstarter is, in my view, dead right in many respects. I will not spend time commenting on or exploring the intricacies of Brookes's argument. Instead, I want to supplement the considerations he presents by exploring some features of the current debates concerning prisons about which he says little but that run parallel to his own efforts. First, I want to situate the discussion in terms of the sociopolitical agendas and audiences it might or might not determine. Second, I want to raise a question about the institutional integrity of the prison and its relation to broader social forces and struggles in modern societies. Third, and lastly, I want to venture some questions about the viability of the discussion given the structural conditions under which it is taking place and the obstacles those conditions present.

First, I would like to characterize Brookes's overall ethical view as a high-theoretical one. What I mean is this: his manner of proceeding suggests that we should first get clear on moral principles, values, and virtues and then appeal to these in trying to sort out our views about specific issues or problems encountered in our daily lives.[2] This is high-theoretic in that it begins with only the most rudimentary, and, it seems to me, preconceived abstract concepts, taken straight out of the mouth of the tradition. That is, Brookes takes aim at the conception of the prison by drawing on what is taken to be our shared conception of human moral worth and dignity. This Enlightenment strategy has, of course, an honorable place in the family mythology of philosophers. But I want to suggest that it serves only to dull the force of Brookes's sharpest critical intentions.

Among other things, this strategy depends on the presumption that if only we do the required intellectual labor aright, we will achieve a consensual clarity of understanding and purpose about how to arrange and reform our social institutions. Brookes's chapter turns this strategy upon itself, in a sense, by arguing that once we have elaborated the correct account of such foundational notions as human moral worth and dignity and have clarified the central function of the prison, we will see that prisons are irredeemably evil and so lie outside the ambit of any ethically oriented reform. Nonetheless, Brookes clearly begins from conceptions taken to be our intellectual inheritance and advances from these positions his attack on the legitimacy of prison and corrections. Although I substantially agree with Brookes's overall view of prisons, I nonetheless want to say that such a battle, no matter how noble the banner under which it is fought, cannot be won. One will never prevail if the attempt is to get everyone to agree, by rational arguments, that human dignity means just so and so or that the central function of prisons is this or that. These are, to use a term first introduced by W. B. Gallie and recently renovated by Mark Tunick, essentially contested concepts.[3] And I think one of the reasons the Enlightenment conception of rational moral discourse has fallen on hard times is the recognition that, because of irresolvable conflicts about the basic moral notions, that conception cannot deliver on its very substantial promises.

One major subtext of Brookes's account is the prominence he gives to slavery, using it as an example to highlight certain general features of institutions and our ethical consideration of them. Slavery is the example he gives of an institution that it would make no sense to try to reform. He uses it as an example of an institution that, though evil, was not all along obviously evil. Finally, he characterizes the ultimate goal of the prison in terms strictly analogous to those he takes to describe the ultimate goal of slavery ("forced captivity" is the operative phrase).[4] This, I take it, is a deliberate and primary textual strategy on Brookes's part.

Anyone who has spent time reading analytic ethical theory will have encountered the use of slavery as an unproblematic, uncontroversial example of a moral evil. It may be that only the figure of Hitler is more ubiquitous as a stock example in that literature. The way Brookes uses the case of slavery as a social institution in his argument sets his strategy apart from that of the stock citations of slavery as evil. For he uses the example in a systematic way, suggesting deep similarities between the two institutions, and positions himself explicitly among the abolitionists. It must be said, however, that despite Brookes's seriousness of purpose, the slavery to which he adverts is the bloodless abstraction of the analytic tradition. I note this fact not as a complaint, but to mark the point of entry for my reading of his slavery analogy.

There are two points on which I want to frame my reading. The first point can perhaps best be made in the words of John Brown, the most ferocious of the abolitionists of old. One hundred and forty years ago, on his way to the gallows at Harper's Ferry, he passed a note to his guard that read, in part, "the crimes of this guilty land will never be purged away but with blood."[5] Brown was widely regarded at the time as a raving maniac, and even to this day he is often dismissed as a murderous religious fanatic. John Brown's note, and his actions, suggest to me the following point: what moral certainty we have now about the evil of slavery was paid for with the blood of tens of thousands—white and black, slave and free—who fought to abolish it. It is to that history that we should look for our bearings. And the very first point to note about that history is that the Emancipation Proclamation Abraham Lincoln signed into law on January 1, 1863, was as much an act of war as it was a response to moral arguments: Lincoln, it seems, though convinced of the immorality of slavery, acted to deny the rebellious Confederates the basis of their power and stimulate resistance from below to the slavocracy.[6] Of course the Emancipation Proclamation of 1863 changed a great deal; many of the leading abolitionists argued after the Civil War that their work was done, that the American Anti-Slavery Society should be disbanded. But some—Frederick Douglass among them—argued that the abolition cause had not yet been won. The Society faded as a result of that fight, but Douglass proved to be right. In that sense, abolition is more a talking point than a full and viable strategy of social change, as far as I can tell. But as a talking point, it can usefully serve to focus attention and frame issues so as to help the prospect of ameliorating the suffering that prisons represent here and now.

I want to make one more point that has to do with the historic struggle for the abolition of slavery. The intensity and difficulty of that struggle largely followed from a crucial feature of U.S. slavery itself—that it was "Negro slavery," "all the more cruel and hideous because it gradually built itself on a caste of race and color," as W.E.B. DuBois put it.[7] Any understanding of slavery, and the battle against it, on American soil would be impossible without taking hold of just that feature—the color of slavery—which is not captured in the philosophical abstractions Brookes considers. And the same can be said of the American prison system, especially today: speaking in the abstract of the morality of the institution considered independently of its social coloring presents a curious case of the divergence of the philosophical and rhetorical that is worth noting.

Now it might be argued that considering the institution of prison in itself provides for the strongest and most damning case against it—one that does not depend upon any contingent features of the actually existing prison system and so offers no hope that its inequities can be ameliorated through reform. There are two problems with this approach to the discussion. First, as already noted, it invites responses that shift the burden of disagreement from issues about the prison system to issues about the best understanding of human worth and dignity, topics that can be contested at any length, removed from the possible intervention of inconvenient details about the actual social world in itself. Second, as should be clear to anyone observing domestic politics in the United States in the last quarter of the twentieth century, disputes around public policy issues often take on coded meanings that are not explicitly articulated by the contending parties but constitute part of the background essential for understanding the dynamics of the debate. I cite only three examples: school busing, welfare reform, and affirmative action. These are all issues that have a racially charged significance that is not captured in the official terms of the dispute.

Absent an account of its functioning in the system of the American "caste of race and color," any evaluation of the prison system will likely strike wide of the most significant determinants of the social dynamic that the public policy discussion tracks. Nor is it by its abstractness more likely to convince, for failing to sound at the level of the subtexts already mentioned—of the legacy of slavery and of the color of that institution and that legacy—it will not address those issues most central to the public debates. And here the issue is crime, not prisons. Prison is presented these days as the answer to crime, and crime is that menace represented largely in the darker hues of the skin-color spectrum. But it is only by addressing the public representations and repressions of a racialized reality that we can hope to articulate fully the functions of imprisonment today.

The very notion of the central function or ultimate goal of the prison on which Brookes depends must be taken not in an a priori way, as if it could be given once and for all independently of the social discourses and struggles raging around its earthly walls. Brookes needs an account of the central function of the prison on which to hang his moral argument: for it is through arguing that the function involves suffering that cannot be justified in principle that Brookes hopes to put moral muscle in his stand against the institution. For his purposes, forced captivity is minimal in withholding any ascription of purpose for the captivity while essential in identifying a feature of imprisonment that does characterize every instance of the institution. The minimalism of his account seems a strength in allowing the argument to skirt what might be considered the side issues of the intention behind enforcing captivity on the principal subjects of the institution or the broader function of the institution in the sociological sense. In that broader, sociological sense, it is unreasonable to expect that there would be one central function of such a complex social dynamic, itself one process in a nexus of social processes constituting an advanced modern society. But it is just that sense that I want to examine for a moment here.

Brookes's account of the central function of imprisonment is itself extremely useful in opening an investigation into the racial significance of the expanding prison system in the United States. Brookes identifies a "purely administrative" function of the prison, namely, to "provide the kind of regime or social system that is required to hold and control a collection of human beings in forced captivity for extended periods of time."[8] This account certainly serves to assimilate the institution of the prison to that of slavery by means of the figure of forced captivity. Indeed, one might ask at this point, what distinguishes the prison from slavery in U.S. society? Presumably the answer would involve at least four points of historical contrast. First, whereas the prison is but one institution in post-1865 U.S. society, slavery was not merely a peculiar institution but the fundamental fact or determinant of a total way of social life, at least in the southern states. Second, whereas the principal subjects of the prisons as a limited function of the criminal justice system are determined by juridically established criminal behavior, the subjects of the slave system came to be determined exclusively by inherited racial identification. Third, and closely related to the first, is the distinction between imprisonment as a state function and enslavement as the result of the economic function of a particular kind of market. Finally, one might point to a difference of motive or social norm—that of the prison being punishment and improvement and that of the slave system being cheap labor and the reproduction and accumulation of wealth.

Each of the points of contrast, however, suggests a closer relation between prison and the slave system if we consider the development of the prison and particularly its current incarnation in the explosive growth of the "prison-industrial complex."[9] Indeed, only the contrast between slavery as a total way of life and the prison system as a particular institution would appear to survive close scrutiny.

Any analysis of the system of representations and discourses in which the public policy discussions of imprisonment are situated would have to foreground the issue of crime as well as its social reality. As Jeffrey Reiman has argued, the issue of crime and the reality of crime are separated from one another by a complex social process in which many institutions, notably the commercial media, elements of the criminal justice system, and the federal, state, and local governments all play their hands.[10] (And it may be a mistake to call this one "social process" rather than the effect of several intersecting processes.) This process results in the representation, legitimation, and reproduction of a crime problem that floats free of actual social conditions yet is constitutive of crime as it figures in public discussions and popular consciousness. Reiman argues that this crime problem serves to legitimate social inequalities and so stabilize and reproduce the domination of social life by an economic elite and its control over the production and accumulation of wealth. And it is this crime problem that fills the prisons of America with young black men and women; indeed, without this factitious crime problem, prisons would be deprived of their central function, and of the legions of principal subjects whose conditions of existence Brookes rightly identifies as the most important criterion of the moral possibility of correctional ethics and of prisons as such. If it is true, as Reiman argues, that the crime problem is artificially reproduced to bolster the fortunes of elites,[11] then the criminality of its principal subjects can no longer be taken as a legitimate differentia of the prison as distinct from the chattel slavery of yore.

Two other of the differentia we identified may also be eviscerated through the progress of the intertwining of private and public signified by the prison-industrial complex. This intertwining of a state-mandated and -sponsored judicial function with an increasingly private, managed-for-profit correctional function throws into question the significance of the public-private distinction. It is not only that prisons are being transformed into money-making enterprises and that prison labor is being used increasingly as a low-cost, union-free alternative to traditional labor markets. If the privatization of prisons means anything, it is that any social significance possessed by the notions of the impartial rule of law and of the function of imprisonment as correction or improvement has become increasingly eroded by the imperative to fight crime and conduct the war on drugs. It is as if—despite the widespread admission that the war on drugs cannot be won and that crime cannot be stemmed as long as the social inequalities that breed it run rampant—the societal consensus is that prosperity is a god that demands sacrifices, and the traditional victims will do just as nicely now as they ever have.

There is one account of the development of imprisonment in America that revolves around a different, less minimal conception of the central function of the prison. This account, elaborated in a number of articles by Angela

Davis, includes as a central function the "involuntary servitude" of the Thirteenth Amendment to the Constitution.[12] That amendment, while famously abolishing slavery and involuntary servitude in the United States, made an exception for "punishment for crime." This connection, in the very law of the land, of involuntary servitude with legal punishment would be taken up, notoriously, in the postbellum and especially the post-Reconstruction South as a central part of the restoration of social conditions very like those of the slavocracy. The convict lease system, the most brutal and well-known penal institution in the postbellum South, involved the conscription and hyperexploitation of a vast army of predominantly black laborers in conditions that were often worse than those of antebellum plantations. What gave this restoration of slavocratic conditions any legitimacy as an institution of penality were the black codes, a standard feature of the legal systems of all the southern states, which in effect created whole categories of crimes for which blacks and blacks alone could be charged and convicted. It was, indeed, these codes and their enforcement through the convict lease system that cemented the symbolic identification of blackness and crime that continues as an unspoken undercurrent in contemporary discourse about prisons and crime. And, for this reason, any critical assault on public policy with respect to crime and prisons of the kind Brookes seems to be embarked on can be successful only to the extent that it exposes and openly confronts that symbolic identification.

Central to Davis's account are two controversial claims summarized in the idea of a punishment industry. The first is that a basic precondition of the return on a national level of a phenomenon analogous to the convict lease system is the widespread ideological equation of blackness and criminality—an equation grounded in its turn in the convict lease system itself. The second is that the prison boom of the last fifteen years does amount to the formation of an industry: central to its function and identity is its role both in bolstering depressed local economies by providing employment as well as in making the involuntary servitude of the prison population the basis of a profitable ultra-low-wage labor pool. Davis further characterizes the prison boom in terms borrowed from the notion of the military-industrial complex of the Cold War period. For, first, the prison-industrial complex presupposes a kind of moral crusade, a war on crime analogous to the Cold War crusade against international communism. Second, the prison boom began gathering momentum, as David Goldberg shows, just as the military budget was scaled back, modestly, from its Reagan-era highs and the military establishment began closing some military bases and facilities.[13] In many cases, abandoned military facilities were themselves used as sites for the construction of correctional facilities. These among other facts lead Goldberg to write of the close connection between the dramatic rise in incarceration and the shifts in the political economy of American society in the last quarter century. Davis, similarly, places the prison boom in the context of the end of the Cold War, the new world order, and corporate globalization.

Another social dynamic also provides a dramatic context in which to see the prison boom. David Goldberg argues that despite—or perhaps because of—the limited gains in political and cultural empowerment achieved by African Americans during the civil rights era, a countervailing process of resegregation—Goldberg writes of "the New Segregation"—has occurred at the same time. This process contributes to the maintenance of fundamental social, economic, and political inequalities between racially identified white suburban and urban professional populations and black and Latino urban populations. Goldberg identifies a logic of segregation as a "totalizing condition": residential segregation leads to educational segregation, which tends to reproduce inequalities in employment and individual income, which in turn reproduce residential segregation once more.[14] This segregation acts to concentrate crimes, especially street crimes, in those neighborhoods that are the poorest and least empowered to begin with. To this must then be added the deployment of crime control policies that overwhelmingly focus on surveillance and control of populations in poor inner-city neighborhoods—which are predominantly black and Latino. From the standpoint of public policy, then, social problems are not addressed at the level of their root social conditions, but are contained in specific socially and racially defined locations based on cost-benefit calculations or the relative political clout and social power of distinct—again racially defined—social strata and populations.

In this context the prison boom can be seen as one of the "cornerstones of the New Segregation, locking poor people of color spatially as much as economically into lives of severe limitation."[15] Now clearly, if the case for prison abolition is tied conceptually to the central function of the prison, then these contextualizations of the prison boom suggest an expansion of the case against prison and for abolition. But they also suggest why the high-theoretic argument for abolition might be counterproductive. For the kind of abstract moral suasion Brookes intends—appealing to the moral worth of human individuals—attempts to fly in the face of those social forces that undercut the purported universal reach of such appeals to undifferentiated abstract humanity. These forces put certain—racially defined—populations beyond the pale of such abstract humanity, making them morally invisible except as criminals and monsters who must be controlled and contained at society's peril.[16] That these forces have converged around—and have been mobilized through—the phenomenon of an extended and expansive penality indicates the real peril to society presented by these criminal justice debates. The stakes are very high indeed. Talking about prison abolition without talking about these forces and dynamics may produce a reflexive affirmative nod in audiences of public policy elites, but only if the issue is set in its real-world context will it serve to promote critical thinking about the panoply of social conditions that make the abolitionist message so relevant in America today.

Notes

1. Derek R. Brookes, "The Possibility of a Correctional Ethic," in this volume, 39–68.

2. Brookes, "The Possibility of a Correctional Ethic," 44.

3. See W. B. Gallie, *Philosophy and the Historical Understanding* (New York: Schocken, 1964); Mark Tunick employs the notion of an "essentially contested practice" in his *Punishment: Theory and Practice* (Berkeley: University of California Press, 1992).

4. Brookes, "The Possibility of a Correctional Ethic," 40.

5. For these "last written words of John Brown," see W. E. B. DuBois, *John Brown* (Armonk, N.Y.: M. E. Sharpe, 1997), 186.

6. See John Hope Franklin, *From Slavery to Freedom: A History of American Negroes* (New York: Alfred A. Knopf), 275–80.

7. DuBois, *John Brown*, 1.

8. Brookes, "The Possibility of a Correctional Ethic," 40.

9. The phrase, which appears to have come into use only during the last decade, is consciously based on one used by President Eisenhower on January 17, 1961, in his farewell address: "In the councils of government, we must guard against the acquisition of unwarranted influence, whether sought or unsought, by the military-industrial complex." See Eric Schlosser, "The Prison-Industrial Complex," *Atlantic Monthly* 282, no. 6 (December 1998): 51–77.

10. Jeffrey Reiman, *The Rich Get Richer and the Poor Get Prison: Ideology, Class, and Criminal Justice*, 4th ed. (Boston: Allyn & Bacon, 1995), especially chapter 2: "A Crime By Any Other Name. . . ."

11. Reiman, *The Rich Get Richer and the Poor Get Prison*, 171.

12. "Racialized Punishment and Prison Abolition"; "Race and Criminalization: Black Americans and the Punishment Industry"; and "From the Prison of Slavery to the Slavery of Prison: Frederick Douglass and the Convict Lease System," in *The Angela Y. Davis Reader*, ed. Joy James (Oxford: Blackwell, 1998), 96–107; 61–73; 74–95.

13. David Goldberg, "Surplus Value: The Political Economy of Prisons and Policing," in *States of Confinement: Policing, Detention, and Prisons*, ed. Joy James (New York: St. Martin's Press, 2000), 205–21.

14. Goldberg, "Surplus Value," 220.

15. Goldberg, "Surplus Value," 221.

16. This need not always amount to the open, bold-faced racism associated with far-right extremism. Consider a recent poll in Texas concerning the death penalty. Whereas 55 percent of respondents agreed that the death penalty is unfair, 75 percent approved of it. *The Village Voice*, July 4, 2000, 36. Although this might be seen as a matter of the public's confusion on the death penalty issue, it can also be taken as evidence of a dissociation between moral scruples and a kind of state-of-nature strategic thinking. Injustice becomes a fact of life in a society in which, as

Angela Davis puts it, "one has a greater chance of going to jail if one is a young black man than if one is actually a law-breaker." "Racialized Punishment and Prison Abolition," in *The Angela Y. Davis Reader,* 107. The high-theoretical approach will not work here.

Chapter 3

Prison Abuse: Prisoner-Staff Relations

Audrey J. Bomse

Introduction

The current state of prisoner-staff relations—in particular, recent increases in the discretionary power of and consequent abuses by staff—is largely a result of legislative and judicial decisions that have eroded the hard-won but short-lived reforms of the 1960s and 1970s. This external decision making provides the framework for this chapter on the ethical issues that confront those who work inside the prison system.

No one in any society has less power than the people that society puts behind bars. And the very nature of incarceration creates a situation that supports the abuse of prisoners. Add the element of race, a factor that cannot be ignored in today's correctional context, and abuse becomes even more endemic. What distinguishes prison systems throughout the world is (1) the degree to which prisoners are dehumanized and their citizenship is forfeited and (2) the level of prison staff/prison official discretion or, conversely, the degree to which oversight of what occurs behind prison walls is monitored by politicians, the judiciary, the press, and the public.[1]

Historically, prisoners in the United States were viewed as "slaves of the State."[2] The Thirteenth Amendment specifically excepts prisoners.[3] Thus, although the country was theoretically founded on a belief in and commitment to individual rights and freedoms, the Bill of Rights has been applied to prisoners only in the past thirty years. In a departure from the prior jurisprudence, the late 1950s Supreme Court, led by Chief Justice Earl Warren, employed an expansive definition of the "cruel and unusual punishment" prohibited by the Eighth Amendment.[4] Largely as a result of the civil rights and prison movements, the Supreme Court later declared the prisoner a citizen, with certain limited rights. In the late 1960s, a series of Court decisions outlined these rights and established the standards for prison conditions and for the treatment and care of prisoners.[5]

In 1974, the Supreme Court held that "though his rights may be diminished by the needs and exigencies of the institutional environment, a prisoner is not wholly stripped of constitutional protections when he is imprisoned for crime. There is no Iron Curtain drawn between the Constitution and the prisons of this country."[6] The rights afforded prisoners by the Eighth Amendment[7] came to include the right to be free of corporal punishment[8] and physical abuse by guards or other prisoners,[9] as well as the right to minimally adequate conditions of confinement, including medical care, exercise, and safe and sanitary living quarters.[10] The First Amendment guaranteed prisoners religious freedom, access to reading materials and correspondence, while the Fourth Amendment extended limited protection from improper cell or body searches, as well as improper seizure of property. Protection from being disciplined or segregated without a hearing, or otherwise being treated arbitrarily and unfairly, was afforded by the Due Process Clause of the Fifth and Fourteenth Amendments. Access to the courts,[11] to a law library or paralegal assistance, and consultation with lawyers was protected by the Sixth Amendment, the First Amendment, or the Due Process Clause.

Before the relatively recent development of federal judicial oversight of our prisons, a reign of terror existed in many prisons in this country.[12] Presented with a litany of abuses, ranging from the merely disturbing to the utterly shocking,[13] and using a totality of conditions analysis,[14] court after court uncovered evidence of systemwide breakdowns and began ordering extensive injunctive relief.[15]

Thereafter, civil rights litigation, much of it pro se, or without an attorney, became a powerful method for forcing improvements in the treatment of prisoners. In the early 1990s, the Supreme Court heard four Eighth Amendment cases.[16] Every one of those cases was filed initially by a pro se prisoner. Two of the cases, *Farmer* and *Hudson*, got to the Supreme Court solely on the basis of prisoner-handwritten or prisoner-typed petitions.

The federal courts were never eager to usurp the task of running prisons. As Justice Brennan said: "The soul-chilling inhumanity of conditions in American prisons [was] thrust upon the judicial conscience."[17] At the same time as the Supreme Court began applying the Bill of Rights to prisoners in the late 1970s, it also began placing limits on the power of federal courts to correct abuse by affording great deference to prison practices and by limiting the scope of what could be considered unconstitutional conditions of confinement. In *Bell v. Wolfish*,[18] then Associate Justice Rehnquist stated: "Prison administrators should be accorded wide-ranging deference in the adoption and execution of policies and practices that in their judgment are needed to preserve internal order and discipline and to maintain institutional security."[19]

Even at the height of federal court intervention, prison abuse continued. Although judicial intervention and oversight succeeded in limiting some of the more serious violations of prisoners' civil and human rights, and also compensated some of those whose rights were violated, it was never able to prevent or eliminate the individual or systemic abuse of prisoners.[20] Recently, however, congressional legislation has sent us racing back to the past as we have witnessed new limits on federal judicial oversight and a narrowing of constitutional protections for prisoners.

The most far-reaching changes have come from the Prison Litigation Reform Act (PLRA),[21] part of a series of actions taken by Congress and President Clinton in 1996 to limit access to the courts by poor people, death-row inmates and other prisoners, undocumented aliens, and even some lawful immigrants. These are the nation's least popular litigants—people who cannot or do not vote. The PLRA has made it difficult, and sometimes impossible, for prisoners and their attorneys to file lawsuits and litigate successfully.[22] It requires indigent prisoners to pay full court filing fees, requires proof of physical injury to raise emotional or mental distress claims, mandates exhaustion of all administrative remedies, even those that may be futile, before litigation can be filed, and drastically limits attorneys fees in prison litigation, providing little incentive for the private bar to represent prisoner plaintiffs. It also prohibits the courts from granting injunctive relief or approving settlement agreements without a finding of a constitutional violation[23] and requires the termination of all prospective relief in prison conditions cases two years after a judgment, unless there are further findings of unconstitutionality.[24] As the *New York Times* reported in a recent front-page article: "Prison officials and lawyers for inmates agree that the statute has significantly shifted the balance in court cases involving prisoners."[25] The impact of the PLRA has been magnified as most states have passed their own version of this devastating legislation.[26]

The second crucial development was the 1996 Legal Services Corporation restrictions on litigation filed on behalf of prisoners, recently upheld by the Ninth Circuit Court of Appeals.[27] These restrictions forbid legal aid groups from representing prisoners if they accept even a penny of federal funding. Since federal funding is essential to the survival of most groups who represent the indigent, there has been little resistance. Most state-funded agencies representing prisoners, such as New Jersey's Office of Inmate Advocacy and New York's Prisoner Legal Services, have also been defunded and eliminated.

The coup de grace was delivered by the Supreme Court itself in *Lewis v. Casey*.[28] This decision gutted what had, until that time, been prisoners' constitutional right of access to the courts, the "right upon which [the Court had recognized] all other rights depend."[29] That case established a new requirement of "actual injury" to allege interference with the right to legal access.[30] *Lewis* limits the legal access obligation of prison officials to their providing prisoners with the tools needed initially to attack their criminal sentences or to file complaints challenging prison conditions. "Impairment of any other litigating capacity is simply one of the incidental (and perfectly constitutional) consequences of conviction and incarceration."[31]

When prisoners lose the ability to litigate, they lose their main mechanism for limiting abuse, redressing grievances, protesting inhumane treatment, and exerting some control over their environment. Today, prisoners who have once again been dehumanized by various law-and-order campaigns no longer have a way to be heard; the prison system is no longer being held accountable. This message has been understood by prison administrators and guards alike. As the area of unfettered discretion on the part of prison officials has increased, so has prison abuse.[32] Thus it appears that the short period of time during which prisoners could turn to the courts for some protection of their civil and human rights is now coming to a close.

Prison Abuse

Prison abuses can be divided into three sometimes overlapping categories, distinguished by their motivation: malicious or purposeful, negligent, and systemic or budgetary.[33]

A taxonomy of prison abuse must also take account of responsibility. Although the immediate focus may be on the actor, the fact that the act can take place often reflects supervisory irresponsibility or complicity and/or failure by top-level administrators to supervise properly or discipline line staff and to develop policies that limit abuse. Prisons are structured as paramilitary hierarchies with clearly differentiated lines of authority and increasingly less discretion the further down one is in the hierarchy. During times of crisis, decision making is completely autocratic.

Although it is clear that prison administrators—as well as policy makers outside the prison system, such as county freeholders or state legislators —are responsible[34] for abuses stemming from budgetary decisions, prison administrators cannot escape responsibility for systemic or even individual patterns and practices of abuse, even when that abuse constitutes criminal behavior. Prison administrators are obligated to establish standards and policies for treating prisoners humanely, respectfully, and without brutality, and must share the responsibility when these standards and policies are not implemented by line staff.

As law enforcement agencies, prisons should uphold high standards of law-abiding behavior. Prison staff should adhere to the law and prison administrators have an obligation to assure that they do so. State and federal prosecutors should prosecute criminal behavior on the part of corrections staff. At least part of the reason for keeping people behind prison walls is to instill in them the belief that transgressions of the law will not be tolerated. When corrections personnel willfully and flagrantly violate the law, without consequence, prisoners will understandably conclude that what matters is not so much whether you violate the law, but who you are when you do so.

The recent trend toward prison privatization has greatly exacerbated the problem of prison abuse. The profit motive together with an inexperienced and undertrained staff have resulted in abuse of all types. The cost conscious private prison industry has little incentive to meet constitutional standards and refuses to accept responsibility for unconstitutional conditions of confinement. Yet deprivation of liberty is the most powerful control the State exercises over its citizens; at the very least, it should be exercised lawfully and free from inappropriate pressures, such as those exerted by monetary rewards.

Malicious/Purposeful/Intentional Abuse

This category of abuse is frequently litigated[35] and is therefore well documented.[36] It also has racial dimensions that cannot be ignored. Despite recent attempts to diversify correctional staff, the vast majority remains white, whereas the majority of prisoners is African American and Latino.

Excessive Use of Force

In many American prisons today, there exists what U.S. District Judge Thelton Henderson recently referred to as "a pattern of needless and officially sanctioned brutality."[37] The incidents litigated differ in the degree of physical force used against prisoners, the amount of injury caused, and the degree to which prisoners were incapacitated and thus able neither to threaten others nor to defend themselves. They range from the assault on a handcuffed prisoner that left no significant lasting injury, presented to the Supreme Court in *Hudson v. McMillian*,[38] to the recent vicious killing of Thomas Pizzuto by jail guards. Pizzuto had been sentenced to ninety days in Nassau County (N.Y.) Jail, but died from a lacerated spleen, apparently after disturbing guards by repeated requests for his methadone treatment. They also differ in the amount of officer self-control and premeditation involved. An example of serious injury inflicted by one out-of-control officer appears in a court opinion holding that "a reasonable prison official should have known that repeatedly striking an inmate's head (20–25 times) on a concrete floor when his limbs were being restrained by four other officers (while two others stood by to assist if necessary) and the inmate offered no resistance would violate clearly established law."[39]

Finally, and perhaps most importantly, responsibility for excessive use of force incidents can be differentially allocated. The responsibility for an assault does not necessarily stop with the assaulter. Other guards and/or immediate supervisors are often present, observing the abuse but failing to intervene.[40] In addition, widespread use of force implies complicity, or deliberate blindness, on the part of prison administrators. Such widespread use of force and intimidation affected the entire prisoner population at Bayside State Prison (N.J.) and led to class action litigation[41] against both prison administrators and line officers when, in the aftermath of the killing of an officer, the Special Operations Group[42] occupied the prison and systematically terrorized its inhabitants over a six-week period. Although investigators from the independent Department of Corrections (DOC) Ombudsman's Office reported a pattern of criminal assault, prison administrators and the DOC commissioner denied the abuse ever occurred.[43] Goon squad activity is rampant and often implicitly tolerated. In one predominantly white rural county jail in New Jersey, the goon squad orchestrated a conflict with an entire housing unit of state-sentenced (largely black and Latino) prisoners being housed there for a neighboring urban county, by insisting that the day room TV be turned off right before Monday Night Football.[44] Specific areas—such as Passaic County (N.J.) Jail's infamous "elevator ride"—are often used for beating and intimidating prisoners.

Excessive use of force can even be official prison policy.[45] For example, the California DOC permitted guards to shoot to kill prisoners fighting in the yard. Since 1994, twelve prisoners have been shot to death in California prisons while another thirty-two have been shot and injured. According to sworn affidavits of corrections officers in Hays State Prison (Ga.), in July 1996, the state commissioner of corrections himself watched, condoned, and even celebrated a mass beating of prisoners, some of whom were handcuffed and lying on the floor.[46] An entire industry of high-tech physical restraints has come into existence as prison officials rush to buy the latest "cruel-and-unusual" equipment, including restraint chairs and wheels and spit helmets (to prevent prisoners from spitting on their jailers). Amnesty International has launched a campaign in the United States to have the stun belt banned as a human rights violation.[47]

Mentally ill prisoners isolated in disciplinary cells are favorite victims for abusive guards, as detailed in *C.F. v. Fauver*,[48] a class action lawsuit in New Jersey by mentally ill prisoners housed in Rahway's Administrative Close Supervision Unit. There, assaults on prisoners were so common that many refused to exit their cells for visits, recreation, or showers until a railing was installed to separate the prisoners from their jailers. In a Lansing,

Michigan, county jail, the forty-year-old mentally ill son of a black minister who had urinated on the floor, causing officers to slip, was hogtied and left lying on his belly in an isolation cell. A videotape produced at his wrongful death trial showed eight white officers restraining and eventually suffocating him.[49]

Although the excessive use of force is a crime, few cases of prison-guard brutality result in criminal prosecutions, let alone convictions, due to the reluctance of both local prosecutors and U.S. attorneys to investigate corrections officials. No action is taken in 96 percent of civil rights criminal cases referred to U.S. attorneys each year by the F.B.I. or other agencies.[50] The F.B.I. investigated the hogtying death of the mentally ill Michigan prisoner discussed above and reported back to federal prosecutors, but they never filed charges against the jail guards.

Rape and Sexual Harassment

Although the sexual abuse of women in prison is not a new phenomenon, the current surge in the female prison population and pervasive use of male guards to supervise them have led to an epidemic of sexual misconduct. Sexual abuse takes many forms in prison[51]—from rape and sexual slavery to sexual harassment[52] and so-called consensual sexual relations.[53]

As a result of the pervasiveness of sexual misconduct, thirty-seven states and the federal government have criminalized sexual contact between correctional staff and prisoners. Still, almost the only way in which this abuse comes to light is if the victim becomes pregnant, in which case the officer is fired and the matter is (occasionally) turned over for prosecution.[54]

An exhaustive 1996 study of eleven states by Human Rights Watch (HRW)[55] revealed pervasive rape and sexual assault throughout the federal prison system, as well as brutal retaliation against prisoners who reported abuse, itself evidence of wider responsibility. Rape and sexual assault were so widespread in Arizona's prisons that the U.S. Justice Department filed suit in March 1997, charging that state DOC officials were "consciously aware of, but deliberately indifferent to" a pattern of sexual abuse.

Beyond these horrors lies an array of subtler abuses. Sex is sometimes used as currency to trade for necessities, such as sanitary products, or for privileges, such as work assignments. According to the HRW report, male officers "have used their near total authority to provide or deny goods and privileges to female prisoners, to compel them to have sex or, in other cases, to reward them for having done so."

Less commonly, women prisoners are left vulnerable to sexual attack from male prisoners,[56] as occurred in the Segregated Housing Unit of the otherwise all-male Federal Detention Center in Dublin (Calif.), when guards opened the cells of three women prisoners at night, giving access to male prisoners. The incident recently resulted in a large settlement[57] by the U.S. Bureau of Prisons (BOP). Although, as part of the settlement, the BOP agreed to remedy the serious deficiencies in policies and procedures for the thousands of women in the federal prison system, the PLRA provisions that limit federal court enforcement of consent decrees and that prohibit attorneys fees for monitoring compliance will likely make it impossible for plaintiffs to enforce the agreed-upon injunctive relief.[58]

Theft and Destruction of Prisoner Property

This frequently accompanies disciplinary conviction and transfer to lockup units. It was so widespread when I worked at the New Jersey Public Advocate's Office that I requested a criminal investigation by the prosecutor's office. Needless to say, no such investigation occurred.

We are not talking here only about food and cigarettes but also about expensive items, such as televisions and word processors. Because prisoners typically file remedy/grievance forms when their property disappears, the prison administration is aware of this abuse, though it appears to be treated as an employment perk.

The three aforementioned abuses are all criminal acts and the bad actors should be prosecuted accordingly. Other abuses committed by correctional staff, listed below, constitute, at least, official misconduct, and should lead to immediate termination.

False Disciplinary Charges

These usually result in a prisoner's placement in disciplinary lockup and are made with apparent impunity. I once had charges written against me for allegedly receiving contraband—a large legal folder containing documents produced by the state during discovery in the criminal prosecutions of prisoners arising out of a riot in the prison mess hall. Although the Appellate Division of the New Jersey Superior Court ordered the file returned to me,[59] no action was ever taken against the complaining officer.

Particularly frustrating to prisoners is the fact that the rules of the game are constantly changing. In New Jersey, prisoners have been disciplined and then placed in the gang unit for possessing literature that came into their possession years before, through normal prison channels.[60] Given the opportunity, prison staff often engage in informal rule making. One professor of criminal justice was told by the mail room at New Jersey State Prison that books on Africa were not permitted to prisoners confined in the Management Control Unit. Not only does such a regulation not exist, it would clearly be illegal if it did.

Outside oversight of this aspect of prison life has always been limited, since the federal courts never looked into the merits of disciplinary decisions, as long as the prisoner's procedural rights were respected.[61] As a result of recent Supreme Court decisions,[62] and the PLRA's requirement that administrative remedies first be exhausted, the federal courts no longer protect even the due process rights of prisoners falsely accused and convicted by kangaroo courts.

Although state courts overturn disciplinary convictions, I am not aware of a single instance in which staff has been discharged or even disciplined by prison administrators for filing what courts have determined to be unfounded charges.

Intentional Denial of Medical Care

This most frequently occurs in the aftermath of incidents of brutality. This form of abuse is especially prevalent in smaller county jails, where medical and correctional staff know each other outside the work environment.

One middle-class Chilean detainee, who was badly beaten in the Sussex County (N.J.) Jail because he had exposed a guard who was selling cigarettes to prisoners, had his medical records falsified by a nurse who came from the same rural community as the officer. She placed false entries on his medical running record, reporting that the inmate, who had extensive surgery performed on his shoulders and knee as soon as he was transferred into the state prison system, was repeatedly seen exercising in the yard.[63] Although the detainee eventually won a $75,000 settlement for the physical injuries that incapacitated him, no action was ever taken against the nurse or the guard.

During the Special Operations Group occupation of Bayside State Prison in New Jersey, some nurses refused to respond to pleas for assistance from prisoners who had been beaten and then locked in their cells, while others performed only the most perfunctory examinations, even when videotaped by Internal Affairs.

Health care professionals who become complicit in activities that have nothing to do with the health care of prisoners obviously violate their professional ethics and should lose their jobs, if not their professional licenses.

Failure to Protect

As a purposeful action, failure to protect occurs when officers know in advance of a threat or actually witness prisoner-on-prisoner violence, but fail to intervene. This official misconduct sometimes happens as retaliation after an officer has been injured. At New Jersey State Prison in Trenton, for example, shortly after an officer was hurt in the prison mess hall, officers removed themselves from the mess hall during an attack on a prisoner, leaving him alone to face three attackers, who beat him into unconsciousness.[64] Another frequent abuse of this type is failure to protect troublemaking, but particularly vulnerable prisoners (because they may be middle class or homosexual/effeminate) from assault by other prisoners.[65] Staff racism is yet another factor in this scenario. For example, a black prisoner in the lockup unit of New Jersey's Northern State Prison was stabbed and beaten by a white prisoner-runner as he walked naked to the shower area. The beating continued for almost ten minutes, in full view of several corrections officers, and was stopped only when a black lieutenant arrived on the scene and ordered the officers to intervene.[66]

Racial Abuse and/or Harassment

This is widespread in prisons. At the penalty phase of the trial in which a black, homosexual prisoner was found guilty of killing a Bayside State Prison corrections officer, the New Jersey jury found as mitigating factors (against imposing the death penalty) rampant racism and homophobia among officers, which often led them to abuse prisoners of color, as well as homosexuals. However, this abuse has usually been reviewed by the courts only when it is closely related to physical abuse or some other constitutional violation. One federal court recently held that, in a prison context, racial slurs and epithets alone are not actionable as civil rights violations.[67] Often it is not until black and Latino prison staff object to rampant racism that change occurs.

Excessive and Humiliating Strip Searches

Although security concerns are clearly legitimate, the circumstances surrounding many strip searches, as well as their sheer number, often create an abusive situation. In fact, these searches have produced almost as much pro se litigation as has the excessive use of force. The practice is particularly offensive when it is performed by or in the presence of officers of the opposite sex.[68] In New Jersey, class action litigation in *Czimadia v. Fauver*[69] resulted in a detailed consent decree that, among other things, called for the construction of "modesty panels" and amended state regulations to limit the circumstances under which the practice could occur.

The largest number of complaints in this area arises from prisoners in control or lockup units and during prison lockdowns. In both situations, increased security concerns are legitimate. Yet the number of such searches often is excessive, and the fact that they are performed repeatedly, for example, to and from escorted window visits, causes a great deal of tension.

At times the threat of strip searches is used to increase the humiliation and harassment of prisoners. For example, during a break in an administrative law hearing of the chairman of the Prisoners Representative Committee at New Jersey State Prison, officers taunted the prisoner—within the hearing of the administrative law judge[70] and placed on the record by the judge— with the strip search he was going to undergo at the end of the day. One former prisoner[71] recalled that his strategy for avoiding repeated strip searches as a prison paralegal was constantly to offer to strip.

Negligent Abuse

This form of prisoner abuse is perhaps less offensive to the courts and others outside prison walls, but it may be just as serious and harmful to those behind the walls and even more pervasive than intentional abuse. These are bad acts that, in extreme cases, warrant disciplinary action of the staff involved, including possible termination of employment.

Negligent Denial of Medical Care

Probably the most frequent complaint in this category, this abuse is the result of malfeasance by either line officers or medical staff. Prisoners in need of close watch because of their medical conditions are frequently neglected. One seven-month pregnant woman in the Camden County (N.J.) Jail miscarried on the floor of the locked cell where she had been assigned to sleep, having been unable to attract the attention of guards in the middle of the night.[72] In another case, following surgery to repair severe facial fractures incurred during a jail altercation, a male detainee in that same jail was forced to sleep on the floor without any way of elevating his head and was not given any medication for the excruciating postsurgery pain.[73]

There are patterns of negligent medical care, either by individual doctors, such as Dr. John Napoleon—whose failure to examine and treat prisoners at one New Jersey state prison, despite being notified of their serious medical needs, resulted in an $80,000 settlement in favor of the prisoner plaintiffs[74]—or by whole medical departments, as was the case in the class action litigation filed by all insulin-dependent diabetic prisoners at the Adult Diagnostic and Treatment Center (ADTC) in New Jersey, alleging that the medical care provided them was "uniformly and grossly inadequate."[75] At ADTC, for example, although the current medical norm is to blood-glucose test three or four times a day, one prisoner's blood was tested only twenty-five times during one year and another's blood was checked only nine times during his seven years of incarceration.

Mentally ill prisoners are sometimes ignored by mental health professionals, dismissed as manipulators, or overmedicated. One New Jersey prisoner, who had experienced audio hallucinations in the form of voices telling him to escape, was labeled manipulative by the sole (unlicensed) psychologist on staff and was turned over to the prison disciplinary system, where he was convicted of planning to escape.[76]

Failure to Protect

In many prisons today, prisoners live in constant fear of being assaulted physically or sexually by other prisoners. These assaults often occur as a result of prison officials' failure to classify prisoners properly or by line officers' failure to take corrective action when they become aware of assaults or assault risks within the prison.[77] In other words, they are the result of either institutional conditions that prison officials have not adequately tried to remedy[78] or of the failure to isolate prisoners who are obvious potential victims.

The "Black Hole"

Total lack of responsiveness to prisoner grievances reinforces prisoners' feelings of powerlessness and unnecessarily exacerbates prison tensions. Close to 90 percent of prison litigation would probably not be filed were there an adequate prison grievance system, instead of the black hole that now exists.[79] What to the outside world seems minor, such as a prisoner's account being charged for a can of peanut butter ordered, but not received from the commissary, in the past ended up as a federal case, simply because there was no other avenue of redress.[80]

Included in this category is lack of ordinary care in handling matters of vital importance to prisoners, such as parole. For example, after one New Jersey prisoner's parole was reinstated, it took almost two weeks for prison parole counselors to forward the necessary paperwork to the appropriate district parole office so that the prisoner could be released.[81] A similar abuse involves ignoring legal access slips, often in the face of known court deadlines.

Frequently, a simple call to jail/prison administrators by an outside agency will immediately resolve problems that the prisoner was unable to resolve with weeks of grievance forms.

Negligent Loss of Property or Mail

This is another unnecessary source of tension. A package containing over $75.00 worth of vitamins ordered by one HIV-positive New Jersey prisoner's wife was misplaced by the mailroom until a prisoner-runner discovered it in a storage room. Regular mail is constantly lost or misplaced. There was so much litigation over lost property in New Jersey state prisons that, until recently, small-claims court judges regularly held court in the prison facilities. The DOC's solution was to promulgate regulations requiring prisoners to pay for the cost of their transportation to small-claims court. Although this new regulation has obviously cut down on the amount of litigation, nothing has been done to reduce the amount of lost property.

Systemic and Budgetary Prison Abuses

This class of abuses has resulted from decisions made at the top, either by high-ranking prison officials or by governmental bodies. It is, therefore, the most insidious category of abuse. Racism makes it easy to dehumanize the prison population and thus to tolerate such inhumane prison conditions.

Overcrowding and Other Consequent Unconstitutional Conditions[82]

The unprecedented growth in the prison population in the last twenty years has created severely overcrowded prison systems. When too many people are clamoring for too few resources and too many people are contained in too small an area, the system inevitably begins to break down. As a result, those dependent on the system suffer.

When society takes away someone's liberty we call it punishment. If we add to that punishment, however, by taking away sustaining services such as adequate food, basic medical care, or any semblance of security, the courts have called it cruel and unusual punishment.[83] A constitutional violation of prisoners' rights in the area of conditions involves denial of the "minimal civilized measure of life's necessities."[84] For example, in *Camden County Jail Inmates v. Parker,* class action litigation in New Jersey that lasted for over a decade and challenged overcrowded conditions, the federal court found that the prisoners' most basic needs for sanitation, recreation, uncontaminated food, minimally sufficient housing space, and personal safety were not met.[85] More recently, a federal district court found numerous conditions of confinement at the San Francisco County Jail—including inmates being forced to spend sixteen to twenty-three hours a day double celled in forty-one-square-foot cells for up to 100 days—violated contemporary standards of decency and the Eighth and Fourteenth Amendments.[86] The court also found that defects in the jail's antiquated water, plumbing, and sewage systems, including sewage leaks, violated public health requirements as well as inmates' constitutional rights, and stressed that prisoners need not await a dysentery attack before obtaining a remedy.

In 1990, forty-one states, along with the District of Columbia, Puerto Rico, and the Virgin Islands, had some portion of their state prison facilities under court supervision, the overwhelming majority for conditions related to overcrowding.[87] From the perspective of a prisoners' rights advocate, however, the problem with conditions litigation is that success is often counterproductive. The most common remedy to antiquated, overcrowded prisons is to build new, larger prisons. What commonly occurs then is that every new bed provided is immediately filled and the overall prison population soars. One of the earliest prison conditions cases, for example, arose in New York

City after a riot in Manhattan's jail known as the Tombs. In 1978, after six years of litigation, the city agreed to settle the case. Under the agreement, the city gutted the Tombs and built a new jail on the site. It also expanded the capacity of the Rikers Island jail from 7,000 to 22,000.

The Supreme Court first attempted to limit federal judicial intervention in state prisons by imposing, in addition to the objective requirement of proving unconstitutional conditions, a subjective requirement, namely, that prisoners must also establish that, in permitting such conditions to exist, prison officials acted with culpable intent.[88] Such a subjective intent requirement could and did permit prison officials to successfully avoid responsibility for objectively cruel and unusual conditions of confinement by claiming a lack of funds despite good-faith efforts to obtain them.

The PLRA's response to successful conditions litigation has been to make it nearly impossible for parties to enter into consent decrees, by prohibiting federal courts from approving settlement agreements without a finding of constitutional violation, by imposing automatic termination of any injunctive relief ordered by the courts within two years, and by limiting attorneys fees and special master's fees in monitoring situations. In an area of litigation characterized by lack of compliance with court orders and settlement agreements, the PLRA's automatic termination provision is particularly deadly.

Provision of Inadequate Medical Care

This always accompanies prison overcrowding. In 1972, in the first challenge to systemwide gross and pervasive neglect of prisoners' medical needs, a district court judge in Alabama concluded that the deaths of a quadriplegic prisoner with maggot-infested wounds, who was left essentially unattended for a month, and of a prisoner unable to eat, who was not provided with any form of intravenous nourishment for three days, "illustrate what can and does occur when too few reasonable men, functioning with too little supportive facilities, undertake what is, in effect, an impossible task."[89] In overcrowded facilities, there are simply not enough doctors to examine properly all detainees who need attention and not enough nurses to adequately provide round-the-clock care for those whose conditions warrant it. Infirmaries in some older jails resemble Civil War facilities.

Privatization of prison medical services (with corporations such as the Correctional Medical Services trying to save money at every turn) and laws that call for co-payments that discourage prisoners from seeking medical care have made a bad situation worse. These developments have potentially disastrous consequences not only for individual prisoners but, from a public health perspective, for the entire class of prisoners, who may be unnecessarily exposed to serious contagious diseases, as well as the communities to which they will return.

With the large number of mentally ill who are incarcerated, budgetary decisions that lead to cutbacks in the provision of adequate mental health treatment can be particularly disastrous. As the result of a state hiring freeze in the early 1990s, Bayside State Prison (N.J.) was left with one unlicensed psychologist (and a psychiatrist borrowed from another prison facility to handle emergencies) to serve 1,500 prisoners. It was during this time that a previously diagnosed schizophrenic prisoner told the psychologist that he was hearing voices telling him to escape. With individual psychiatric treatment and group therapy no longer available at the prison, the overworked psychologist turned him over to the disciplinary system, and he was found guilty of attempting to escape and placed in solitary for six months. Not surprisingly, his mental condition deteriorated still further, and he remained psychotic when he was released from prison soon after his return to the general prison population.[90]

Although the decision to make sufficient resources available lies with policy makers inside and outside the prison system, responsibility for inadequate health care must also lie with correctional health care professionals. Medical health professionals cannot accept responsibility for the health care of prisoners if they are not provided with resources adequate to enable them to discharge that responsibility. The final judgment about what professionals need in order to do their work must be a professional judgment. To accept less is unethical and should have professional consequences.

Failure to Protect

Overcrowding is inevitably accompanied by a raised ratio of prisoners to staff, leading to a cutback in programs and services and to a rise in the level of violence. Failure to protect prisoners from violence by guards or other prisoners is an inevitable consequence of overcrowding, understaffing and/ or underfunding.

Elimination or Reduction of Visits and Other Programs

This is frequently seen as an easy way to reduce the cost of corrections, by cutting staff overtime, even though these programs are not the cause of the spiraling overtime costs. In New Jersey, for example, the projected 1999 overtime costs at state prisons were $72 million, $20 million more than was budgeted. Some $84 million was spent in overtime in 1998, largely because of round-the-clock prison lockdowns at two state prisons. Bowing to pressure from the new commissioner of corrections, who had promised the state legislature to rein in overtime costs, every New Jersey state prison superintendent reduced the visiting program, one eliminating all daytime weekend visits. In 1997, overtime was cut by ending visits on Thanksgiving, Christmas, and New Year's Day.

Cutbacks in programs, such as higher education, which was eliminated in New Jersey in 1994, are nonsensical from any perspective other than that of preserving custody positions.

Co-payments and Surcharges

Although it is hard to oppose society's desire to make convicts share the cost of their incarceration, charging pretrial detainees, who are guilty only of not having enough money to pay their bail, for medical services or room and board is abusive. Furthermore, prisoners will soon be paroled with huge debts for such prison services as rent, medical care, and legal copying, making their reintegration into society even more problematic. Contracts with telephone companies that set exorbitant rates for collect calls by prisoners are an accepted way to bring revenue to the departments of corrections or other state agencies.

Use of Isolation Units to Cage Prisoners

Caged isolation for up to twenty-three hours a day, with almost no contact with other human beings, is becoming increasingly common. There are two types of isolation units: (1) disciplinary lockup, to which people are sentenced for finite periods for rule violations and (2) control units, considered nonpunitive administrative units, in which people are placed for open-ended periods of time, often with vague or no exit criteria.

Although there are obviously valid security concerns at stake, the inevitable subjectivity[91] involved in decisions to place more and more prisoners, overwhelmingly black and Latino, in administrative control units lends itself to abuse.[92] The subjectivity can originate with the line officer, and be directed against an individual prisoner, or from Internal Affairs or prison administrators, and be directed against whole groups of prisoners. The decision to rely increasingly upon such lockup units in order to run the prison clearly comes from the top.

The use of confidential informants and confidential information is routine in hearings for placement in administrative control units, as well as disciplinary hearings. Except in the most extreme cases, courts have refused to order disclosure of the identity or even the statements of confidential informants.

There is an inherent potential for abuse when reliance is placed on hearsay statements by informants without guarantees of reliability. Since courts have often held that the prisoner need not be informed even of the dates and details of the alleged acts lest it expose the informant's identity, there is typically no way for the prisoner to defend himself against the conclusory allegations. In August 1990, for example, in the wake of an attack on officers in the yard of New Jersey State Prison, approximately ninety prisoners with

African names were all placed in the Management Control Unit (MCU) as members of a supposed revolutionary prison organization, the African National Ujamaa (ANU). Each of them received the exact same Special Report, stating that a confidential informant reported him as being a member of the ANU, whose aim was to murder officers and wreak havoc throughout the entire New Jersey prison system. No dates, no names, no specifics were given. How does one possibly defend oneself against allegations like that?

The courts have never offered much oversight in this area of prison life, deferring instead to the real or imagined security concerns of administrators.[93] One of the very few successful suits in this area, *Chavis v. Holvey*,[94] challenged New Jersey's MCU, in which politically conscious and articulate prison leaders, over 98 percent of whom were black, had been confined for up to twelve years. The New Jersey prisoners argued successfully that their placement was racially discriminatory, in that white prisoners with similar records had not been placed there. After years of solitary confinement, many MCU residents are now being released as a result of a review of their placement by a court-appointed special master, and the DOC has agreed to pay the sum of $17.50 per day to each prisoner found to have been wrongfully confined. However, soon after that victory, the DOC opened a new and much larger control unit to confine alleged gang members,[95] who, once again, are overwhelmingly black and Latino.

Housed alone for long periods of time, prisoners in isolation are often driven crazy. Charles Dickens said of solitary confinement: "I hold this slow and daily tampering with the mysteries of the brain to be immeasurably worse than any torture of the body. . . . [I]ts ghastly signs are not so palpable to the eye . . . and it extorts few cries that human ears can hear; therefore I the more denounce it as a secret punishment which slumbering humanity is not roused up to stay."[96] Celled together, prisoners in isolation cells often become violent. In one twenty-five-month period, Pelican Bay Prison in California reported three cellmate slayings in its Special Housing Unit.[97]

When mentally ill prisoners are placed in isolation, their mental state deteriorates further, and they are often taunted and tormented by staff. New Jersey's Office of Inmate Advocacy reported on one prisoner housed in disciplinary lockup who was forced to get on all fours and bark like a dog for cigarettes. The successful class action challenge to such practices, *C.F. v. Fauver*,[98] resulted in an agreement by the New Jersey DOC to make a major financial commitment to the mental health screening and care of mentally ill prisoners caught up in the disciplinary process.[99]

Prisoner Abuse of Officers

In his chapter in this volume, Kevin Wright states that individuals "who end up in prisons have demonstrated a proclivity for using violence and disrespecting the rights of others and the use of violence. Incarceration enhances this tendency, and many prisoners therefore resist their keepers. Some lie and manipulate, verbally and physically attack staff, disobey the rules, insult, and even throw feces at staff."[100] Although I am cognizant of the fact that prison abuse is not a one-way street and that all sorts of indignities are heaped upon staff, as an advocate of prisoners' rights, I am less familiar with and unable to analyze these largely intentional, but often irrational acts, which are arguably caused by feelings of total powerlessness.

Conclusion

At its best, judicial intervention limited prison abuse, but it never provided sufficient principled guidance or adequate means of enforcement to prevent such abuse. Indeed, it could not. It is within the context of endemic and systemic abuse that external oversight becomes the key predictor of the extent of prison abuse. Thus, it is no coincidence that as judicial oversight over prisons has been limited in recent years, we have witnessed an increase in the level of abuse. Ninety years ago, in *Chambers v. Baltimore & Ohio Railroad*,[101] the Supreme Court concluded that "the right to sue and defend in the Courts is the alternative of force." With the limiting of federal judicial oversight of prisoners' rights to take their grievances to court, prisoners are left with few alternatives for seeking redress from the exercise of what is often totally arbitrary authority. Twenty-eight years after Attica, riots and rebellions are no longer front-page news; they are routine.[102] In 1999 alone, there were significant disturbances in prisons in eight states, including New York, where prisoners in Sing Sing and Green Haven spent the two weeks before the Attica settlement locked in their cells for twenty-four hours a day, as prison officials reacted to a nonviolent demonstration of collective distress with parole inaction. The prisoners had worn only prison clothing for several days and had remained silent outside their cells.[103]

External oversight of what occurs behind our prisons' walls has come from sources other than our courts. As the courthouse doors have closed to prisoners, segments of civil society, including academics, leaders in the communities from which prisoners come and to which they will return, and families and friends of those incarcerated, are attempting to exert a greater impact upon what goes on behind the walls.[104] Human rights organizations, such as Amnesty International and Human Rights Watch, have launched investigations into brutality and abuse in American prisons and are demanding that prisons in the United States conform to international human rights norms. Now that prisoners in the United States have lost many of their civil rights, or at least the means of enforcing those rights, protection of their universal human rights is of vital importance.[105] Every year the Human Rights Committee of the United Nations reviews complaints brought before it and finds that some parties have violated the 1976 International Covenant on Civil and Political Rights by allowing, among other things, ill-treatment of prisoners and inhumane prison conditions. Article 53 of the Covenant protects such rights as the right to life, liberty, and security of person and prohibits torture, slavery, and forced labor. Among the remedies imposed are compensation and commutation of sentence. (HRC Communication No. 750/1997). To be reviewed, however, complaints must come from citizens of states that are parties to the Optional Protocol to the Covenant. To date the United States is not one of those states.

However, if we remain unable to eliminate what we all agree is ethically unacceptable behavior, then it is time to reevaluate the prison system as we know it.

Notes

1. In the United States, for instance, organizations such as the American Friends Service Committee, the American Civil Liberties Union, Human Rights Watch, and Amnesty International have all attempted, sometimes with success, to influence policy and practice regarding prisoners' rights.

2. The phrase was used by the Supreme Court of Virginia one hundred years ago, in *Ruffin v. Commonwealth*, 62 Va. 790 (1871). That court went on to hold that "[t]he bill of rights is a declaration of general principles to govern a society of freemen, and not of convicted felons and men civilly dead."

3. The Thirteenth Amendment provides: "Neither slavery nor involuntary servitude, except as punishment for crime whereof the party shall have been duly convicted, shall exist in the United States."

4. According to Chief Justice Warren: "The Amendment must draw its meaning from the evolving standards of decency that mark the progress of a maturing society." *Trop v. Dulles*, 356 U.S. 86 (1958).

5. Another factor that figured in the timing of the courts' involvement in our nation's prisons was their growing willingness, after *Brown v. Board of Education*, 349 U.S. 294 (1955), to grant broad injunctive relief against various public institutions.

6. *Wolff v. McDonnell*, 418 U.S. 539, 555–56 (1974).

7. The Eighth Amendment does not apply to pretrial detainees, but the Due Process Clauses of the Fifth and Fourteenth Amendment have been held to prohibit conditions that amount to "punishment" for persons who have not been convicted.

8. The Arkansas prison system was the first to come under federal judicial scrutiny. Quickly prohibited were the long-standing practices of whipping prisoners with large leather straps and using the "Tucker Telephone" to administer electric shocks to prisoners' bodies. On appeal, the Eighth Circuit prohibited all forms of corporal punishment. See *Talley v. Stephens*, 247 F. Supp. 683, 689 (E.D. Ark. 1969), and *Jackson v. Bishop*, 268 F. Supp. 804, 815 (E.D. Ark. 1967), *vacated*, 404 F. 2d 571 (8th Cir. 1968).

9. The Alabama prisoner classification system was the first to be held unconstitutional after a twenty-year-old prisoner, with the mind of a five year old, was

assigned to the maximum-security general population where security was so inadequate that he was raped by a group of fellow prisoners on his first night and practically strangled by two others on the second night. *Pugh v. Locke*, 406 F. Supp. 318 (M.D. Ala. 1976).

10. In 1970, a district court in Arkansas was the first to hold that "confinement within a given institution may amount to a cruel and unusual punishment prohibited by the Constitution where the confinement is characterized by conditions and practices so base as to be shocking to the conscience of reasonably civilized people." *Holt v. Sarver*, 309 F. Supp. 362 (E.D. Ark. 1970). In 1978, the Supreme Court for the first time directly addressed the relationship between the Eighth Amendment and prison conditions of confinement and completely upheld the challenged aspects of the district court's order, that is, its use of broad injunctive remedies.

11. The importance of prisoners being able to bring cases alleging cruel and unusual conditions of confinement to federal courts cannot be emphasized too strongly, as the federal courts cannot act until there is a case or controversy before them.

12. This terror was recounted in films such as *Murder One*, the story of Alcatraz's dungeons and the people who were held there for years without any contact with the outside world, and *Brubeck*, about Angola State Prison and the bodies of prisoners buried beneath its walls.

13. In *Holt v. Sarver*, 309 F. Supp. 362 (E.D. Ark. 1970), which would become the paradigm for all other prison conditions cases, prisoners described the system of security, called the "trusty system," which gave certain prisoners, designated trusty guards, the power of life and death over other prisoners. In one instance, a trusty guard fired his rifle into a crowded barracks because the prisoners would not turn off the television when asked.

14. It should be noted that in 1991 the Supreme Court replaced the totality of conditions standard, whereby the Court asked whether the conditions of confinement "alone or in combination . . . deprive inmates of the minimal civilized measure of life's necessities," *Rhodes v. Chapman*, 452 U.S. 337, 347 (1981), with a more exacting one requiring that conditions "have a mutually enforcing effect that produces the deprivation of a single, identifiable human need such as food, warmth, or exercise" before they constitute cruel and unusual punishment. *Wilson v. Seiter*, 501 U.S. 294, 111 S. Ct. 2321, 2327 (1991).

15. Staff-prisoner ratios were established; meaningful classification systems were imposed; limits were placed on the length of time a prisoner could spend in isolation; food, medical, and dental services were overhauled; repairs to ancient facilities were ordered; and caps were placed on the prisoner population, or minimum requirements set out for the amount of space to be allotted to each prisoner. See, for example, *Ruiz v. Estelle*, 679 F. 2d 1115 (5th Cir. 1982).

16. *Wilson v. Seiter*, 501 U.S. 294 (1991), dealing with prison conditions; *Hudson v. McMillian*, 503 U.S. 1, 112 S. Ct. 995 (1992), which involved prison brutality; *Helling v. McKinney*, 509 U.S. 25, 113 S. Ct. 2475 (1993), a second-hand smoking case; and *Farmer v. Brennan*, 511 U.S. 825, 114 S. Ct. 1970 (1994), involving the rape of a prisoner and the standard of proof of notice to prison officials.

17. *Rhodes v. Chapman*, 452 U.S. 337, 354 (1981) (Brennan, J., concurring).

18. 441 U.S. 520, 547–48 (1979).

19. In a more recent attempt to limit the parameters of federal court review of prison conditions, the Supreme Court added a new requirement for establishing an

Eighth Amendment claim, that is, that prison officials acted with culpable intent ("deliberate indifference") in permitting such conditions to exist. *Wilson v. Seiter,* 501 U.S. 294 (1991).

20. This point was not clearly articulated in an earlier draft of this chapter. As a result, it was possible to misunderstand my position, as William Heffernan did in his response, as an argument for judicial oversight as the solution to the problem of prison abuse, rather than as an indictment of the prison system itself—albeit advocating more extensive court intervention to prevent a return to conditions of the past. To Heffernan's question whether I believe that civil rights litigation, brought either by pro se prisoner litigants or by public interest lawyers, can have a dramatically beneficial effect on correctional institutions, my response is "yes." However, I agree with Heffernan that litigation will never eliminate prison abuse, nor fundamentally change the nature of incarceration. I submit, however, that his own solution, namely, well-designed administrative schemes, will be even less effective at preventing systemic prison abuse.

21. Title VIII of the Omnibus Consolidated Recissions and Appropriations Act of 1996, Pub. L. No. 104–134, 110 Stat. 1321 (April 26, 1996).

22. Even during the "best of times," fewer than 2 percent of federal petitions filed by prisoners were decided in their favor. See Bureau of Justice Statistics, *Prisoner Petitions in Federal Courts 1980–1996* (October 1997).

23. Settlement agreements or consent orders, by their very nature, are approved without findings by the court, in order to save both sides the time and expense of long trials. By eliminating any possibility of settlement, the PLRA forces the parties in all future prison conditions cases into costly litigation and thus lessens the likelihood that such litigation will be filed.

24. This despite the fact that, as all sides in prison litigation are well aware, it takes far longer than two years for unconstitutional conditions to be remedied.

25. John Sullivan, "States and Cities Removing Prisons from Courts' Grip," *New York Times,* January 30, 2000, 1-1.

26. See, for example, New Jersey's version, *N.J.S.A.* 30-11.

27. *Legal Aid Society of Hawaii v. Legal Services Corp.,* 145 F. 3d 1017 (9th Cir. 1998).

28. 518 U.S. 343, 116 S. Ct. 2174 (1996).

29. *Bounds v. Smith,* 430 U.S. 817 (1977).

30. For example, a prisoner now must allege that her meritorious litigation could not be filed, was dismissed, or was otherwise negatively impacted because she could not get to the law library to find proper forms or case law. The mere fact that she could not get to the law library or obtain legal assistance (even if she is illiterate or non-English speaking) is no longer sufficient.

31. 116 S. Ct. at 2182 (1996).

32. Two other external factors have combined with the limitations on prisoner access to the courts to impact negatively upon prisoner-staff relations: (1) the huge influx of prisoners within last twenty years has seriously overburdened the system and necessitated the hiring of young, inexperienced officers and (2) the growing acceptance of social Darwinism—denigration of compassion—which has caused people to turn their backs on all groups at the bottom, including the homeless, welfare mothers, and prisoners.

33. Denial of adequate medical care, for instance, could fall into all three categories.

34. Responsibility is clearly separate and distinguishable from legal liability.

35. This type of litigation does not generally result in the courts' issuing detailed injunctions concerning the minutiae of prison administration; compare Heffernan's preoccupation with this concern in his response.

36. Such litigation will surely become less frequent in the future, as federal courts of appeal have begun holding that excessive force is a "prison condition," and thus, under the PLRA, a prisoner must first exhaust all administrative remedies before bringing a civil rights action alleging guards' intentional acts of violence. See, for example, *Booth v. Churner*, 2000 WL 251627 (3d Cir. 2000).

37. *Madrid v. Gomez*, 940 F. Supp. 247 (N.D. Calif. 1996), the Pelican Bay Segregated Housing Unit litigation. The legal standard for brutality is whether the force was "applied in a good faith effort to maintain or restore discipline, or whether it was applied maliciously and sadistically for the very purpose of causing harm." See *Hudson v. McMillian*, 503 U.S. 1 (1992); *Whitley v. Albers*, 475 U.S. 312 (1986).

38. 503 U.S. 1 (1992).

39. *Estate of Davis v. Delo*, 115 F. 3d 1388, 1395 (8th Cir. 1997). The officer had argued he was entitled to qualified immunity.

40. Such was the case in *Hudson v. McMillian*, 503 U.S. 1 (1992).

41. *White v. Fauver*, 19 F. Supp. 2d 305 (D. N.J. 1998).

42. A SWAT-like team of corrections officers specially chosen from prisons throughout the state and trained in paramilitary operations.

43. The assistant superintendent asked one investigator how she could be certain that the many injuries had not been inflicted by other prisoners.

44. *Hahne v. Ziolkowski*, Civil Action No. 95-614 (D. N.J., DRD), resulted in a settlement with Sussex County jail officials, including a total payment of $373,000 to plaintiffs and injunctive relief, including installation of video surveillance cameras throughout the jail.

45. The $12 million settlement just awarded the Attica prisoners and their attorneys is the result of a bloodbath that cost the lives of thirty-two prisoners and eleven corrections officer hostages and injured hundreds. Yet the responsibility of Governor Rockefeller and other top state and prison officials has been ignored. Recently, the American Correctional Association (ACA) published a purportedly definitive chronicle of America's prison system. Of Attica, the ACA says only that "the riot cost the lives" of corrections officers and prisoners, as if no one pulled the triggers, there was no chain of command leading up to the governor, and no vengeance-seeking guards who forced prisoners to crawl naked over broken glass.

46. According to the deposition filed in federal district court by Lt. Ray McWhorter, a riot squad lieutenant at the prison, Commissioner Wayne Garner watched as the prisoners were punched, kicked, and stomped until blood streaked the walls. Later, Garner applauded the guards at a celebratory chicken dinner. "Everybody was high-fiving and shaking hands and congratulating each other and patting each other on the back and bragging about how much butt you kicked," stated Lt. McWhorter. See Rick Bragg, "Prison Chief Encouraged Brutality, Witnesses Report," *New York Times*, July 30, 1997, A12.

47. Stun guns are nonlethal electroshock weapons used to subdue a person by applying high voltage pulses to his/her muscles, causing instant fatigue, weakness, loss of balance, and disorientation. See Amnesty International, *Raise the Roof* (USA's Legislative Update), March 1999, which details how these weapons are sometimes

used to gain compliance from passively resisting prisoners or even prisoners already restrained.

48. Now called *C.F. v. Terhune*, Civil Action No. 96-1840 (D. N.J., AET).

49. Martha Mendoza, "Civil Rights Complaints Only Rarely Make It Past US Attorneys," *Star Ledger*, March 28, 1999, section 1, 45.

50. Mendoza, "Civil Rights Complaints Only Rarely Make It," 45.

51. Here I concentrate on the sexual abuse of female prisoners. But the harassment and sexual abuse of homosexual prisoners is also prevalent. See, for example, *Farmer v. Brennan*, 511 U.S. 825 (1994).

52. Courts have sometimes refused to intervene in sexual harassment cases, holding that while serious sexual abuse of a prisoner by a guard violates contemporary standards of decency, "simple" unwarranted touching and sexual harassment are not sufficient to constitute an Eighth Amendment violation. See, for example, *Boddie v. Schneider*, 105 F. 3d 857, 861 (2d Cir. 1997).

53. Given the power imbalance between prisoners and guards and the inability of prisoners to escape from abusive situations, genuinely consensual sex is extremely rare.

54. The State of Washington paid $110,000 in 1996 to one former female prisoner who was raped and impregnated by a guard who had previously been found to have sexually assaulted other women prisoners, yet remained on the job.

55. The report is entitled *All Too Familiar: Sexual Abuse of Women in U.S. State Prisons.* Another HRW report, *Nowhere to Hide: Retaliation against Women in Michigan State Prisons,* charges that Michigan prison officials have not stopped guards and staff from committing acts of sexual assault and abuse against female prisoners and, moreover, that because of reprisals against women who report abuses, the conditions in which women prisoners are held continue to be brutal and are getting worse.

56. This abuse could fall within the category of failure to protect.

57. A $500,000 settlement terminated the litigation in *Lucas, Mercadel and Douthit v. White*, Civil Action No. 96-2905 (N.D. Ca. 1998).

58. The PLRA's requirement that a prisoner prove physical injury in order to raise emotional or mental distress claims will further limit future litigation in this area.

59. *Valentine v. Fauver*, Docket No. A-2139-90T5 (N.J. App.Div. 1991).

60. Several months later, after many had already been sanctioned, the DOC belatedly complied with its obligation to publish proposed rule changes. See *N.J.A.C.* 10A:5–6.1 et seq.

61. All that is required in terms of due process is notice, a hearing, and written statement of the evidence that the decision is based on and the reasons for the decision taken. *Wolff v. McDonnell*, 418 U.S. 539, 556 (1974).

62. *See Heck v. Humphrey*, 512 U.S. 477, 487 (1994) (prisoner's claim is not cognizable under § 1983, the civil rights statute, if a judgment in favor of the plaintiff would necessarily imply the invalidity of his conviction); and *Edwards v. Balisok*, 520 U.S. 641, 117 S. Ct. 1584 (1977).

63. The litigation, *Camprubi-Soms v. Untig*, Civil Action No. 92-3334 (D. N.J., HAA), resulted in a settlement of $75,000 in favor of the plaintiff.

64. *Ortiz v. Fleming, et al.*, Civil Action No. 91-417 (D. N.J., MLP).

65. *See Farmer v. Brennan*, 511 U.S. 825 (1994), the Supreme Court's decision establishing the standard in this area.

66. *Sholomo David v. Blevins, et al.*, Docket No. L-1414-94, Superior Court of New Jersey, Essex County.

67. *Brown v. Crocea*, 967 F. Supp. 101 (S.D. N.Y. 1997).

68. This complaint is raised particularly by Islamic prisoners of both sexes.

69 Civil Action No. 88-786 (D. N.J., GEB). The decree was later codified by regulation, namely, *N.J.A.C.* 10A:3–5.7(d), (e).

70. The hearing took place during the appeal of the prisoner's disciplinary conviction for incitement to riot, an appeal that eventually was resolved in the prisoner's favor. *Valentine v. Fauver*, Docket No. A-2139-90T5 (N.J. App. Div. 1991).

71. Charles Holman, administrator of the Prisoners Self Help Legal Clinic, Newark, New Jersey.

72. Testimony was taken from this woman as part of class action litigation in *Camden County Jail Inmates v. Parker*, 123 F.R.D. 490 (D. N.J. 1988).

73. *Ingalls v. Florio*, 968 F. Supp. 193 (D. N.J. 1997).

74. *White v. Napoleon*, Civil Action No. 88-0497 (D. N.J., JBS). After years of malpractice and prisoner complaints, Dr. Napoleon, who worked at both Bayside State Prison and the Cumberland County Jail, had his license to practice revoked by the State of New Jersey in 1997.

75. *Rouse v. Plantier*, 987 F. Supp. 302 (D. N.J. 1997).

76. *Torres v. Neubert*, Civil Action No. 95-3435 (D. N.J., MLC).

77. Although the courts have held that prison officials are under a legal duty to protect prisoners from assaults by other prisoners, to prove a constitutional violation, prisoners must show that officials displayed "deliberate indifference," "gross negligence," or "reckless disregard" for their safety. "Mere negligence," defined as failure to exercise reasonable care, does not make them civilly liable.

78. An example would be if, despite numerous assaults occurring in the gym, prison officials fail to assign a guard to the gym when it is open to use by prisoners.

79. The PLRA's solution is to require the exhaustion of all administrative remedies, whether or not they can provide the prisoner-plaintiff with the desired relief. According to most circuit courts of appeal, there is no "futility" exception. See, for example, *Nyhuis v. Reno*, 2000 WL 157531 (3d Cir. 2000).

80. The solution of the Prison Litigation Reform Act was to close the courthouse doors to what was perceived as frivolous litigation, leaving the prisoner with absolutely no avenue to redress such grievances.

81. The prison claimed that its fax machine had not been working for a week. Apparently, it had not occurred to anyone that the paperwork could be mailed.

82. Prison conditions are violative of prisoners' constitutional rights if they "shock the conscience." *Rhodes v. Chapman*, 452 U.S. 337 (1981). Much of this pre-PLRA case law was based on what the Court called "the evolving standards of decency that mark the progress of a maturing society."

83. Overcrowding and its consequences have been the main concern of most prisoner rights agencies, which filed numerous class actions, with the possibility of large attorneys' fees. Only such agencies had the resources to engage in this type of protracted litigation and produce the kind of detailed injunctions that so concern Heffernan. Cf. his response in this volume, 105–12.

84. *Rhodes v. Chapman*, 452 U.S. 337, 347 (1981).

85. 123 F.R.D. 490 (D. N.J. 1988). The challenged conditions included four to six inmates confined in a cell built to house one or two persons, with at least two forced

to sleep on the floor, either under a cellmate's bed or beside the cell toilet.

86. *Jones v. City and County of San Francisco*, 976 F. Supp. 896 (N.D. Cal. 1997).

87. The National Prison Project of the ACLU Foundation, *Status Report: The Courts and Prisons* (January 1, 1990). In other states, such as New Jersey, whose state system was not the subject of a court order, the overflow of state prisoners was transferred to the county jails, which then became overcrowded and subsequently came under court supervision.

Although litigation resulting in detailed injunctions is a major concern of Heffernan, most prison litigation is not of this variety. It is far more limited and is initiated by or on behalf of individual prisoners seeking to implement their constitutional rights, to limit abuse, and redress grievances. Thus, the issue of the optimality of judicial oversight via detailed injunctions is not my focus.

88. *Wilson v. Seiter*, 501 U.S. 294 (1991).

89. *Newman v. Alabama*, 349 F. Supp. 278, 285 (M.D. Ala. 1972).

90. See *Torres v. Neubert*, Civil Action No. 95-3435 (D. N.J., MLC).

91. The almost meaningless standard for placement is "some evidence" that the individual poses a threat to the safety of others, of damage to property, or of interrupting the operation of a correctional facility. In New Jersey, the criteria for determining the appropriateness of such placement include "evidence of an attitude which indicates an unwillingness to follow rules and obey orders." See, e.g., *N.J.A.C.* 10A:5–2.4.

92. Involuntary interstate transfer is another abusive way in which political and/or activist prison leaders and prison paralegals are removed from their base of support without much process, a result of the subjective discretion of prison officials. This occurred in New Jersey when three leaders of the African National Ujamaa, which had functioned openly in New Jersey State Prison, were transferred to states such as New Mexico and Utah, after it was alleged that the organization had orchestrated an attack on officers in 1990, though none of the three was ever accused of participating in the attack. For the legal basis of this practice, see the Supreme Court decision in *Crawford-El v. Britton, et al.*, 523 U.S. 574, 118 S. Ct. 1584 (1998).

93. The Supreme Court has held that there is no constitutionally based liberty interest in remaining in the general prison population and out of administrative segregation, even though it assumed that conditions were about the same in administrative and disciplinary segregation. The Court stated that "administrative segregation is the sort of confinement that inmates should reasonably anticipate receiving at some point in their incarceration," and held that an informal non-adversarial evidentiary review is all that is necessary. *Hewitt v. Helms*, 459 U.S. 460, 103 S. Ct. 864, 870, 874 (1983).

94. Civ. No. 91-3884 (D. N.J., AET), subsequently entitled *Lumumba v. Holvey*.

95. The Security Threat Group Management Unit, the 300-plus bed unit at New Jersey's Northern State Prison. Again, the designation of what groups and individuals present a security threat is almost totally subjective and is made by Internal Affairs, which overwhelmingly comprises white males. In the company of an administrative law judge, in 1992 I visited the IA office in Trenton State Prison, where we observed a large confederate flag prominently displayed on the wall.

96. American Friends Service Committee, *Struggle for Justice* (1971) (quoting Charles Dickens, *Pictures from Italy and American Notes* [London, 1867], 283).

97. *Sacramento Bee,* December 1998.

98. Civil Action No. 96-1840 (D. N.J, AET).

99. That litigation was filed by the Office of Inmate Advocacy, which has since been defunded and disbanded, leaving no agency in the state with the resources to litigate similar actions.

100. I disagree, however, with Wright's implication that such prisoner behavior is a major factor in causing prison staff to drift toward disrespect for and abuse of prisoners. See his "Management-Staff Relations: Issues in Leadership, Ethics, and Values," in this volume, 214–15.

101. 207 U.S. 142, 148 (1907).

102. Little is known about these rebellions because prison authorities, learning perhaps from the Attica experience, now keep the media away. In Virginia, California, and other states, reporters are now banned from routine interviews with prisoners.

103. "Despite Inmate Strike Threat, No Disruptions," *New York Times,* January 4, 2000, B5; and "Restrictions Are Lifted at Two Prisons," *New York Times,* January 14, 2000, B5.

104. Conferences such as Critical Resistance at the University of California–Berkeley and Race-ing Justice at Columbia University and the Boycott Crime Campaign in Newark, New Jersey, are prime examples of this recent development.

105. Article 5 of the Universal Declaration of Human Rights states: "No one shall be subjected to torture or to cruel, inhuman or degrading treatment or punishment."

Response to Chapter 3

Correctional Ethics and the Courts

William C. Heffernan

Two different themes are discernible in Audrey Bomse's thought-provoking chapter on prison abuse. First, the chapter contains a fairly detailed catalogue of abuses of power by officials in American prisons. Second, it indirectly addresses legislative issues by bemoaning passage of the Prison Litigation Reform Act of 1996 (PRLA), suggesting that this legislation will bring us "back to the past" as far as judicial oversight of corrections is concerned.[1] These two themes can be harmonized. In criticizing PLRA's adoption, Bomse can be understood to argue for strong judicial oversight of prisons; such oversight, she can be understood to say, is essential to eliminating abuses of power by correctional officials. Harmonizing the themes does not, however, eliminate the questions that can be asked about them. The abuses Bomse catalogues occurred in pre-PRLA days, so why, one wonders, was the more extensive judicial oversight of those times not sufficient to prevent them? And if substantial judicial oversight is so important, then should not Bomse provide a standard by which to assess its value? Judicial oversight of school officials may be worthwhile, but many reasonable people are worried that court rulings in the area of school discipline have undercut the authority of school officials. Surely similar concerns are possible in the context of corrections. At the very least, one would like Bomse to explain what level of oversight is optimal and why her desired level would not undercut security concerns in prisons.

In this response, I address each of the themes in Bomse's chapter. I begin by considering the issue of judicial oversight, an issue on which Bomse and I may disagree. I then turn to the catalogue of abuses she mentions. I note here why I agree with her and then consider the significance of our agreement.

Judicial Oversight of Corrections

Where does Bomse stand on the question of judicial oversight of law enforcement? Does she believe that tort litigation, brought either by prisoners pro se or by public interest lawyers can have a dramatically beneficial effect on correctional institutions? Does she think that the issuance of detailed injunctions will substantially alter prison life? After reading her chapter with some care, I think, though I am not sure, I know her answer to these questions. I suspect she believes that tort lawyers can make a substantial difference; I also suspect that she favors detailed injunctions for corrections facilities. Her chapter is so much a report from the trenches, however, that I am not sure of her position on general questions of strategy. In particular, I am not sure what her position is on the issue of optimality. Does she believe that more litigation is always better? Or does she think that there is an optimal level of litigation beyond which the benefits it generates are exceeded by its costs? It seems to me that anyone writing in this area must consider this optimality issue. I would like to hear Bomse's thoughts on it.

Let me illustrate the importance of the optimality question by reviewing a 1996 Supreme Court decision, *Lewis v. Casey*,[2] that Bomse deplores. In *Lewis*, the Court reviewed an injunction issued by a federal trial judge concerning the library facilities for inmates operated by the Arizona Department of Corrections. Finding the facilities constitutionally inadequate, the judge issued a detailed injunction, specifying, among other things, "the times that [prison] libraries were to be kept open, the number of hours of library use to which each inmate was entitled (10 per week), the minimal education requirements for prison librarians (a library science degree, law degree, or paralegal degree), [and] the content of a videotaped legal-research course for inmates."[3] In all, the injunctive decree extended over twenty-five pages. In examining it, we can see that the judge—operating through a special master—had become involved in the minutiae of prison administration. Looking beyond *Lewis*, one cannot help but note that it portends the possibility of judicial micromanagement of large sections of prison life. Indeed, just as *Roe v. Wade*[4] gave constitutional standing to the legislative program of Planned Parenthood of America, *Lewis* holds out the possibility of giving constitutional standing to the administrative program of the American Correctional Association.

I am not advancing a per se argument against prison injunctions. I am not even arguing against some kind of injunctive intervention in a case such as *Lewis*. Rather, I am simply pointing to the extraordinarily detailed injunction in *Lewis* to suggest that the concept of optimality is essential when thinking about prison litigation, just as it is essential when thinking about a strategy to reform schools or the police. And, of course, I am suggesting something else as well. I am suggesting that, however detailed the scope of injunctive relief, however penetrating the barrage of tort litigation, legal reforms are unlikely to eliminate many abuses in a prison system. Bomse's catalogue of abuses tends to support this point. Many of the abuses she mentions occurred prior to passage of PRLA. If legal and equitable remedies were unable to prevent occurrence of abuses in the pre-PRLA era, it seems reasonable to conclude that litigation alone is unlikely to be effective in this context. Is this where ethics comes in—as a need to supplement what the law cannot create with its threat of sanctions? My answer to this is "yes"—or at least "yes" as long as one is concerned with ethics in its most elementary sense, ethics without the casuistry of ethicists. I am certainly not arguing that ethicists should be hired to run training programs that will enhance the moral sensitivity of corrections officials. Rather, I think there are certain patently obvious wrongs committed by prison officials that the law may be unable to prevent but that can, perhaps, be prevented by well-designed administrative schemes. Let me expand on this argument by considering the points on which I agree with Bomse.

Points of Agreement

Bomse provides a detailed, carefully thought-out account of abuses of authority by contemporary corrections officials. I agree with her that such abuses exist. I also agree that they are serious in the sense that they are morally grave. I share, for example, her concern about the excessive use of force in prison settings. I am also worried about intentional and negligent denial of medical care to inmates. And I certainly agree that given the power possessed by corrections officers in prison settings, steps should be taken to prevent sexual exploitation of prisoners by corrections officers.

This much is easy. Now for a harder question. What is the basis for my agreement with Bomse? I do not think it is attributable to the fact that we are both lawyers; special training in the law is not needed to denounce the kind of behavior that concerns Bomse. Nor, I think, can it be said that our agreement hinges on some special expertise in moral philosophy. Unprovoked assaults on prisoners can, and should be, denounced as immoral, but no training in moral philosophy is needed for someone to reach a conclusion about their immorality. But if expert knowledge is not critical to our agreement, then what is the basis on which it rests? Is it simply that Bomse and I share broadly held intuitions about the wrongfulness of unprovoked assault, official corruption, and sexual extortion? If only the latter is needed to account for our agreement, then no appeal to expertise is needed when dealing with her cases of prison abuse. These involve patently wrongful conduct, conduct whose wrongfulness is intuitively, and immediately, obvious.

In my opinion, this latter hypothesis best accounts for my agreement with Bomse. Needless to say, there are many controverted ethical issues relevant to corrections—the legitimacy of the death penalty, for example, or the legitimacy of prison privatization. The issues Bomse raises in her chapter are not, however, among them. She raises what I shall call "easy cases" in correctional ethics—"easy" because they involve paradigmatic instances of wrongful conduct, not because they are easy to prevent. Standing in contrast to these are "hard" (or at least "harder") cases—"hard" in the sense that they cannot be classified as paradigmatically wrong and so may well be appropriate subjects for analysis by ethicists. It is helpful, I think, to consider the subject matter of correctional ethics along this hard-easy continuum, helpful in part because we can better understand the different senses in which people appeal to ethics and helpful as well because the distinction between hard and easy cases has important implications for action. I shall develop these points while discussing further the continuum between hard and easy cases.

The Continuum

My suspicion is that most members of the public, if asked about the meaning of the term "correctional ethics," would respond that it deals with clear-cut rights and wrongs in the administration of punishment. It is because of my experience with the term "police ethics" that I advance this suggestion. More than ten years ago, I co-edited a book entitled *Police Ethics: Hard Choices in Law Enforcement*.[5] The book dealt with issues such as police officers' obligations to adhere to statutes requiring full enforcement of the law, the desirable limits (if any) of police undercover activities, the moral legitimacy of affirmative action programs in police departments—in short, it dealt with police practices that generate substantial controversy among the public at large and among experts on policing. The scholars who contributed to the book seemed to enjoy the chance to take on controversial questions. However, when I mentioned to nonacademics (in particular, to police executives) that I had just published a book on police ethics, the reaction was uniform. "Oh, that's important," I was told, "you'll contribute to the fight against corruption and brutality." To nonacademics, the term "police ethics" had an obvious ring. "Ethics" refers to what is unambiguously right and wrong. The challenge, nonacademics assumed, is not to work on borderline questions about wrongfulness—rather, it is to make sure that people do not violate clear moral prohibitions in their daily conduct.

Because of my work in preparing the book, I had already learned that professional philosophers viewed the subject matter of police ethics quite differently. Trained to analyze controverted issues, philosophers contributing to the book made it clear that they had little interest in matters such as corruption and brutality—or, at least, that they had little interest in such matters unless a fine point of moral theory was at stake. The philosophers with whom I worked were quite willing to accept public funding for their work. They showed no inclination, however, to find out whether public agencies were providing financial support for work on police ethics under the mistaken assumption that this would contribute to the reduction of flagrant wrongdoing. And actually working for the reduction of such wrongdoing did not interest the philosophers at all. They thought of this as someone else's job—the job of a pastor, for example, or of an editorial writer.

As I have suggested, my agreement with Bomse is understandable in terms of this category of easy cases. I mean nothing by way of disparagement in characterizing brutality and corruption as easy cases. If there were not some easy cases—some settings that provide a starting point for reasoning about the requisites of morality in the institutions of punishment—it would be very difficult to proceed to controverted issues. I am simply drawing a contrast, then, between cases that elicit broad agreement among members of a society and cases that generate controversy among those same people. The former type of case provides a foundation for the latter since examination of it can provide principles useful for considering hard cases. Even when core principles are agreed upon, however, special skills are required when approaching such cases.

In particular, expertise in three subjects is essential when thinking about hard cases in correctional ethics. First, a commentator must be familiar with long-standing debates about the justifiability of punishment. Second, a commentator must also be acquainted with the institutional complexity of contemporary corrections—the commentator must understand the nature of prisons and jails, the function of parole and probation, the role of halfway houses, and so forth. And third, the commentator must also understand the legal rules that govern corrections.

It is these last two points that distinguish reflection on the hard cases in correctional ethics from philosophical reflection on punishment. Someone approaching controverted issues in corrections must of course have a plausible theory as to why punishment is justified; in this respect, the commentator on controverted issues in correctional ethics must be every bit as well-informed as someone who ventures into philosophical debates about justifications for punishment. But more is required of such a commentator precisely because institutional arrangements are at stake. Someone writing about correctional ethics must address not only "thin" philosophical theories concerning the justifiability of punishment but also "thick" institutional facts relevant to its administration. Indeed, the commentator must go beyond this, for one asks of the commentator a considered judgment—a criterion—for assessing institutional performance and also the performance of officials operating within the institution. I assume that this is what is at stake when one speaks of discretion in a closed setting. To speak intelligently about such discretion, one must understand the institutional arrangements, including the legal rules, under which prisons and jails operate—and one must then offer a plausible criterion for determining when these officials should exceed the minimum legal standards imposed on them and when they should not.

The Significance of the Continuum

Given the points just made, we can say that it is no coincidence that Bomse and I agree on the wrongfulness of the conduct she describes. Whatever our position on hard cases in correctional ethics, we can agree that what she describes are abuses. Had we met as strangers sitting next to one another on a long plane flight, we could have agreed that brutality and corruption in prison settings must be stopped, and we could have agreed on this even while disagreeing about matters such as the death penalty or the justness of patterns of wealth distribution in America today.

If this point is correct, then perhaps there is a moral to be drawn from it. Perhaps we should take a vow to denounce conduct of the kind Bomse describes and then hand matters over to experts on public administration to devise schemes that will minimize the kinds of evils that concern her. As far as easy cases are concerned, then, we should close up shop. Important work remains to be done—not by us, however, but by people who think carefully about the ways in which malfunctioning organizations can be set straight. What about hard cases? The case for keeping the shop seems much stronger here; disputing hard cases is just what experts in moral philosophy are trained to do. If I may, however, I would like to conclude by noting two difficulties that have to be considered when thinking about hard cases. The first has to do with the strategic value of seizing the label "ethics." Once we turn to hard cases, we must realize how important it is to avoid final conclusions about what is and is not ethical. Nothing is easier in discussions of applied ethics than to deliver a series of ad hoc remarks about a subject and to conclude with a pronouncement about what is and is not ethical. Capital punishment? Easy—that is morally wrong, or at least morally questionable. Prison privatization—morally wrong. The disproportionate incarceration of the poor and racial minorities—morally wrong as well. The ethics label comes in handy on such occasions. Attitudes, deeply felt but poorly articulated, can be converted into reproaches with the dismissive remark, "That's immoral." I am not suggesting, of course, that this will inevitably happen. I do worry, however, that it *can* happen. As a procedural matter, I suggest that this danger is best avoided through careful attention to the three prerequisites, mentioned earlier, to discussion of hard cases.

One other danger that arises with the discussion of hard cases deserves to be noted, a danger both subtler than the one just mentioned and, to my mind, even more serious. This second danger is associated with moral complacency. It may seem peculiar to raise a worry about moral complacency when ethics is the subject of discussion. Reconsideration of the distinction between easy and hard cases will make clear what I have in mind. When I finally succeeded in explaining to police executives that the subject "police ethics" was concerned with controverted issues in law enforcement, the executives began to take great pleasure in what I had said. I had just made the case, they began to think, for treating their blue collar occupation as a profession. Just as doctors face troubling choices in the course of their work, police officers face troubling ones in theirs—choices so troubling that professional philosophers must actually take the time to address them.

At first, I was pleased that I had finally made the distinction clear to police executives and pleased that the executives felt flattered by the attention. Over time, though, I began to experience misgivings. To the extent that executives felt flattered by the distinction, I realized, they were distancing themselves from the easy cases. And easy cases, I further realized, are so classified not simply because there is broad consensus about their wrongfulness, but because they involve serious harm to other people. I gradually concluded that concentration on hard cases can have a numbing effect on a target audience. In fact, I have come to the conclusion that a set of clear priorities is needed in applied ethics. As far as policing is concerned, I am not particularly interested in hard cases until I see strong evidence that a department has taken extensive steps to try to eliminate brutality and corruption. As far as corrections is concerned, I think the same point is in order. In this sense, I think Bomse's agenda is exactly right. It may be that philosophers are unwilling to discuss the easy cases she mentions, but I am skeptical about the value of discussion of hard cases when so much remains to be done about the easy ones.

Notes

1. Audrey J. Bomse, "Prison Abuse: Prisoner-Staff Relations," in this volume, 81.
2. 518 U.S. 343 (1996).
3. 518 U.S. 343, 349 (1996).

4. 410 U.S. 113 (1973).

5. William C. Heffernan and Timothy Stroup (eds.), *Police Ethics: Hard Choices in Law Enforcement* (New York: John Jay Press, 1985).

Chapter 4

Health Care in the Corrections Setting: An Ethical Analysis

Kenneth Kipnis

Ethics may have the most to learn at societal interfaces. Where differing cultural values and social practices brush up against each other in ways that force accommodation, the collision of normative systems can sometimes provide the ethical theorist with fascinating data even as it affords the ethicist-practitioner with an opportunity to participate creatively in a process of principled reconciliation. Such an interface can be found at the boundaries of medicine and corrections. For health care professionals who work in prison settings—nurses and psychologists as well as doctors—and for the corrections officers who sometimes work alongside them, there can be a sense of working at the margin. It will be the purpose of this chapter to characterize the types of normative conflict that arise for correctional health care professionals (CHCPs) and to set out some strategies for engaging them. I will, in the process, make some observations about how to understand the generic nature of these insufficiently studied ethical issues.

The Incarcerative Backdrop

Much of the appeal of *M.A.S.H.*, both the film and the television series, was in its surrealistic foregrounding of a close-knit team of devoted healers against the grim backdrop of a vast military organization, optimized to inflict death and serious injury upon an enemy. The drama, with its regular doses of black humor, drew heavily on the value conflicts inherent in that context. It was easy to appreciate why most of these well-meaning doctors and nurses were cynically alienated from military life, and why they drank.

In some ways, the social responsibilities of prison health care professionals are comparable to those of the military in wartime. Like the army, prisons do not serve to promote health care. The constituting task of penal institutions is readily grasped when we recollect that those convicted of sufficiently grave offenses are, as we say, remanded to the warden's custody. In doing so, the judicial system solemnly entrusts prison administrators to carry out the penal sentences imposed by the courts. Aside from the restrictions placed on probationers, retributive loss of liberty is the predominant form that judicial punishment takes: there are about two million persons in American jails and prisons.

Although more philosophical work needs to be done on the nature and justification of imprisonment as a form of punishment, we should not be surprised, in our society, to see retribution take the form of loss of liberty. For it is common for those reared in liberal democracies to celebrate personal freedom as the preeminent political good. Liberal democratic societies are, perhaps by definition, informed by the value that rational persons are presumed to place on liberty. So the first of John Rawls's two principles of justice reads: "each person is to have an equal right to the most basic liberty compatible with a similar liberty for others."[1] And Joel Feinberg has devoted much of his career elaborating the Millian view that, unless there are good reasons to the contrary, individuals should be at liberty to do as they choose.[2] Accordingly, if liberty is embraced as a preeminent political good, then official punishment, as a societally imposed form of hard treatment, might well take the form of imprisonment: that is, an officially imposed, systematic suspension of liberty. Not only could loss of liberty be reasonably supposed to be, broadly, undesirable enough to deter rational malefactors, but additionally, its imposition upon those convicted of serious offenses could persuade law-abiding citizens that, so retributed, crime does not pay.

Accordingly we do not take issue here with the premises that wrongdoers should be punished; that the forfeiture of liberty is, here and now, a societally appropriate punishment in many cases; and that the prison—more or less as we understand it—is an appropriate means of implementing such a punishment. So conceived, prisons are institutions in which the presumption in favor of liberty is in large measure reversed: that is, unless there are good reasons to the contrary, inmates should not be at liberty to do as they choose. So conceived, prisons exist as societally constituted institutions for the purpose of systematically and generally denying opportunities to those convicted of serious offenses.

Jurisprudentially, the prison's implementation of this inverted liberal principle has historically taken the form of judicial deference to experienced prison administrators. Adopting a hands-off policy, courts have generally given wardens broad latitude to implement institutional policies that further proper penal purposes. But these purposes—a motley agglomeration of goals, some perhaps central to the prison's mission and others more or less peripheral to it—are often controversial. Along with prison's role in implementing a retributive forfeiture of liberty, commentators have spoken of the value of rehabilitation, encouraging repentance, incapacitating convicted wrongdoers, deterring extramural crime, making available a population of tightly controlled research subjects, generating revenues through the use of a monitored labor force, promoting institutional efficiency, earning profits, reducing an excess labor force, administering suffering, and so on. Hence the need, noted earlier, for further philosophical inquiry.

But notwithstanding this variety, there is one salient fact that sharply narrows a warden's focus: prisons are, by their very nature, coercive institutions. The inmates have been arrested, their sentences have been imposed on them, and, from the moment a prisoner first hears the heavy steel doors slam shut, the elements of everyday life are palpably shut off. Accordingly, those who are remanded to the warden's custody are presumed to be (1) intent on taking their leave should the opportunity arise and (2) unenthusiastic at best about deferring to the prison's de jure authority. Thus, the rights that inmates will surely forfeit are those that must give way to the warden's responsibilities for prison security: the twin duties to prevent escape and riot. In this regard we point to the authoritarian model of management, the thick walls, the razor wire, the locked doors, the armed guards, the regimentation, and the secondary penal systems that are set up within the penal system. Philosophically, administratively, and physically, these familiar elements of the prison betoken an absence of trust.

The Mandate of the Correctional Health Care Professional

Although it is relatively easy to discern the warden's ethical situation in the context of prison life, the role responsibilities of the correctional health care professional are somewhat hazier. Notwithstanding the systematic suspension of liberty, it is useful to distinguish between two types of right that inmates can claim.[3] There are, first, what we might call residual rights that properly survive the sentence to prison. The general right to legal counsel, for example, cannot be abridged by wardens, though it is commonly contoured to comport with penal regimes. And second, there are other rights that flow from the status of being in custody: rights, for example, to food and to other living conditions that measure up to our "evolving standards of decency."

Although prison medicine has had a long but not entirely illustrious history in the United States, courts have only occasionally scrutinized the sources and scope of the duty to treat. In 1926, for example, a North Carolina court opined in *Spicer v. Williamson*: "it is but just that the public be required to care for the prisoner, who cannot, by reason of the deprivation of his liberty, care for himself."[4] However it was not until 1973 that the Supreme Court saw fit to set what one might take to be a minimum requirement. Appealing to the constitutional prohibition of cruel and unusual punishment, the Court ruled, in *Estelle v. Gamble*, that

> deliberate indifference to serious medical needs of prisoners consti-
> tutes the "unnecessary and wanton infliction of pain" . . . proscribed
> by the Eighth Amendment. This is true whether the indifference is
> manifested by prison doctors in their reponse to the prisoner's needs
> or by prison guards in intentionally denying or delaying access to
> medical care or intentionally interfering with the treatment once pre-
> scribed. Regardless of how evidenced, deliberate indifference to a
> prisoner's serious illness or injury states a cause of action under Sec.
> 1983.[5]

Thus, surprisingly and thanks to *Estelle*, convicted felons are the only population in the United States with a constitutional right to health care.

It is perhaps useful to tease apart these two quite distinct arguments for the prisoner's right to indicated medical treatment. *Estelle*—the more recent Supreme Court case—bases it on the constitutional prohibition against cruel and unusual punishment. Since "deliberate indifference" to the inmate's medical needs adds an extra and illicit measure of suffering to that which is already incident to the licit penalty of imprisonment (that is, loss of liberty), the warden (and therefore all those accountable to that office) have derivative duties to respond to evident medical requirements. It is unconstitutional cruelty to withhold needed health care. No longer merely an element of good penological practice, responsiveness to the inmate's medical requirements has evolved into a constitutionally mandated entitlement.

On the other hand, *Spicer*, the North Carolina case, derives the right from custodial obligations derived from the prisoner's societally imposed deprivation of liberty. In this context, inmates resemble children, at least jurisprudentially. Although there are differences, it is revealing to observe how the legally narrowed liberty rights of children are comparably paired with a reciprocal prohibition against parental neglect. It is, in part, because children—like inmates—are systematically denied the legal powers needed to provide for themselves, that parents and guardians—like wardens—are properly charged with a legal duty to make needed medical services available to those in their custody. In Hohfeldian terms, the constriction of the standard range of liberty-rights is tolerable, in part, because of the presence of special claim-rights. Upon emancipation or completion of a sentence, both the legal adult and the parolee enjoy an immediately enhanced liberty just when they lose their claims to bed, board, and various other necessities of life.

On either of these two jurisprudential analyses, what brings health care professionals into prison are, first, the legal requirement that prison administrators attend to the serious health needs of inmates and, second, the legal prohibition on the unlicensed practice of medicine and nursing. Legally, wardens are under a duty to provide needed health care. But—equally legally—they are generally not licensed to provide it themselves. When we add the duty to make appropriate medical and nursing services available (following *Spicer* and *Estelle*) to the fact of health care licensure, what precipitates is the warden's special obligation to retain health care professionals in the corrections setting.

Health Care in the Corrections Setting

Now, by their very nature, health care professionals are committed to putting the patient's interests first: striving above all never to harm them, treating decisionally capacitated patients only with informed consent, and scrupulously preserving patient confidences. At the root of this attentive deference, so antithetical to the prison's punitive ambience, is the understandable vulnerability that the ill generally experience when compelled to rely on health care professionals. Infirmity can force us to tell uncomfortable truths to doctors, requiring that we open ourselves in ways that, in other settings, would be embarrassing, shameful, and imprudent. This trust in the integrity of health care professionals is an indispensable element of the therapeutic alliance. It is largely because of these distinctive professional commitments (coupled with the profession's distinctive knowledge and skills) that, first, we as a society have delegated to duly licensed health care professionals the exclusive responsibility to deliver their distinctive services (unauthorized practice being a criminal offense) and, second, that the infirm are as willing as they are to seek out, to trust, and to utilize these specialists.

But although these health care providers serve the needs of the inmate population, they are nonetheless working, directly or indirectly, for prison administration. We have noted how the elements of prison administration betoken both the coercion of and the absence of trust in the inmate. Against this background, the CHCP's foundational duty to nurture the trust and confidence of the inmate/patient runs directly counter to the prevailing ethic in the institution.[6]

In systematically representing a profession's normative commitments, it is often useful to organize them according to the discrete social roles encountered in generic professional practice. Preschool teachers, for example, characteristically have professional dealings with children, parents, colleagues (including supra- and subordinates), specialists in other fields (psychologists and social workers, for example), and, occasionally, with the public. One way of conceiving of a profession's ethics is to try to specify and array the various obligations that practitioners have toward those who occupy each of these generic roles so that, in the end, the obligations are consistent with each other.

In the present context, it is a useful oversimplification to regard the responsibilities of the generic correctional health care professional as vectored toward three discrete parties. As noted earlier and as with all health care professionals, there are the familiar clinical obligations toward the inmate/patient: centrally, a duty of beneficence toward the patient within the parameters of the patient's consent. Because privacy is largely and commonly forfeited upon conviction, the CHCP's obligation of confidentiality is best seen here as derived from the duty of beneficence. A clinician who is known to reveal medical information to the detriment of patients will soon find that the resulting distrust makes it more difficult if not impossible to respond promptly and appropriately to the medical needs of inmates. A second set of obligations involves duties as an employee of the warden/employer and, derivatively, toward other correctional officers also accountable to the warden. And, finally, there is a third set of public health obligations for the well-being of the inmate population taken as a whole. Quite unlike the clinician's focus upon an autonomous patient, public health concerns may require that a doctor impose treatment for the benefit of a larger group of persons. This third perspective manifests itself in a variety of strategies devised to prevent or slow the spread of illness through a population, strategies that can sometimes pit collective interests against the interests of individuals. In the most dramatic cases—for example, an outbreak of multiple drug resistant tuberculosis in an institutionalized population—infected persons, if they refuse to cooperate, can be properly quarantined against their will.

Many of the ethical dilemmas of correctional health are understandable as conflicts arising out of these three potentially competing sets of obligations: clinical, employee, and public health. Here are four representative examples.

Case 1 illustrates a characteristic clash between clinical and employee obligations.

> 1: You are director of health services for a large correctional facility. The warden has received reliable information from an informant that a certain inmate is sequestering a gun in his rectum. The warden insists that he has probable cause to perform a search and directs you to have it carried out. The inmate will not consent to examination. Except for members of your staff, no correctional personnel are qualified to do X rays or perform body cavity searches.

Cases 2 and 3 illustrate the tension between clinical and public health obligations.

> 2: Following an outbreak of five cases of hepatitis B in one of your units, your investigation points to a prisoner tattooist as the possible source. Though it violated prison regulations, all the infected inmates had recently been tattooed. The tattooist is unwilling to cooperate, refusing to be tested for hepatitis B. Do you test him against his will? If he is a carrier, what do you do then?

> 3: Inmate Richard Wong is a diabetic who has been placed on a special diet by order of the medical staff. He has been hospitalized three times with life-threatening diabetic ketoacidosis following ingestion of candy bars obtained from the inmate canteen. The expenses generated by these unnecessary hospitalizations are forcing you to trim expenditures on other parts of your program, with detrimental results to other inmates/patients. You can initiate disciplinary procedures that will result in his loss of canteen privileges.

Case 4 illustrates a tension between public health obligations and employee responsibilities.

> 4: The encouragement and facilitation of condom usage is a standard and effective public health intervention for managing a sexually active population with HIV seroprevalence. Though condoms do not prevent disease in every instance, their usage significantly reduces the spread of the AIDS virus. Despite evidence that the transmission of HIV (and other STDs) occurs in prison, common administrative policies barring inmates from having sexual relations have been invoked to justify derivative prohibitions on the distribution of condoms to inmates. These restrictions on inexpensive public health efforts contribute to the spread of a deadly and expensive-to-treat disease as they draw heavily on the financial and staff resources of fixed-budget correctional health services. Should health care professionals distribute condoms anyway?

It is useful to distinguish between problems involving conflicts of obligation and those involving conflicts of interest. One has a conflict of obligation when, for example, one owes it to A that one do R but also owes it to B that one not do R. A surgeon, for example, who happens to be a Jehovah's Witness might be the only doctor on duty when an injured non-Witness enters the emergency room in need of an immediate blood transfusion. As a doctor, the surgeon has a clear duty to transfuse, but as a Witness, the surgeon has an equally clear obligation not to. In retrospect, the mistake was to be alone and on duty. The best advice would be scrupulously to avoid placing oneself in situations in which such a conflict could arise. Accordingly, in dealing with potential conflicts of obligation, professionals need to be, first, alert to the possibility of ethical conflict and, second, empowered to configure their responsibilities in advance so that conflicts cannot arise. All four cases can be construed as involving conflicts of obligation.

In contrast, a conflict of interest occurs when, first, the practitioner's role essentially involves some type of fidelity and, second, when some fact reasonably calls that fidelity into question. There is nothing wrong with refereeing a soccer game and nothing wrong with being a parent. But there is something wrong with refereeing a game in which one's own child is a player. While each role is legitimate, one cannot discharge both at once. For we expect parents to be partial to their own children, and that simple fact calls into question the impartiality we want to see in a referee. Given a close call, the parent/referee can be suspected of bias if he favors his child and can be suspected of bending over backward to avoid the appearance of favoritism if he does not. In medicine, fidelity to the patient involves an acknowledgment of the inmate's humanity. Doctors are not supposed to betray, coerce, or harm their patients. A responsible physician honors the duty of fidelity to the patient; this relationship is remarkable in the correctional context, and yet it is the only way to engender a therapeutic alliance, the only way to be a doctor.

Taking these cases as illustrative, what then do health care professionals owe to the inmate/patient, what do they owe to the prison population conceived as a whole, and what do they owe to their prison-administrator employers? While I do not claim to be able to pronounce the final word on this issue, let me propose the following principles as, perhaps, a place to start.

1. *Health care professionals must have the necessary resources and latitude that they need in order to perform their job.*

Correctional health care professionals have the responsibility to provide health services to inmate/patients. Since wardens are not licensed health care professionals, they cannot discharge that responsibility themselves and so they must delegate it to doctors and nurses. Additionally—and crucially important in this context—they must provide these professionals with what they need to do their job. The point that needs making here is not that prison administrators are required to provide health care professionals with everything that they need. From the perspective of professional ethics, it is rather that it is improper for professionals to accept responsibility for the health care of inmates unless they are provided with a level of resources that is adequate to discharge that responsibility. There is a difference between honestly doing one's job and maintaining an illusion of concerned attention.

In the final analysis, the judgment about what professionals need in order to do their work is a professional judgment. Nonprofessionals are typically not competent, for example, to decide what drugs should be in a clinic's formulary. Likewise, because health care professionals need the trust of their patients if they are to discharge their responsibilities to them, prison administrators may not require health care professionals to act in ways that appear to betray that trust. What doctors do to inmate/patients must be done within the framework of the doctor/patient relationship. This line of reasoning supports the second principle.

2. *Health care professionals should scrupulously avoid enlisting in or being conscripted into activities that are not required as part of health care. They must especially avoid complicity in activities that would take advantage of their professional skills to promote prison security or other penal purposes.*

A doctor or nurse is not acting as a health care professional if he or she carries out a body cavity search, conducted against the will of the inmate, for reasons that have nothing to do with the health care of that inmate. The concern here is to keep the two spheres of responsibility—security and health care—separate. Only in this way can doctors and nurses continue to be seen as independent health care professionals rather than as agents of the prison administration. Prison administrators may want to enlist health care providers into the incarcerative mission of the institution, to recruit them, so to speak, into secondary roles as security personnel. But they need to remember that success in this endeavor is likely to undermine the credibility of correctional health care professionals and, as a consequence, damage the prison's ability to discharge its responsibility for inmate health care.

It may be difficult to discern the line that separates the normal practice of medicine from illicit complicity in the punitive mission of the institution. Consider, for example, the use of physicians to pronounce death following executions. At one level, this is merely reliance upon doctors to do what they commonly do every day outside of the penal setting. But notice that when, during the course of a hospital examination and pronouncement, a physician discovers that a patient thought to be dead is, on the contrary, really alive, energetic efforts are characteristically and immediately made to save that patient's life. Contrast that health care response with what happens when a physician discovers, following a penal electrocution, that the condemned has somehow survived the electric chair. The response there is to re-electrocute until death can finally be pronounced. Because the execution is not over until the doctor says it is over, the health care professional in that context is serving as an integral part of a punitive process. Accordingly, even though it may resemble what physicians do elsewhere, wardens should not be able to rely on correctional health care professionals to carry out that task.

But just as wardens must respect the working space that health care professionals require, so too must health care professionals bear in mind the incarcerative mission of the prison. Reciprocally, doctors and nurses must remember that their work is to be carried out within procedures that ensure prison security. This leads to our third principle.

3. *While health care professionals should strive to be independent of the incarcerative function of the prison, they must defer to rules and procedures intended to further institutional security.*

Assuming that such rules and practices do not make it impossible to discharge their health care responsibilities, health care professionals need to appreciate the overriding responsibility that wardens have for prison security. Both health care professionals and prison administrators need to work together to reach a modus vivendi, coordinating the health care and incarcerative responsibilities of prisons. While health care in the corrections setting should not be compromised because of the prison administration's concern for security, the health care staff should nonetheless scrupulously respect reasonable security requirements.

Applied to case 1, these principles would suggest that prison administrators find alternate ways of dealing with the suspected firearm. Perhaps prison security could be adequately provided for if the inmate were placed in restraints and under guard in a dry room for several days. Were the inmate eventually to request medical attention, health care professionals would then be at liberty to provide it, with the procedure being protected by physician-patient confidentiality. (I assume that the procedure will be carried out in such a way as to ensure protection of the health care staff. Restraints might be used if general anaesthesia is not required.) However once the sequestered firearm comes into the possession of the health care professional, he or she would clearly be ethically prohibited, under principle 3 above, from returning it to the inmate. The health care professional could conceivably convey the gun to the warden. But because of principle 2 above, and apart from conveying the firearm to the inmate, the physician should not be asked to testify against the inmate.

At bottom, this approach depends upon the abilities of wardens and health care professionals to draw a line between, on the one hand, health care activities that respect reasonable rules that ensure prison security and, on the other hand, activities that constitute complicity by health care staff in the incarcerative mission of the prison. While the former behavior can properly be required of health care professionals, doctors and nurses should uniformly refuse, as a matter of professional ethics, to participate in the latter. Faced with these conscientious refusals, prison administrators should accede to them out of a concern for the effectiveness and professional integrity of their health care staff.

From a public health perspective, condom availability is a standard intervention in dealing with a sexually active population with some HIV seroprevalence. It seems very likely that there will be significant morbidity and mortality, not only in prisons but outside of them as well, as a consequence of our current prison policies. What all people need is education in the use of prophylactic measures. It could be argued that health care professionals commit professional neglect if they withhold the means for inmate self-protection where condoms are not available from other sources and where high-risk sexual activity occurs and is expected, often, to be less than fully consensual. It could be argued that, in failing to assist in the inexpensive prevention of HIV infection where the ensuing disease can result in costly drains on scarce medical resources, CHCPs are allocating scarce resources unwisely and therefore failing to honor their obligations to respect the claims of other non-HIV-positive inmates with health problems of their own. It could be argued that it is manifestly improper to assume responsibility for the health care of a population when one's employer explicitly prohibits interventions that are known to be effective in preventing the spread of deadly diseases within that population.

In the early decades of this century, university professors, under the aegis of the American Association of University Professors, carried on debate and political struggle over the proper dimensions of professional autonomy in higher education. There was broad agreement that it was manifestly improper for a university administration to hire a capable scholar to pursue responsible judgment in some academic arena and then to specify the conclusions that that scholar could and could not defend. It was plain that if one is going to have scholarship, then one has to allow scholars to pursue arguments wherever they lead, even if they support conclusions that run counter to received doctrine. The academic freedom that is so essential to responsible scholarship is a secured limitation on the employer's right to determine the conditions of employment. Trustees and presidents cannot fire academicians merely because they disapprove of the substance of the work they publish.

If the analysis above is correct, then correctional health services professionals are at a point today that compares to the one that professors occupied prior to 1919. There is some emerging awareness that if health care professionals accept the responsibility to provide care to a population, then they must be free from administrative restrictions that seriously impair their abilities to do that job. Alas, there are also many CHCPs whose professional commitments are evaporating as they align themselves with the incarcerative imperatives that prevail in prison. It is always a political-ethical struggle to retain integrity within institutions that see it as a threat. But lest we think of this problem as one that merely discomfits a criminal element that does not invite our sympathy, we would do well to consider the meteoric ascendancy of managed care. As medicine moves away from its independent fee-for-service transactions toward large-scale, for-profit enterprises in which physicians increasingly think of themselves as employees, the very health of health care will depend on the profession's competence in managing similar

124   *Kenneth Kipnis*

pressures. But all of us will be affected then. The lessons of prison medicine (and, for that matter, military medicine) are eminently worthy of philosophical attention.

Notes

1. *A Theory of Justice* (Cambridge, Mass.: Harvard University Press, 1971), 60.

2. See, for example, his *Social Philosophy* (Englewood Cliffs, N.J.: Prentice-Hall, 1973).

3. Hugo Bedau, "Prisoners' Rights," *Criminal Justice Ethics* 1 (Winter/Spring 1982): 38.

4. 191 N.C. 487, 490 (1926).

5. 429 U.S. 97 (1976).

6. Nancy Dubler and B. Jaye Anno, "Ethical Considerations and the Interface with Custody," in *Prison Health Care: Guidelines for the Management of an Adequate Delivery System,* ed. B. Jaye Anno (Washington, D.C.: United States Department of Justice, National Institute of Corrections, 1991), 55.

Response to Chapter 4

First, Do No Harm

Heather Barr

The intersection of health care and corrections does indeed, as Kipnis points out, create an enormous culture clash.[1] Not only does the role of health care providers (to heal) bear no relation to the duty of corrections (to punish), but the corrections setting also robs health care providers of their power, making them navigate institutions in which healing is never the central mission and is often, in fact, regarded as a necessary evil. In other settings, health care providers have great power and control over the lives of their patients (although, admittedly, this power is increasingly circumscribed by managed care companies and billing departments). Doctors decide when a patient will enter and leave the hospital, whether an individual is entitled to disability or worker's compensation, when the patient must return to the clinic, and, in the case of people with mental illness, whether the person should be confined to a hospital and even medicated against her or his will. In a community setting, a doctor is overruled very rarely and then only by a judge.

In corrections, this whole order is turned on its head. The correctional health care professional's ability to do his or her job is drastically circumscribed in three ways: (1) by the tensions between prisoners and corrections staff that are inherent to the prison environment, (2) by the tension between health care staff and corrections staff created by needs of the institution (to control prisoners, to maintain security, to use staff time efficiently) and the attitudes of individual corrections officers, and (3) by tensions that the correctional setting creates between treatment providers and prisoner-patients.

My central critique of Kipnis's analysis is a disagreement with his foundational assumption that incarceration is "a societally appropriate punishment in many cases."[2] I would like to suggest that the conflicts inherent in providing health services in correctional settings are, in fact, excellent examples of why, in most cases, incarceration is not societally appropriate.

The Purpose of Punishment

Kipnis begins by articulating the importance our culture attaches to loss of liberty. He suggests that this societal value makes incarceration a societally appropriate response to crime, and uses the fact that there are two million people in U.S. jails and prisons to illustrate the point. At the outset, I would like to note that although the loss of liberty may be an appropriate response to crime in our society, loss of liberty need not mean incarceration; while two million Americans are incarcerated, another four million are losing their liberty while living in our communities under the supervision of probation or parole. Incarceration is not our society's only means of punishing.

The debate over the purpose that punishment is intended to serve is a rich one amply discussed by others. But many theories of punishment have, I believe, a common theme. Whether we talk in terms of deterrence, rehabilitation, encouraging repentance, offering time for reflection, or incapacitating wrongdoers, the central purpose of these approaches to punishment is crime prevention. Surveys show that the general public believes that the purpose of prison is to rehabilitate or to prevent crime (with retributive punishment being a distant third purpose);[3] in either case, to take a person who has injured society somehow and make sure that this injury is not re-inflicted. If the purpose of the criminal justice system is indeed, as the general public believes, to prevent crime, then the obstacles to providing adequate health care in prison offer an excellent example of why incarceration is not, in most cases, a rational, societally appropriate response to crime.

Incarceration prevents crime, but for the most part only through incapacitation. Deterrence, the notion that an individual will weigh the benefits of a crime against the possibility and severity of punishment and make a rational choice, requires rationality on the part of those one wishes to deter. The people we send to jail and prison are very sick; a large majority of those who are incarcerated for committing crimes suffer from substance abuse or mental illness or a combination of the two. For example, at Rikers Island, New York City's jail complex (and the largest penal colony in the world), approximately 75 to 80 percent of inmates have substance abuse problems, and 15 to 25 percent are seriously mentally ill.[4] Another 10 percent of inmates require some type of mental health services while at Rikers Island, where the average length of stay is only about forty-five days.[5] These statistics are mirrored nationwide.[6] Kipnis writes that the "loss of liberty [could] be reasonably supposed to be, broadly, undesirable enough to deter rational malefactors,"[7] but people who are mentally ill and/or addicted to drugs often do not make very rational choices.

Philosophers seem to be increasingly convinced that the sole purpose of the criminal justice system is retributive—to express to wrongdoers, and perhaps potential wrongdoers, our disapproval of a set of choices. This argument, while it seems to ignore what most of the public (including, presumably, the majority of crime victims) wants, is also vulnerable to attack if one examines it through the lens of the health needs of prisoners. I would argue that imbedded in a discussion of the difficulties inherent in treating the medical needs of prisoners is evidence that the retributive use of incarceration is misdirected in that most of the decision making it punishes can hardly be called rational, or even, often, volitional.

Incarcerating people who commit aberrant acts as a result of psychosis or addiction fails to accomplish any practical goal (except incapacitation); instead it wastes money while failing to address the cause of the behavior. The decision to incarcerate sick people, I would argue, also fails to accomplish an expressive goal, in that the general public seems to understand that, for addicts and the mentally ill, shame usually comes only with recovery, and recovery does not occur in prison. If we accept that crime prevention and punishing an individual for making foolish choices are the main goals of the criminal justice system, then an analysis of how that system deals with the sick demonstrates clearly the futility of incarceration.

The Incarceration of the Sick

Kipnis suggests that the imposition of loss of liberty "upon those convicted of serious offenses could persuade law-abiding citizens that, so retributed, crime does not pay."[8] This statement seems to harbor two misconceptions: first, that incarceration is used only to punish serious offenses, and, second, that the public believes, and that empirical reality confirms, that all criminals are equally likely to be caught and punished.

Most crimes for which people are incarcerated today (72 percent in New York State last year) are nonviolent. Hence, the crimes we seek to protect ourselves from or to express condemnation for are usually not people hurting us or our loved ones, but rather things that fall into the category of aggravating—people using or selling drugs on our street, unarmed people breaking into unoccupied buildings.[9] In order to protect ourselves from these aggravations, we sentence people to terms of incarceration that have for many years been substantial[10] and are now becoming even more onerous as we move toward the complete abolition of parole in New York State and other states pass "three strikes" laws. I would like to suggest that incarcerating sick people for nonviolent offenses is not only fiscally wasteful, but also, because of the conflicts inherent in correctional health care, no way to prevent or express condemnation of crime.

Not all criminals are equally likely to be caught and incarcerated. I will not suggest that all crime is the result of addiction or mental illness (though much of it is), but I do believe that the small proportion of criminals who are apprehended and incarcerated are not representative of offenders generally. As a law student, I spent two years working with public defenders at the Legal Aid Society. I was surprised at the apparent ineptitude of most of the offenders with whom I worked. They appeared consistently to have committed foolish offenses in ways that were almost guaranteed to get them caught. At first I thought that all criminals must be inept. Then I realized that the court sees only the smallest proportion of offenders—the more competent criminals must be the ones who remain out there.

Class clearly plays a role in who is arrested and prosecuted; a stark example of this was the impact of New York City's recent emphasis on "quality-of-life" crime enforcement. Many of the offenses for which people were being diligently arrested are acts that only poor people, and especially homeless people (whose entire lives our mayor may view as quality-of-life offenses), typically commit—for example, public urination, public alcohol or drug consumption, minor drug possession, jumping subway turnstiles, and subway panhandling. At the time of their arrest, 20 percent of the people at Rikers Island, and 43 percent of the mentally ill people there, were homeless.[11]

Those of us with money and homes can generally pay for the subway, have no desire to subject ourselves to the humiliation of begging, and urinate, drink, or, if we wish, smoke crack in the privacy of our own homes. "Quality-of-life" arrests do not lead immediately to incarceration, but they increasingly lead to community service sentences that the homeless, the mentally ill, the addicted, and those who cannot afford the subway fare to get to community service are unlikely to complete. Quality-of-life offenders who do not comply with community service, or who are arrested repeatedly, go to jail.

The addicted and the mentally ill are also more likely to be arrested and incarcerated for serious offenses than less disenfranchised people committing the same offenses. Crime victimization surveys consistently show that most criminals are not caught; surely it is persuasive to argue, when confronted with the pathologies of inmates at facilities like Rikers Island, that the people there were caught because their crimes were done foolishly and sloppily. The offenders who end up in jail are either very unlucky or, more often, the ones who were too messed up to be competent criminals.

Being addicted or mentally ill, especially if one is also homeless, does nothing to improve one's chances of being released pending trial. In New York at least, bail decisions focus primarily on the offender's community ties, an area in which few addicts and mental patients are rich. When bail is set, these offenders are unlikely to be able to pay it; sometimes Rikers Island plays host to detainees charged with relatively minor offenses who cannot make a $500 bail. It is well known that when one is incarcerated pending trial, this incarceration correlates with a more severe sentence at disposition.

Thus, we send people to prison not just in spite of the fact that they have health care needs, but very often *as a result* of their health care needs. As noted above, the vast majority of people in jail and prison have drug problems, or are mentally ill, or both. Substance abuse and mental illness are health problems. Substance abuse is often considered to be more of a character flaw than an illness, but the medical profession has embraced it as its own.[12] Treating health problems is the duty of the health care profession, and when people behave in aberrant ways as a result of their health problems, it is not an appropriate response to shift responsibility to an institution for which provision of the needed services is an unwelcome burden, not a priority. This is always true, but never more so than when the aberrant behavior arising from the illness endangers no one (except perhaps the person with the illness).

We incarcerate people for their illnesses not only in situations in which individuals have refused to deal with their problem, but also in situations in which they have sought help but help has evaded them. Access to community health and mental health care for poor people in New York City is catastrophically limited. Welfare reform has brought with it huge barriers to accessing Medicaid, and without Medicaid there is no health care for poor people except that which is available through emergency rooms, and sometimes not even that. Substance abuse treatment is extremely difficult to access in the community as well. Without Medicaid it is impossible to get substance abuse treatment, and even with Medicaid it is not readily available, especially, for special populations such as pregnant women, women with children, people who also have a mental illness, people with physical disabilities, or people with serious medical needs. The rise of managed care and recent efforts to move Medicaid recipients into managed care plans have done nothing to improve access to services for people with mental illness.[13]

Many people go to jail or prison as a direct result of the fact that they were unable to access the health services they needed. This is particularly true of people with mental illness. At my office, we hear stories about people who went to more than one clinic or hospital seeking help for psychiatric symptoms and were turned away, before intentionally committing a crime in order to gain admission to jail and the mental health services the person knows (through prior experience) are available there. We also talk to parents of mentally ill people who have called the police and had their child arrested because they have been told that it is the one sure way of getting the person help.

Sick People Do Not Fare Well in Correctional Settings

Most of the people in jail and prison are there because their drug addiction or psychiatric problems made them irrational.[14] Incarceration does not assist these people to make rational choices. Once people with substance abuse or mental health problems enter correctional settings, the consequences for which the illness put them at risk in the community (poverty, homelessness, social isolation) are replaced by new and, perhaps, even worse consequences. Substance abusers do not get drug treatment promptly (or perhaps ever) and they continue to have access to drugs, but are now subjected to random urinalysis. They continue to feed their untreated addiction with drugs, and as a result are punished through loss of privileges and segregation.

The mentally ill fare even worse. All of the recent research in mental health points to the importance of coordinated services, integrated mental health and substance abuse treatment, and client-centered services and psychoeducation that encourage compliance with medication.[15] None of these innovations is available in the vast majority of correctional settings. Deprived of access to effective treatment, save, perhaps, psychopharmacology, the mentally ill prisoner can remain in an acutely psychotic state for years, unable to conform to the elaborate rules that govern correctional facilities and spending more and more time isolated in segregation units that confine the illness without controlling it. Unable to be "good prisoners" and cut off from good mental health services, these prisoners are not only very frequently denied parole, but may also be convicted of new offenses while incarcerated. Consider the following case, the son of a woman who called me seeking help in having him moved from punitive segregation to a mental health unit within the prison system:

> At age 20, after a childhood marked by learning disabilities and serious emotional disturbance, M had full-blown schizoaffective disorder. His erratic behavior had begun to frighten his mother, who asked him to move out of her house and, on the advice of friends, took out an order of protection against him. One night, in a psychotic state, M came to his mother's house, pounded on the door, and refused to leave. M's mother called the police who came and arrested him. That night, at the county jail, M tried to hang himself. Several officers rushed in to stop him and he bit one of them. For this assault on the guard, M was sentenced to one to three years in prison. After five months in prison, M's psychiatric condition had not improved and he was at last referred to the mental health staff of the prison. He assaulted the psychologist sent to talk to him, holding her hostage, and was charged with assault and kidnapping. He was sent to punitive segregation awaiting disposition on this new case. In punitive segregation, his psychiatric condition became worse and he was moved to an observation cell where he could be monitored to prevent suicide.

While in that cell he assaulted a guard, was charged with assault and sent back to punitive segregation. On this assault case, he went to trial and was found not guilty by reason of insanity, but on the previous case he pled guilty and took a four-year sentence. He was then transferred to a special housing unit for the mentally ill, but after three months there his urinalysis tested positive for marijuana and he was sentenced to three months punitive segregation.[16]

As Kipnis notes, the people who go to prison are disproportionately those who were socially stigmatized and medically underserved in the community, so their health is often poor when they enter corrections custody. In some cases, particularly for the homeless and the uninsured, the correctional setting offers the first access to health care they have had for a long time. It would be a mistake, however, to assume that this means that going to prison or jail is good for one's health. New ailments, both physical and mental, can arise as a consequence of incarceration. Infectious diseases are spread through sexual contact or needle sharing, or simply as a result of having hundreds of people (many of whom entered the system in poor health) living together in close quarters, often with poor ventilation. The psychiatric impact of incarceration is well documented; in fact the New York State Office of Mental Health is currently in the process of developing several training programs to teach mental health professionals how to help ex-prisoners overcome the residual effects of the traumas inherent in incarceration.[17] There is nothing therapeutic about the correctional environment.

Tensions between Corrections, Doctors, and Prisoners Make It Impossible to Heal the Sick

In any case in which a patient in a correctional setting requires treatment for a medical condition, whether the condition is a physical one, a mental illness, or a substance abuse problem, there are always three key parties involved in the decision making and who determine the adequacy of the treatment that the patient receives. These decision makers are, of course, the patient, the treatment provider, and the institution.[18] Tensions among all three have detrimental effects on the capacity of correctional health care providers to offer prisoners adequate care.

Tensions between Corrections Staff and Prisoners

As Kipnis notes, tensions among corrections staff, the administration of a prison, and the prisoners is inherent to these relationships, and these tensions play a direct and major role in reducing the effectiveness of health care provided behind bars. Correctional facilities are toxic settings in which the desperation of the imprisoned and the power dynamics between the keepers and the kept poison not only those in the cage but also those guarding the cage. Everyone who spends time in these settings—prisoners, guards, or health care workers—cannot help but become institutionalized to some extent. Being a corrections officer is unquestionably a difficult job; how can it be healthy to spend most of your waking hours in the company of people who hate you for being the symbol and enforcer of their loss of liberty?

Guards may resent that fact that prisoners get free health care, or they may have such negative perceptions of prisoners that they presume malingering and delay prisoners' access to medical care through their control of prisoner movement within the facility. Administrators, perhaps sharing some of these attitudes, almost certainly view security as a higher priority than the provision of health care services, and allocate resources and staff time accordingly. Even in a system such as New York's in which many of the health and mental health services are provided by health care agencies rather than by the entities operating the correctional facilities,[19] health care providers cannot get services to patients in a timely fashion without the cooperation of facility guards and administrators. A prison could have the most lavishly funded medical facility in the world and prisoners would not benefit if the prison administration and staff did not choose to make those services available to the prisoners.

Tensions between Corrections and Health Care Staff

It is not only the tension between prisoners and their keepers that undermines the efficacy of correctional health care. Often there is also great tension between treatment providers and corrections staff—and attempts to resolve this tension almost always have a detrimental effect on the quality of patients' care. Corrections staff sometimes view correctional health care providers, especially those who not only serve inmates well but also advocate for inmates, as coddlers who do not understand the importance and difficulty of corrections officers' work.[20]

The majority of people who spend time in correctional settings are either inmates or guards—their roles are clear, as is the adversarial nature of their relationship. The role of health care professionals, who are staff but not guards, creates ambiguity. These workers may find themselves in the worst possible situation—allied with neither side, distrusted by the patients they must treat, yet viewed as "inmate lovers" by the guards with whom they must work side by side.

While I certainly do not mean to say bad things about everyone who works in corrections, corrections staff can, and sometimes do, make health care staff's lives miserable and place great obstacles in the way of their doing their jobs. Correctional health care workers, naturally, respond by trying to make their work environments more congenial, or at least bearable. Unable, except in the most egregious situations, to force corrections officers to be more supportive of prisoners' access to health care, health care workers are forced to choose between allying themselves with their patients (against the guards) and developing a better relationship with guards. Since guards and corrections staff possess most of the power in a correctional facility, and prisoners possess almost none, it is not surprising that many correctional health care workers ally themselves, consciously or not, with guards. When this alliance forms between health care professionals and guards, it does not go unnoticed by the prisoners; it is duly noted and plays a great role in destroying what shaky trust may have existed between health care worker and patient. The inevitable result is worse health care for prisoners.

Tensions between Health Staff and Prisoners

The ultimate, and tragic, consequence of the tensions between corrections staff and health care staff, and between prisoners and guards, is that correctional health care providers lose the ability to form the therapeutic alliance with their patients to which Kipnis refers. As he rightly says, "trust in the integrity of health care professionals is an indispensable element of the therapeutic alliance,"[21] —but integral aspects of the correctional environment make this trust near impossible.

At the heart of tensions between prisoners and their health care providers are perceptions on both sides about malingering. If you or I go to our doctor and report that we are experiencing, for example, sharp stomach pains, then, unless we have offered unfounded complaints in the past, we can assume that the doctor will take our distress at face value and work immediately to fix the problem. Prisoners have a completely different experience. Rather than there being a presumption that prisoner-patient complaints are truthfully reported, there often seems to be a presumption that, when they discuss symptoms, they are lying.

Like guards, correctional health care professionals often presume malingering when a prisoner reports or displays medical or psychiatric symptoms. Correctional health care systems differ from health care systems in the outside world primarily in the gatekeeping mechanisms built into them to screen out malingerers. Managed care is increasingly building gatekeeping mechanisms into health care in the outside world, but if they have insurance normal citizens can still at least be assured of seeing a primary care physician whenever they feel they should. For a prisoner, getting to see a doctor often involves signing up for sick call repeatedly, convincing a nurse that the ailment is real and that Tylenol will not cure it, and even risking punishment.[22] The suspicion with which health care professionals regard the health complaints of prisoners taints the entire relationship, leads health care workers to miss real illnesses, and encourages prisoners to mistrust health care workers and believe that they must exaggerate their symptoms if they are to get any help.

Why do correctional health care workers so often suspect prisoners of malingering? In part, I suppose, because prisoners sometimes do malinger. Prisoners fake illness more often than people in the outside world for several reasons. First, life in prison is an unpleasant existence and prisoners, rationally enough, use whatever means are at their disposal to make this existence more bearable. Prisoners may malinger in search of protection from dangers in the correctional environment. A prisoner who knows that other prisoners mean him harm, who simply fears the risks inherent in many correctional environments, or who is being punished in punitive segregation, may seek refuge in the infirmary or in a segregated housing unit for people with special needs. For example, at Rikers Island, where many parts of the jail are very dangerous, but the segregated mental health units are safer, some inmates undoubtedly fake psychiatric symptoms in attempts to get into a segregated unit. Similarly, in the past, policy dictated that inmates with psychiatric problems not be held in the "bing"—the punitive segregation unit; perhaps some inmates faked mental illness to get out of the bing.[23]

Prisoners may also create symptoms as a cry for help with another problem, often a psychiatric one. Or they may malinger in order to spend a few minutes talking to a health care professional they hope will be caring (and perhaps female). Perhaps some prisoners overuse health services simply because the imposed helplessness of prison breeds hypochondria, or because one of the very few choices they get to make is the decision to sign up for sick call. Malingering, however many prisoners do or do not engage in it, has terrible consequences for the adequacy of the health care all prisoners receive. Malingering antagonizes health care workers and makes them (as well as the corrections officers with whom they work) less responsive to all medical complaints by prisoners. When health care workers seems nonresponsive to prisoners' needs, the antagonism is returned. Most health care workers in the outside world, I would guess, feel not only that their work is important, but also that it is appreciated; very few health care workers in correctional settings seem to feel appreciated.

It is important to realize, however, that malingering is not the only distortion of the clinical picture created by the stressors of the correctional environment. For every prisoner with an imaginary illness, there may be another prisoner who suppresses symptoms because of the consequences the correctional environment imposes on the sick. In the outside world, if we are sick, we go to the doctor, we assume she or he will protect our privacy, and that if we are ill the doctor will help us to make educated decisions about what to do next. Prisoners know that they do not have this much control; fears about loss of confidentiality and autonomy drive many prisoners away from seeking medical assistance.

Prisoners who worry or know that they are HIV positive may not seek medical attention for fear that everyone in the facility will come to know of their status. Lack of confidentiality is a particular concern for non-English speaking prisoners who may have to rely on other inmates to act as interpreters. Tuberculosis testing is now frequently mandated, but prisoners with symptoms of other infectious diseases may wish to avoid a quarantine that could cost them work assignments and the few freedoms they enjoy.

The mentally ill, because of stigma and the lack of insight that sometimes accompanies mental illness, are often reluctant to be diagnosed and treated in the outside world. Behind bars, they are likely to be more so, because many facilities do nothing to protect their confidentiality[24] and being identified as a "loony" is likely to subject them to abuse not only from other inmates, but also from guards. Being mentally ill also does not necessarily get you better living conditions; prisoners removed from punitive segregation in New York State prisons because of mental illness are moved to solitary observation cells where they are kept naked with no mattress, no blankets, and no property—conditions far worse than those in punitive segregation.

The tensions in relationships between prisoners and their health care providers create great, often insurmountable, barriers to the provision of good health care. Prisoners fake and suppress symptoms, health care workers view every complaint with skepticism, and there is no semblance of a therapeutic alliance. Layer on top of this a lack of resources and staffing that often makes it impossible for a correctional health care worker to do a good job and you get some sense of what a hopeless treatment milieu this is. In correctional settings, doctors and patients cannot trust each other, and any healing that takes place does so over tremendous obstacles. As long as prisons and jails are what they are, I can think of no way to improve things significantly.

Health care workers, "institutionalized" and working in hostile environments treating hostile patients, either quit or adapt. Adapting usually means accepting the fact that you are not able to do what would be regarded as a good job in the outside world, but carrying on anyway. Health care workers in this position do what they can and let the rest go. What this usually means in practice is an exclusive focus on preventing death, through illness or suicide, and on treating acute illnesses. Although it can be hoped that the big catastrophes will be avoided, small ones happen every day. Less dramatic work that is nevertheless essential to good medical practice—for example, discharge planning and creating a continuum of care—goes completely by the wayside.[25]

Why Have a Smart Policy When You Can Have a Really Stupid One?

In spite of our ever-harsher sentencing laws, almost everyone still gets out of prison someday, and those who went in sick, especially the mentally ill and the substance abusers, often come out sicker. Our prisons and jails fail in that they do not do what the public asks of them—to rehabilitate and to prevent crime. But they fail on other grounds too. They fail because they waste our money and because we substitute them for alternatives that we know *do* help to rehabilitate and prevent crime.

New York City and New York State again provide excellent examples of remarkably stupid public policies. New York State prisons cost a relatively modest $32,000 per prisoner per year, but Rikers Island, at $69,000 per inmate per year, may be the costliest correctional facility in the world.[26] Both systems shudder under the impact of overcrowding generally and specifically under the burden of caring for the increasingly sick inmates that corrections is being asked to care for. The numbers of mentally ill in particular are swelling, attracting attention in the national media[27] and taxing resources.

New Yorkers know how to help people with mental illness. In 1990, the city and state jointly funded 3,600 supportive housing beds for mentally ill homeless people in New York City. These housing programs cost $12,000 per year per client and they unquestionably work; they provide not only a roof, but also twenty-four-hour supportive services and supervision. An evaluation of one program found that 88 percent of clients, all formerly homeless mentally ill substance abusers, most with criminal records, remained housed five years later.[28] Unfortunately, all of the supportive housing beds are now full and vacancies are so rare that intake coordinators may receive 200 applications for one bed. Downsizing of both acute care and long-term psychiatric hospitals has forced seriously mentally ill people out of these settings, and with no vacancies in supportive housing, these people have nowhere to go. There are approximately 12,000 mentally ill homeless people in New York City.

Faced with this situation—rising numbers of mentally ill prisoners straining corrections resources, and a shortage of spaces in cost-effective community mental health housing—New York Governor Pataki responded in the most irrational way possible. His proposed budget for 1999 did the following: (1) It downsized state psychiatric hospitals by another 470 beds, and (2) allocated $360 million dollars for two new maximum-security prisons with psychiatric units.

New York's current situation is a useful illustration of the policy choices that are forcing our country's jails and prisons to become the primary health care providers for some of our neediest citizens. Only when we acknowledge that correctional settings are the worst places to treat the sick—from a financial perspective, from an ethical perspective, and from the perspective of efficiency—will we be able to make an accurate assessment of the impact of these policies. Only then will it become clear that incarcerating the sick, and making doomed efforts to heal them behind bars, wastes resources and wastes lives.

Notes

1. Kenneth Kipnis, "Health Care in the Corrections Setting: An Ethical Analysis," in this volume, 113–24.

2. Kipnis, "Health Care in the Corrections Setting," 114.

3. Bureau of Justice Statistics, "Correctional Populations in the United States, 1996," NCJ 171684 (March 1999): Table 2.53.

4. "Assessing the Care of the Mentally Ill and Mental Health Services in New York City Correctional Institutions: Hearing before the Subcommittee on Mental Health, Mental Retardation, Alcoholism and Drug Abuse Service," statement of Dr. Arthur Lynch, Director of Mental Health Services for the NYC Health and Hospitals Corporation before the New York City Council Mental Health Subcommitee, April 22, 1998, 2. On file with author.

5. *City of New York, Mayor's Management Report: Preliminary Fiscal 1998*, vol. 2, *Agency and Citywide Indicators*, 15.

6. Paula M. Ditton, "Special Report: Mental Health and Treatment of Inmates and Probationers," Bureau of Justice Statistics, NCJ 174463 (July 1999).

7. Kipnis, "Health Care in the Corrections Setting," 114.

8. Kipnis, "Health Care in the Corrections Setting," 114.

9. Last year, 47 percent of the people who went to prison in New York State were sent there for drug offenses. Only 28 percent were sentenced for offenses considered violent under New York's Penal Law. The 28 percent figure, low as it is, is somewhat elevated by the fact that the Penal Law takes a relatively broad view of what acts are violent. For example, breaking into an unoccupied dwelling is considered a violent crime, as is breaking into an unoccupied building while armed. N.Y.S. Penal Law § 140.25.

10. For example, under New York's "Rockefeller Drug Laws," the minimum sentence for some nonviolent drug possession and sale charges is fifteen-years-to-life—even for first-time offenders.

11. David Michaels et al., "Homelessness and Indicators of Mental Illness among Inmates in New York City's Correctional System," *Hospital & Community Psychiatry* 43 (1992): 155; David A. Martell et al., "Base-Rate Estimates of Criminal Behavior by Homeless Mentally Ill Persons in New York City," *Psychiatric Services* 46 (1995): 596.

12. *Diagnostic and Statistical Manual of Mental Disorders: DSM-IV,* 4th ed. (Washington, D.C.: American Psychiatric Association, 1994), 175–272.

13. The following excerpt is from a suicide note the author, a man suffering from major depression, left for his sister:

> When I moved here, I contacted my mental health doctor in Pennsylvania for a referral to someone to see in Massachusetts. He was not able to provide one. I tried to find a doctor on my own but didn't want to pick one

out of the phone book (not that it would do me any good, I later discovered). I called the Massachusetts psychiatric referral line. It was not in service due to "staff turnover." With no other number to call, I called the local hospital referral line. I got voice mail. I made an appointment with a general physician. I tried to get a referral from him. His office tried to set me up with an affiliated doctor, but their mental health care doctors didn't take my insurance. I said I would pay CASH! They said they didn't take cash, because it is too expensive. I called the HMO. They had four doctors. I called each one. The earliest appointment I could get was a month away. I called my GP back to see if he knew any of these doctors. He said, No, sorry, I can't help you.

So that is my story. I know I am sick. I tried to get help. No one wanted to help me. It is no wonder that there are so many suicides in this country. My only hope is that my death will awaken the health care community and that lives will be saved in the future.

Reproduced in "Managed Despair," *Harper's Magazine* 298 (January 1999): 26.

14. See, generally, E. Fuller Torrey et al., "Criminalizing the Seriously Mentally Ill: The Abuse of Jails as Mental Hospitals," *Innovations and Research* 2 (1993): 11; Linda A. Teplin, "Criminalizing Mental Disorder: The Comparative Arrest Rate of the Mentally Ill," *American Psychologist* 39 (1984): 794.

15. See, e.g., Roger H. Peters and Holly A. Hills, *Intervention Strategies for Offenders with Co-Occurring Disorders: What Works?* (Delmar, N.Y.: The GAINS Center, 1997), 46; D. C. Chandler et al., "Client Outcomes in a Three-Year Controlled Study of an Integrated Service Agency Model," *Psychiatric Services* 47 (1996): 1337; Kim T. Mueser et al., "The Course and Treatment of Substance Abuse Disorders in People with Severe Mental Illness," in *The Treatment of Drug-Dependent Individuals with Comorbid Mental Disorders,* ed. Lisa S. Onken et al., National Institute on Drug Abuse Research Monograph 172 (Rockville, Md.: U.S. Dept. of Health and Human Services, 1997), 86–109; Roger D. Weiss and Lisa M. Najavits, "Overview of Treatment Modalities for Dual Diagnosis Patients: Pharmacotherapy, Psychotherapy, and Twelve-Step Programs," in *Dual Diagnosis and Treatment: Substance Abuse and Comorbid Medical and Psychiatric Disorders,* ed. H. R. Kranzler and B. J. Rounsaville (New York: Marcel Dekker, 1998), 87.

16. On file with author.

17. These training programs include the SPECTRUM (Sensitizing Providers to the Effects of Correctional incarceration on Treatment and Risk Management) training developed by staff at Bronx Psychiatric Center. Another New York State Office of Mental Health initiative is through the Howie T. Harp Advocacy Center in New York City; this program is a forensic peer advocacy training program that is preparing mental health consumers who are also ex–state prisoners to go into the community and teach mental health providers how to work with ex-offenders.

18. The patient's family members and/or previous community treatment providers are sometimes, especially in cases of mental illness, involved in treatment decision making, but they often face great obstacles in becoming involved. I spend a great deal of time helping family members and community mental health providers who are attempting to get patient information to correctional treatment providers in New York City and State—and who often feel that no one within the system is interested in hearing from them.

19. In the New York City jail system, all health and mental health services are provided, directly or through contract, by the city's Health and Hospitals Corporation. In the state prison system, mental health services are provided directly by the state Office of Mental Health, whereas nonpsychiatric health services are provided, directly or through contract, by the state Department of Correctional Services.

20. Interview with Jennifer Wynn, Director, Prison Visiting Project, The Correctional Association of New York.

21. Kipnis, "Health Care in the Corrections Setting," 117.

22. Jennifer Wynn, "Healthcare in New York State Prisons," the Correctional Association of New York, February 2000.

23. The city's Department of Correction recently addressed this issue by building a new "mental health bing" exclusively for inmates sentenced to punitive segregation who have mental health problems, so that they can be punished (as opposed to being merely incarcerated) and treated at the same time.

24. For example, in the Los Angeles County jail, mentally ill inmates were forced to wear colored jumpsuits that differed from those of other inmates. In many facilities, psychiatric medications are dispensed publicly and on a different schedule from that of medical medications, making it obvious to everyone who the psychiatric patients are.

25. For example, though the mental health services at Rikers Island compare relatively well with those available in other jails, the staff there make almost no attempt to contact outside treatment providers who were working with inmates at the time of their arrest or to arrange for the patient to be able to access treatment after release. When their release date arrives, seriously mentally ill inmates who have been receiving psychotropic medication daily while incarcerated are put on a bus with other inmates and dropped off at Queens Plaza at 4 A.M. with three subway tokens, no medication, no referral to outpatient services, and (if they are homeless) no referral to a shelter.

26. New York State Department of Correctional Services 1996–97 per Capita Cost Report, Fiscal Year 4/1/96–3/31/97. The exact figure for New York State prisons is $32,035.55. Dean M. Mead, *The State of Municipal Services in the 1990s: New York City Department of Correction* (The Citizen's Budget Committee, June 1997). This report cites a cost of $63,725 per inmate per year for the New York City jail system. However, this figure does not include the cost of providing health and mental health care to an inmate. These services add an additional $5,521 per inmate per year bringing the total cost of jail incarceration in New York City to $69,246 per inmate per year. Conversation with Andrew Rein of the Citizen's Budget Committee, August 4, 1998.

27. Fox Butterfield, "Prisons Replace Hospitals for the Nation's Mentally Ill, *New York Times*, March 5, 1998, A1.

28. Michael Winerip, "Bedlam on the Streets: Increasingly the Mentally Ill Have Nowhere to Go. That's Their Problem—and Ours," *New York Times Magazine*, May 23, 1999, 42.

Response to Chapter 4

Brokering Correctional Health Care

John Kleinig

It is a rare person for whom the jail or prison experience could be deemed a pleasant one. Indeed, it is almost a principle of punitive incarceration that the custodial experience be less desirable than noncustodial experience. The rationale need not be one of deterrence. If punishment—as retributively deserved—is to be punishment, it must be intended (and normally experienced) as an imposition, as hard treatment. Not only is the experience not pleasant but, as Kipnis notes, the public overseers of jails and prisons do not have the psychological and physical well-being of their clientele among their most significant priorities. Even though the incarcerative institution must have a restorative or reintegrative function if it is to be publicly justifiable,[1] those in control of prisons generally see their role as custodial and incapacitative rather than as educative and reintegrative.

It is understandable therefore that those who are incarcerated will be tempted to seek ways of making their lives a little more comfortable, a little less unpleasant. Exploitation of prison medical facilities may present one such opportunity. Boredom may be relieved, company may be briefly changed, attention may be given. Awareness of such exploitative possibilities might be the most generous explanation for the reluctance of custodial personnel to be responsive to the health care requests of inmates.

That said, it is also likely to be the case that those who are incarcerated will suffer greater infirmities—both psychological and physical—than the general population, even if not always greater than the populations from which they are drawn. If their incarceration is drug related, there is a reasonable chance that they have compromised immune systems or that nutritional deficits have had other health-related sequelae. If their crimes have been violent, there is also a reasonable chance that they have suffered from residual damage themselves. And the conditions of incarceration may generate or exacerbate health hazards of various kinds—the spread of infection, psychological stress, inmate violence, and so on.[2]

Professionalism Undermined

The body of Kipnis's chapter focuses on the tension that may exist between the professional needs of the health worker and the liberty-limiting and security demands of the jail or prison. And I agree that this tension generates an important cluster of ethical problems for the provision of health care in correctional settings.[3] I am sympathetic to much of what Kipnis says in this connection, adding only that besides the problematic involvement of health personnel in death penalty situations, in which the purpose is not to further the security interests of the prison, but instead to advance its punitive or retributive purposes,[4] he might have also considered their problematic involvement in the management of hunger strikers,[5] in assessments of the suitability of a prisoner for parole,[6] and in judgments about malingering.

Moreover, I think the professional tension that he points out may be more complicated than he indicates—sometimes because of decisions made externally to the correctional institution. The problems that emerged in New York as a result of the contract between St. Bamabas Hospital, Rikers Island jail, and the Manhattan Detention Complex suggest that, by virtue of their interest in profitability, private hospitals may contribute to the ethical problems confronting correctional health care.[7] If health care services are put out for tender, the result may be profit-driven agreements that jeopardize inmate welfare independently of the security needs of the correctional institution.

In yet other cases, ethical problems in correctional health care may have had their primary origin in the health care providers themselves. The provision of correctional health care has little prestige attached to it, and in order to satisfy the demand for health services, correctional institutions have sometimes employed health care personnel who have been found guilty of criminal and/or unprofessional conduct.[8] Even if the health care providers have not previously come to attention for unprofessional conduct, they may still provide medical care that is manifestly substandard, either because, though qualified, they are poor practitioners or because they are poorly qualified.[9] Another source of problems, probably greater in the past than now, is that health care personnel may have research interests that conflict with their care provider interests.[10]

The Brokers of Correctional Health Care

But there is a further dimension to the issue of health care in a correctional setting. It is referred to—but Kipnis leaves it uncommented on—in the quotation he takes from *Estelle*. Speaking of the "deliberate indifference" that violates the provisions of the Eighth Amendment, the Court there noted that the indifference in question is not limited to that "manifested by prison doctors in their response to the prisoner's needs," but extends to "prison guards in intentionally denying or delaying access to medical care or intentionally interfering with the treatment once prescribed."[11]

I suspect that the ethical problems surrounding health care in a correctional setting may be even more critical in these latter cases. Inmates do not have automatic or immediate access to health care facilities, but are dependent on the discretion—or, if not discretion, the power[12]—of corrections officers. Officers who presume that prisoners are—or that a particular prisoner is—likely to seek access to health facilities for essentially nonmedical reasons or believe that the medical reasons are not serious enough, or see the use of discretion as an opportunity for showing who is in control, will be minded to refuse requests for medical attention or at least to delay compliance until the need for such attention is more manifestly displayed. By then, of course, it may be too late or, if not too late, the problems may have worsened and treatment will need to be prolonged or will be less successful.

Furthermore, prison officers almost certainly see their role as executors of societal retribution with a special responsibility for institutional security needs. If security is given a near-overriding significance, the importance of health care needs is likely to be underplayed. Their responsibility is seen solely as one of containment and warehousing, and not as including preparation for the inmate's eventual return to and productive involvement in the wider society.

Even if officers see their responsibility in broader terms, as ensuring that a social debt is paid, they may consider it important that prisoners "pull their weight" or work and thus place physical and other demands on inmates even when these are medically or psychologically contraindicated.[13]

But why should correctional officers be as responsive to the medical requests or needs of inmates as health professionals? They are not health care professionals, nor are they employed to be health care professionals. How should they, as gatekeepers to the health care professional, as brokers of health care, act in an ethically responsible way? What should an inmate's health care rights be?

Principles of Brokerage

We can, I think, start with a principle that has been enunciated by the courts but which also makes good moral sense. It is that because an incarcerated

individual "becomes both vulnerable and dependent upon the state to provide certain simple and basic human needs,"[14] it is therefore incumbent on
the state's agents to ensure that those basic needs are adequately met. The
needs in question include not only food, shelter, and sanitation, but also
medical care. Whatever onus may ordinarily lie on the individual to look
after his or her own medical needs, it is shifted to the state when the person
is incarcerated: "restrained by the authority of the state, the individual cannot himself seek medical aid or provide the other necessities for sustaining
life and health."[15]

That principle of course rests on a much more fundamental principle
about the inherent dignity of the human individual, a dignity that is not lost
or forfeited by wrongdoing even if considerations of desert, justice, and public danger make it appropriate that a person suffers a diminution of the
benefits of social life.[16] An incarcerated person has a legitimate expectation
that he or she will be provided with the basic human needs compatible with
his or her maintenance of dignity and self-respect.

Given this principle, I would suggest that until an individual pattern of
behavior shows it to be otherwise,[17] there should be an initial presumption
of good faith on the requesting inmate's part, and prison staff should take
appropriate steps to provide timely access to professional health care services,[18] or be otherwise responsive to an inmate's health care needs.[19] Morally, this requires more than an absence of deliberate indifference. In a prison
situation, with its dependency and vulnerability, it demands an active concern with inmates' health needs, even if they are not always obvious.

Correctional officers are not generally in a position to judge the legitimacy of a request for medical services. Those judgments should normally be
left to trained health care personnel who will then exercise their professional
judgment. It should be the responsibility of correctional officers and officials
to ensure that—compatible with the security needs of the custodial institution—inmates requesting medical assistance are provided with the access
they need.

Although the provision of such services might sometimes result in a
slight diminution of security, it should generally be possible to provide access to medical services without there being significant compromise, and the
inmate's medical interests should normally prevail over any relatively small
diminution in security.[20]

Other factors might also be taken into account. If, for example, an inmate
requests medical assistance in the middle of the night, when regular health
care personnel are not available, some judgment may need to be made as to
whether acting on the request can wait till morning. In some cases delay
might be appropriate; if, however, the distress appears genuine and serious,
prison personnel ought to be under an obligation to respond to it. Doubt
should be interpreted in the inmate's favor.[21]

Account should also be taken of the special medical needs of inmates who are under medical supervision. In her chapter, Bomse refers to several cases in which inmates whose medical needs had already been recognized by health care personnel were subjected to conditions that compromised their treatment.[22]

Should the health care personnel—after an appropriate diagnostic investigation—consider the request to be groundless and should a pattern of apparently groundless requests develop, then greater circumspection might be justified and some delay initiated. I say "delay" because, as in the story of the boy who cried "Wolf," it is not unreasonable to assume that medical problems will at some time manifest themselves in a prison or jail setting and that even those who seek to exploit the system will be vulnerable to illness.

Perhaps the most difficult—but also most common—situations in which health care may need to be brokered will concern the mental health needs of inmates. If inmates do not have significant mental health problems before they are incarcerated (and many of them do, often as a factor in the criminality that has led to their incarceration), the custodial environment will itself foster and aggravate such problems.[23] There is a tendency among correctional officers to ignore signs of mental disintegration as long as it does not become a management problem. Barring specific inmate requests, such pathologies are not viewed as treatable so much as manageable. There is some evidence that health care personnel may look at it in the same way, thus reinforcing the status quo and the dehumanized relationship that too often exists between correctional personnel and inmates.[24]

Although, as Kipnis notes, inmates are the only citizens to have a constitutional right to health care, there is an ironic and often tragic gap between this privileged status and reality.[25]

Notes

1. Even if punishment is retributively deserved, its embodiment in a public institution must have some teleological justification. The reintegrative aspect of custodial care is usually assigned to program/civilian staff rather than to correctional officers. Indeed, there are often deterrents to the latter taking an educative interest in inmates.

2. Consider the spread of HIV—through prison sex/rape—hepatitis, and tuberculosis. In this context, there are important ethical questions concerning screening and segregation. See Leo Carroll, "AIDS and Human Rights in the Prisons: A Comment on the Ethics of Screening and Segregation," in *Correctional Theory and Practice*, ed. Clayton A. Hartjen and Edward E. Rhine (Chicago: Nelson-Hall, 1992), 162–77. Consider also claims about the hazardousness of the enclosed prison environment as a result of environmental tobacco smoke. Here the concern is as much with future as with current health. Though initially one of administrative discretion, the smoking issue has now been settled externally by a Supreme Court deci-

sion, *Helling v. McKinney,* 509 U.S. 25, 113 S. Ct. 2475 (1993). See Lisa Gizzi, "Smoking in the Cell Block—Cruel and Unusual Punishment?" *American University Law Review* 43 (Spring 1994): 1091–134. Note, however, the possible link between non-smoking regulations and increased prison violence, discussed in Matthew C. Leone, Patrick T. Kincade, and Mark Covington, "To Smoke or Not to Smoke: The Experience of a Nevada Jail," *American Jails* (January/February, 1996): 46–52.

3. For a valuable overview, see Michael Puisis et al. (eds.), *Clinical Practice in Correctional Medicine* (St. Louis: Mosby, 1998). The book is insightfully reviewed by David Kent in the *New England Journal of Medicine* 340, no. 12 (March 25, 1999): 972.

4. See C. Michalos, "Medical Ethics and the Executing Process in the United States of America," *Medicine and Law* 16 (1997): 125–67; Physicians for Human Rights, American College of Physicians, National Coalition to Abolish the Death Penalty, and Human Rights Watch, *Breach of Trust: Physician Participation in Executions in the United States* (Boston: Physicians for Human Rights, March 1994). The problems here may extend to psychiatric determinations that a prisoner is sufficiently "competent" to be executed. See Richard Bonnie, "Dilemmas in Administering the Death Penalty: Conscientious Abstention, Professional Ethics, and the Needs of the Legal System," *Law and Human Behavior* 14, no. 1 (1990): 67–90.

5. See Lubor Neoral, "Ethical and Medico-Legal Problems Concerning So-Called Hunger Strikers," *Forensic Science International* 69, no. 3 (1994): 327–28; D. Silove, J. Curtis, C. Mason, and R. Becker, "Ethical Considerations in the Management of Asylum Seekers on Hunger Strike," *JAMA* 276, no. 5 (1996): 410–15.

6. See Michael Decaire, "Ethical Concerns within the Practice of Correctional Psychology," <www.uplink.com.au/lawlibrary/Documents/Docs/Doc93.html> (July 25, 2000); cf. also Linda E. Weinberger and Shoba Sreenivasan, "Ethical and Professional Conflicts in Correctional Psychology," *Professional Psychology: Research and Practice* 25, no. 2 (1994): 161–67.

7. Jim Dwyer, "Inmates Suffer for Profits?" *New York Daily News,* October 6, 1998, 8. In this case the contract (essentially a managed-care one) was awarded by the city's Health and Hospital Corporation. But economic factors may also come to play a role in another way. Some prison systems—as part of an attempt to curb what is seen as excessive inmate use of medical facilities—have begun to charge for prison medical services by deducting amounts from what inmates have earned while engaged in prison work. See Wesley P. Shields, "Prisoner Health Care: Is It Proper to Charge Inmates for Health Services?" *Houston Law Review* 32, no. 1 (Summer 1995): 271–302. Consider also the early case of *Tolbert v. Eyman,* in which a prison doctor, skeptical of a prisoner's claim that he suffered from diabetic retinopathy (which was being treated successfully prior to his incarceration), told him he could have the treatment only if he paid for it. 434 F. 2d 625 (1970). In the particular case, however, not even this sufficed to convince the prison authorities to permit him access to it.

8. Andrew A. Skolnick, "Prison Deaths Spotlight How Boards Handle Impaired, Disciplined Physicians," *JAMA* 280 (October 28, 1998): 1387–90, and "Critics Denounce Staffing Jails and Prisons with Physicians Convicted of Misconduct," *JAMA* 280 (October 28, 1998): 1391–92.

9. Although the courts have been rightly reluctant to second-guess medical judgments—at least as constitutional rather than tortious issues—they have not closed that door entirely. See *Tolbert v. Eyman,* 434 F. 2d 625 (1970); *Martinez v.*

Mancusi et al., 443 F. 2d 921 (1970) (a case in which a prison doctor conformed his judgment to institutional convenience—in disregard of the surgeon's instructions); and *Williams v. Vincent,* 508 F. 2d 541 (1974) (in which a doctor chose the "easier and less efficacious treatment" of discarding the inmate's ear and stitching the stump).

10. Edna Erez, "Randomized Experiments in a Correctional Context: Legal, Ethical, and Practical Concerns," *Journal of Criminal Justice* 14 (1986): 389–400. During the heyday of psychosurgical experimentation, prison inmates were frequently induced to "consent" to operations. See Samuel Chavkin, *The Mind Stealers: Psychosurgery and Mind Control* (Boston: Houghton Mifflin, 1978), chapter 5.

11. *Estelle v. Gamble,* 429 U.S. 97, at 104–05 (1976)(notes omitted).

12. Discretion, as I understand it, is a prerogative, an authority to exercise judgment, rather than merely a power to decide.

13. Consider, for example, *Campbell v. Beto,* in which the inmate, Campbell, who suffered documented heart problems, was sent to work in the fields, and whose heart medicine was withheld from him while he was at work. Subsequent to a heart attack, when Campbell initiated a suit against the prison authorities, he was placed in solitary on a restricted diet without mandated medical attention. 460 F. 2d 765 (1972). This case shows the potential for punitive responses should an inmate protest decisions that are made concerning health care. See also *Wilbron v. Hutto,* in which the inmate complained that he was denied medically indicated surgery on an injured hand and was forced to work in the fields, thus aggravating the injury. 509 F. 2d 621 (1975).

14. *Fitzke v. Shappell,* 468 F. 2d 1072, at 1076 (1972)—harking back to *Spicer v. Williamson:* "it is but just that the public be required to care for the prisoner, who cannot by reason of the deprivation of his liberty, care for himself." 191 N.C. 487, at 490, 132 S.E. 291, at 293 (1926). This is not quite the paternalistic principle that I think Kipnis construes it to be: the emphasis is on provision rather than imposition.

15. *Fitzke v. Shappell,* 468 F. 2d 1072, at 1076 (1972). In sufficiently serious cases of denial, the denial may constitute a constitutional violation—either as cruel and unusual punishment (Eighth Amendment) or as a denial of due process (Fourteenth Amendment). Since *Estelle,* the former has predominated.

16. Here I prescind from debates about the compatibility of capital punishment with human dignity. Suffice it to say that opponents generally consider them incompatible and proponents believe them to be compatible.

17. There is a tendency among correctional officers to see inmates as chronic malingerers and to use this profile as a reason for being less than appropriately responsive to individual inmate requests. Although—as I mentioned at the beginning—there are factors in the prison environment that encourage malingering, using a profile to make decisions in an individual case cannot be justified.

18. The courts do not, as far as I can tell, wish to go this far, though I believe it to be ethically required. In *Fitzke v. Shappell,* the court states that constitutional due process does not require that "every request for medical attention must be heeded" but "only where the circumstances are clearly sufficient to indicate the need of medical attention for injury or illness." 468 F. 2d 1072, at 1076 (1972).

19. In *Westlake v. Lucas,* the inmate, Westlake, indicated on admission to the Wayne County jail that he suffered from an ulcer and required a special diet and medication. But jail personnel denied his request until they were ordered to grant it by a doctor, even though they knew that Westlake had received a special diet and

medication at another institution. 537 F. 2d 857 (1976). Had the admitting personnel not known about the special treatment Westlake had received at the other institution, they might have had some reason to demur, though even then an expedited medical examination should have been expected. Westlake had to wait eight days before he received appropriate medical attention.

20. Exceptions can be contemplated. Suppose inmate A has been wounded by inmate B, who is still armed and dangerous. Inmate A's cries for medical assistance may go unheeded while inmate B remains a threat to any who would approach A. But this is an extreme case. Even if an inmate wounds himself as part of an elaborate escape attempt, this would be reason for increased security rather than the denial of health care. See Ted Conover, *Newjack: Guarding Sing Sing* (New York: Random House, 2000), 161.

21. See, in particular, *Fitzke v. Shappell,* where the court noted that "the case before us illustrates the fallacy of the oft-made assumption that one who is dazed or exhibits the symptoms of drunkenness and who may have alcohol on his breath, or who may in fact be intoxicated, requires the 'drunk tank' and not medical attention." 468 F. 2d 1072, at 1079 (1972).

22. Audrey Bomse, "Prison Abuse: Prisoner-Staff Relations," in this volume, 79–104.

23. See, for example, Heather Barr, "First, Do No Harm," in this volume, 125–39.

24. Conover notes the tendency in Sing Sing to refer to mentally disturbed inmates uniformly as "bugs." *Newjack*, 116, 138–51.

25. There is more appearance than reality in this formal privilege. The constitutional right is simply a negative protection against deliberate indifference to a medical condition, gained via a Supreme Court interpretation of cruel and unusual punishment. Those outside prison settings generally have legally secured access to treatment in public hospitals in cases of emergency. This might well serve them better than the constitutional protection possessed by prisoners. My thanks to Margaret Smith.

Chapter 5

Ideology into Practice/Practice into Ideology: Staff-Offender Relationships in Institutional and Community Corrections in an Era of Retribution

Joseph V. Williams

Ideology into Practice

Introduction

Within the social institution of corrections, many factors influence the ethical dimension of staff-offender relationships. In this chapter I discuss a number of factors that, over the last fifty years, have been influential in changing those relationships. My particular concern is with the ethical character of the staff-offender relationship as it is mediated by retributive ideology and the incapacitation that appears to flow from that ideology.[1] In this regard I wish to distinguish my focus on ideology from the classic conservative-liberal debate in which conservatives usually favor imprisonment and liberals usually favor alternatives to imprisonment. My intention is to show how and why one ideology (retribution) has become dominant (over reform, rehabilitation, or reintegration) and has been translated into the normative practices of correctional personnel.

I recognize that the relation of retributive ideology to correctional practices has not been a lockstep one but relatively dynamic, depending on the perceptions of the various external and internal groups who comprise and therefore influence corrections as a social institution. Overlaying the dynamic features of ideological change and practices are the historically constraining features that ensue from economic and racial stratification. That is, we should not dismiss the idea that corrections is an extension of society's attempt to control those labeled as socially deviant, depraved, despised, and dangerous.[2] It is my contention that we must therefore

- examine the recent ebb and flow of correctional ideology, noting how it has influenced the practices of correctional personnel;
- provide specific examples of ideological-function transitions; for example, retributive practices and their contrast with rehabilitative practices;
- observe how various organizational structures of corrections have hindered or helped correctional personnel in adapting to the changes in correctional ideology;
- discuss the impact of the ideology (or era) of retribution on the restorative function of corrections for offenders and their communities; and
- consistently keep in mind how the effects of class, race, and gender are correlated with ideological changes and correctional practices.

Correctional Ideology and Functional Changes

It will aid our understanding if we distinguish correctional ideology from functionality. Correctional ideologies are beliefs held by members of interest groups in the larger society. Correctional functions, by contrast, though they may originate in ideology, are the practices of members of correctional organizations. Broadly speaking, four correctional ideologies have prevailed. At times they have counterbalanced one another; at other times they have been in direct conflict. Sometimes one has predominated. They are:

Reform: the belief that through reflection, repentance, and hard work within prison an offender will be forced to change;

Rehabilitation: the belief that through intensive treatment of the offender over an unspecified length of time, he or she will be cured of his or her deviancy;

Reintegration: the belief that recidivism will be reduced through various preparation strategies addressed to offenders who are returning to their communities ; and

Retribution: the belief that offenders should be imprisoned for punishment instead of as punishment.[3]

Major correctional functions are:

Custodial: perhaps the primary function of prisons, underscored by the fact that they do it so well. Escapes from prisons worldwide are minuscule in comparison with the overwhelming number of offenders who are held to the end of their sentences.

Restorative: the expressed secondary function of most, if not all, prison systems worldwide. Without at least some tangible evidence to inmates that rehabilitation could and does take place, the management of prisons systems would become nearly impossible.

Controlling: makes the custodial and restorative functions problematic. For it should be more than a relationship in which the authority figures say, "Jump!" and the inmates respond, "How high?"

Maintenance: as a relatively closed community, the prison must provide a range of services, from food to medicine. Indeed, for this reason many prison systems are referred to as departments of correctional *services*.[4]

It should be understood that the custodial, restorative, and controlling functions in particular overlap in part or whole depending upon the level of security (whether maximum, medium, or minimum), the commitment of the correctional leadership to a particular ideology, and, of course, the relative level of cooperation of the offenders.[5] In this regard, both offenders and staff bring with them anticipatory socialization factors conditioned by their respective community environments (such as an expectation by inmates that physical punishments will occur, and by officers that physical punishments should occur) that will influence the prison environment and therefore affect the prison functions. Indeed, there will be manifest and latent class and power differences with and between staff as well as inmates, such as those between the warden and corrections officer, between officers and inmates, and among the inmates themselves.

In addition and in particular, staff and inmates' perception of the quality of the maintenance services, is critical to the smooth operation of the prison system. These services are tangible and nontangible for both staff and offenders. On the offender side, for example, it has been very important that they perceive, as well as actually experience, that the disciplinary procedures are conducted fairly or that some level of self-management is allowable. On the staff side, it is equally important that they perceive and actually experience some social distance between themselves and inmates lest they be accused of overidentifying with offenders. Intra- and intersocial differences among staff and inmates, then, create the dynamic fluid in correctional relationships and contribute to the problematic character of control within prisons.[6]

The Demise of Rehabilitation and the Reaffirmation of Retributive Ideology

The ebb and flow of correctional ideology has affected correctional functions and, in turn, staff-offender relationships. Prior to the 1970s (pre-Attica), reformative ideology and practices were prevalent, given the type of inmates and the relatively small number of persons in prison.[7] This could be seen in the organizational structure of most prisons, including New York's, in which there was unilateral custodial supremacy over all staff and strict control over offenders. It was not until the prison riots of the late 1960s and early 1970s that prison organizational changes began to create the necessary infrastructure for rehabilitative practices.[8]

In the New York State Department of Correction, a significant post-Attica organizational structural change was the shift in title from the Department of Correction to the Department of Correctional Services. As well, the titles of Warden and Deputy Warden were changed to Superintendent and Deputy Superintendent. These and other changes symbolized a reinventing of corrections to reflect an array of services of which custody and control were only parts of a larger whole. At a minimum they were indicative of a movement from unilateral custodial direction to trilateral directional structures. These tridirectional structures comprised equally ranked department heads referred to as Deputy Superintendents of Security, Programs, and Administration. They resulted in a perceived, though not actual, balance of power between the authority components, especially Security and Programs. Rehabilitation-oriented personnel began to feel a sense of empowerment, a sense of empowerment that unfortunately could not reach its fullest potential because of the legacy of custodial supremacy, distracting power struggles between custodial and treatment staff, and a growing external sense that prison cannot, and should not, constitute more than a punitive environment.

Thus, long before Martinson declared or discovered that "nothing works,"[9] many practitioners (myself included) were discovering that there was a lack of both external and internal support for significant rehabilitative efforts.[10] This could easily be discerned internally through differential budget allocations to the various departments and externally through movements to end indeterminate sentences.

Two primary factors contributed to the end of indeterminate sentences and their related ideology, rehabilitation. First, internally, there was the harm that emanated from doing nothing or doing wrong to offenders while under indeterminate sentences[11] and the failure of programming staff to document that something works.[12] For example, idleness reduction among the inmates often served as a justification for the inmate activities that had no redeeming value or rehabilitative worth other than that of reducing boredom. It is also known that, because they were a captive audience, many inappropriate experiments were done on inmates with or without their consent. Program staff either acquiesced in the face of a more powerful custodial staff or did not care enough to fight for the right type of programs. Most importantly, perhaps, those program staff who were doing the right thing failed to note those programs in the records that mattered. There is now, therefore, little support for rehabilitation as a viable ideology and, in consequence, as a primary correctional practice. In fact, the current strategy is to claim that offenders are much more problematic than they were in the past and in dire need of longer, fixed sentences.[13]

Secondly, there were external groups who felt that indeterminate sentencing was not proving effective over time. To be sure, these external groups differed ideologically about the need to end determinate sentencing. On the one hand, there were those who felt that there should be certainty of lengthy punishment (that, for example, a life sentence should mean life in prison with no parole). On the other hand, there were the just deserts folks who agreed with certainty of punishment but felt that punishment should be as short as possible within the least restrictive correctional sanction. The former group have won the day decisively, as we practitioners have seen unabated changes in sentencing structures that signal the demise of rehabilitative ideology and the ascendancy of retributive ideology.

The most obvious reason has been the enormously increased use of incarceration to solve social problems such as drug addiction and poverty. A less obvious reason, perhaps because it has been so consistent, is the use of incarceration to control minority—and particularly black—social mobility.[14] In any case, this incapacitative strategy is driven by the public's fear of an escalation in crime.[15] Politicians have willingly accommodated this fear—at the national level by passage of the Violent Crimes Control and Law Enforcement Act of 1994, which contains truth-in-sentencing legislation, at the state level with three-strikes-you're-out legislation, and at the local level through quality-of-life legislation.[16] America now finds itself the world leader in the number of its citizens who are under some form of correctional supervision—5.5 million as of 1996 and still growing. Although the negative impact of this growth is evident at every level of the correctional continuum, from probation to prison to parole,[17] it is in prisons that correctional overcrowding (defined as an excess of population over resources) most easily has deadly consequences for both staff and inmates.[18]

Tonry noted the disproportionate incarceration of minorities in English-speaking countries worldwide when he compared the ratios of black-white imprisonment in Australia, Canada, and the United Kingdom with the United States.[19] In the United States, minority disproportionality also extends to inmates on death row. At the end of 1998, for example, thirty-four states and the federal prison system held 3,452 prisoners under sentence of death, 4 percent more than at the end of 1997. Of these, 1,906 were white and 1,486 were black.[20]

Given the demise of rehabilitation as a viable ideology, the rise of retributive ideology, the political—and therefore public—support for a more punitive approach,[21] the resultant overcrowding, and the disproportionate minority populations in most of our prisons, it is hard not to conclude that:

- we cannot build enough correctional institutions to accommodate the growth, and
- we should not redesign community corrections as an extension of punishment.[22]

On the first point, it could be argued that one way of solving the problem of prison overcrowding would be to increase the number of capital crimes and then to accelerate executions. This strategy, fortunately, has not received wide support.[23]

On the second point, more intensive monitoring of offenders in the community has resulted in more offenders returning to prison for technical violations. When one considers that fully one-third of the prison population comprises inmates who have violated the conditions of their probation/ parole, as opposed to committing new crimes, the prospects for rehabilitative success are poor indeed.[24]

Practice into Ideology

Changes in Correctional Supervisory Techniques: A New Penology

The dominance of retributive ideology has forced a change in judicial and correctional practices. In particular, ideological change has resulted in the narrowing or curtailing of discretionary power.[25] Although this curtailment may have had its positive features—such as minimizing sentencing disparities—there have also been negative features. To quote Allen: "[T]he preoccupation becomes pathological when it nourishes the belief that discretion can be avoided or when it prompts opposition to the programs and policies of social institutions solely because they rest in some measure on discretionary exercises of authority . . . for what needs to be done may unavoidably entail the exercise of discretion by public functionaries."[26]

Attempting to "do the right thing" in the face of discretionary restrictions has had obvious ramifications for those who were predisposed to do and say the "right things." Most judicial and correctional practitioners, however, have supported retributive ideology and have conformed to the "new penology."[27] Judicially, it goes without saying that an increasing number of offenders is being sentenced to determinate and lengthy periods of incarceration. On the one hand, at the institutional correctional level, we find refined classification assessments that rate security risk over treatment needs and view case management as an offender-control mechanism. At the community corrections level, on the other hand, there are correctional supervisory techniques that stress greater control over offenders. This is made evident by the contemporary refocusing of traditional probation, parole, and imprisonment into so-called intermediate sanctions. Staff-offender contacts are maximized and there is more drug testing and greater surveillance.[28] This method of offender supervision is best described as case management and purports to be a multifunctional approach ranging from monitoring to advocacy. Although I have observed that some case managers have successfully combined these functions to the benefit of offenders, most have not, especially in the light of large case loads. Large case loads are the norm in correctional practice. Accordingly, the advocacy and service aspects of case management often fail to be demonstrated in the staff-offender relationship. Thus control rather than change of offenders is more apparent in both institutional and community corrections.[29]

It is evident that heretofore laudable objectives that shaped the perspective of rehabilitation ideology, such as provision of continuity of offender services from the institution to the community, development of community resources to lessen offender recidivism, and offender-family reunification efforts, have become mired in the more influential objectives of control and monitoring that characterize retributive ideology.[30] In this manner, corrections has become a revolving door: releasing offenders usually after they have served the major part of their sentence and then returning them to prisons, usually for technical violations rather than their commission of new crimes.[31] Ironically, the return of offenders to prison has become an accepted indicator of corrections' efficiency and effectiveness rather than of its failure.[32]

Traditional Institutional Corrections and Community Corrections: Pre-Attica

How did corrections come to be such an ineffective institution when measured by its role in recidivating offenders? The answer can be found by looking at the context of traditional (pre-Attica) institutional corrections and the castelike officer-offender and treatment staff–offender relationships that prevailed until the mid-1970s.[33] On the one hand, there were manifest and objective differences between officers and offenders that created the tension that moved them to their respective subcultural group norms. On the other hand, treatment-offender relationships were seriously hampered by the fact that offenders were involuntarily confined. Indeed, given the involuntary nature of the relationships (at least for the offender), it was exceptional for a trusting and cooperative relationship to form between an offender and either custodial or treatment staff.[34]

The mission of corrections—to hold persons involuntarily until the expiration of their sentences—led to prisonization.[35] This included adoption of the so-called inmate code, which required overt loyalty to the inmate group and opposition to the direction of prison staff. Under traditional correctional conditions, the process of prisonization (that is, internalization of prison norms and values) was, to some degree, nearly impossible to resist. Nevertheless, there were variations in how individuals and groups of inmates responded to the process. Wheeler states that it was "lowest for those inmates who have had 'positive' and 'socialized' relationships during prepenal life, those who continue their positive relationships with persons outside the walls, those whose short sentences subject them to only brief exposure to the universal features of imprisonment, those who refuse or are unable to affiliate with inmate primary groups, and those who by chance are placed with other inmates not integrated into the inmate community."[36]

The most important aspect of prisonization became the degree of affiliation the individual inmate had with the dominant inmate group. The degree of affiliation in turn depended on where the inmate was in time and place. That is, was he or she far away from or close to release? Was he or she in the maximum- or minimum-security wing of the facility? It should be noted at this point that there were only a few so-called medium-security prisons before the 1970s and minimum-security prisons did not exist at all. Therefore, most maximum-security prisons developed a small cell block in which to place inmates who were nearing release, utilizing them for workgangs outside the prison. Time and place, then, determined the receptiveness of offenders to staff in general and in particular the ability of treatment staff to deliver treatment. For example, in the more secure wing of the facility custodial concerns would always be more dominant than treatment concerns, treatment staff were present for only one shift whereas custodial staff were present for three shifts, and treatment staff were not very well trained in ways of changing offenders.[37] It was thus nearly impossible to treat offenders effectively within the environment of a maximum-security prison. To do so would have required that offenders relinquish their adherence to the inmate code and custodial staff their overt control over offenders.[38] Inmate adherence to subcultural responses was more definitive of outcomes than officers, due, as I have suggested, to the involuntary nature of their role in the prisons. From a cultural perspective, the inmates' acculturation and adaptation began the moment they were assigned an inmate identification number. That and other "degradation ceremonies" helped to reinforce the inmate's commitment to the inmate code.[39]

Did there also exist an endurable subculture in the social world of the guards?[40] Subcultures usually form as a result of reactionary negative perceptions to the host culture, in this case the prison organization. Included in this was the stress of realizing the formalized objectives (reform and/or punishment). Officers in traditional corrections had a sense of the danger-ousness of their work and that their ability to carry it out was circumscribed and compromised by others internal and external to the organization (for example, administrators, minorities, and women). As was the case with in-mates, officers resorted to different strategies to cope with their perceived occupational frustrations. The most salient of these adaptation strategies were:

> "Retreatism," wherein officers adapted by moving to the perimeters of the prison and minimizing interaction with offenders; "Quitting," wherein they adapted by either leaving the organization altogether or took a support or treatment job within the organization; "Active Opposition," where they joined the union and became active leaders; or "Professionalism," which assumes they would demonstrate be-havior and attitudes that showed a search for continual improve-ment toward the ideal Correction Officer.[41]

The situation in traditional community corrections has not been too dissimilar in respect of factors that impact negatively on staff-offender rela-tionships. It is interesting that the number of adults under traditional proba-tion supervision has been much larger than the number of adults in prison or on parole.[42] It is for this reason perhaps that probation officer case loads have been excessive and have left little time for the rehabilitative or reintegra-tive needs of offenders.[43] Indeed, as it is within the prison and parole, the operative condition in the probationer–probation officer relationship is one of overcrowding. Although it is not clear why probation has failed, the rea-sons for parole failure are much clearer. Put simply, parole's failure is di-rectly related to institutional corrections' failure. Prison experience made offenders too dysfunctional to survive in the community. In addition, given their degraded status as public offenders,[44] "they may [have returned] to associations with other ex-offenders not so much to continue a criminal career as to find a supportive social setting."[45]

Nontraditional Institutions and Community Corrections: Post-Attica

In traditional institutional corrections and community corrections, relation-ships between staff and offenders appeared to be static, and expectations were well understood by everyone. Under these pre-Attica circumstances, the authority of the warden was inviolate, and the inmate generally dis-played an overt compliance while being covertly committed to the inmate code. I would also suggest that features of the so-called deprivation model forced the offenders to develop means of surviving through banding together with their fellow inmates.

Post-Attica, however, we find that these relationships have come to be based on different expectations because of the changes resulting from judicial interventions, media attention, and the offenders themselves. To put these changes in perspective, Stastny and Tyrnauer could now pose a question that would have been unthinkable in pre-Attica days, namely: "Who rules the joint?"[46] They concluded that it depended on who held the power at any particular time—administrators, guards, or inmates! In New York State Prison System there were numerous general strikes by inmates with Attica serving as the epicenter.[47] It is a given, based on these forced changes, that the problem of control has stemmed from a pluralization of American prison culture. From my perspective, contemporary prisons can be viewed only as open communities. The warden is no longer the sole authority, either formally or informally, and inmates import many of their subcultural values and behaviors. There are now very few prisons that can be viewed as closed communities or total institutions.[48] Perhaps those that come closest to being total institutions are the new Supermax prisons. Even here we find that, though some atrocities have taken place behind closed doors, the goings-on are mostly open secrets and we rather quickly come to the point that something must be done about it. This, of course, contrasts with pre-Attica times when, in the so-called Big Houses, many such atrocities were never exposed.

The open prison, however, has meant an openness to new ideas and new possibilities for meeting the dual objectives of restraining and restoring offenders. The introduction of such concepts as "reintegration"[49] and more recently "restorative justice"[50] have opened wide the correctional door by creating the possibility for correctional reform and concern about the communities to which offenders will be returning.[51] This reform at the institutional level has come about, on the one hand, out of a recognition that the majority of offenders will be released at some point and that they will fare better if released from a minimum-security setting that approximates the communities to which they will be paroled.[52] On this note the transfer of inmates to facilities specifically designated as medium or minimum security has become a common post-Attica correctional practice.

On the other hand, correctional reform at the community level has come about because of the high level of actual failures of offenders under community supervision.[53] Basically, high offender failure may be found in the character and criminal history of most offenders. On a more superficial level, however, offender failure can be attributed to the inability of probation officers—given their excessive case loads—to supervise, counsel, and guide offenders properly, particularly felons as opposed to misdemeanants.[54] To the extent that funding has allowed, this high failure rate has prompted reforms that have included (under the umbrella of what has been called intensive supervision programs [ISPs]) a reduction of case loads close to the ideal of thirty offenders per line officer. Necessarily, due to their higher cost, ISPs have also had to be sold to the public, judges, and offenders. It has been argued that ISPs have a greater deterrent effect than either traditional probation or imprisonment.[55] An extreme case has been the community supervision of sex offenders—aptly called a containment approach[56]—which rests on a philosophy and goal of community and victim safety. It has three different supervisory components: specialized probation/parole officers, a treatment therapist, and a polygraph examiner. The supervisory components work in a coordinated manner to contain the sex offender.

Contemporary Changes in Staff-Offender Roles: Post-Attica Reactions

Given pre- and post-Attica dynamics, staff-offender relationships have been reformulated in a manner that reflects the two major ideologies: one is decisively proactive and the other reactive. Reactive correctional practices are evident in the responses of practitioners who often speak and behave as though correctional managers have lost control of their operations. Much like the growth of the so-called take back the streets from the criminals movement, a large number of correctional staff, custodial staff in particular, have dedicated their efforts to "take back the prisons" from inmates. In New York State and City corrections, the intense correction officer union activity, leading to protests and strikes in the late 1970s and throughout the 1980s, were and are indicative of a concern that inmates have too many rights and that management has made too many concessions to inmates. From their perspective, this has resulted in inmates being co-managers, possessing a power that they felt should be their own. As a group that had actual power based on authorization, however, corrections officers did force correctional practices toward more and better control of offenders. All other internal groups (that is, management, inmates, and civilian staff) have been influenced to follow their lead by seeing control as the key to staff-offender relationships.

The dominance of controlling practices in contemporary corrections is, of course, consistent with its historical belief that incapacitation is a primary raison d'être for corrections as a social institution.[57] This has been understood by all staff, whether they are correctional officers or correctional counselors and regardless of the prevailing operational ideology. Contrary, then, to the notion that so-called treatment staff, especially in the institutional corrections environment, may have had or must have experienced role conflict, it was always understood by treatment staff that they needed to resolve their cognitive dissonance, if any, in favor of control.[58]

At the community corrections level, this may be less evident, for there custodial and treatment staff are often identical and they perform the dual roles of cop and social worker. On this point, however, I have to agree with Meyerson that it was never the role of correctional supervisors to be either cops or social workers but to assist offenders to live a crime-free life style. Meyerson's formal definition of the community correctional practitioner's role is "to authoritatively assist persons under supervision in living a crime-free life and in successfully completing the conditions of their sentence in a manner consistent with obligations to public safety and obligations to the sentencing authority."[59] This account distinguishes community correctional supervisors from both police and social workers. Whereas correctional supervisors are concerned with offenders' return to criminal behavior, police are concerned with crime prevention and social workers with change of the whole person. In addition, the correctional supervisor-offender relationship is, as I have underscored, an involuntary one, which makes all the difference between the police, who need probable cause to intervene against the free citizen, and the social worker, who cannot be effective without a significant degree of client voluntariness. Thus, it is most important that the relationship cultivated between corrections practitioners and offenders be one of referral to therapeutic services rather than of attempting to administer therapy themselves. Otherwise, there may indeed be a moral and functional conflict with the practitioner who is then forced to send an offender to or back to an institutional setting.[60] Although this may be unacceptable and certainly unpleasant from the offender's perspective, it was always a real dimension of the practitioner-offender relationship.[61]

It could be suggested, then, given the diametrically opposed objectives of offenders and staff—the former to maximize freedom and the latter to maximize control—that the relationship must be inherently conflictual as opposed to cooperative. For a number of reasons, the validity of this perception is unfounded. Observationally, most practitioners and offenders manifest a symbiotic relationship so that they can get through the days, the weeks, or months that their forced relationship will last.[62] In this regard, it is probable that their relationship varies between the extremes of overt conflict and cooperation, but is most likely to be moderately accommodating. Individual staff-offender relationships within institutional and community correctional settings may lean toward cooperation. At the institutional custodial and treatment level, we are easily reminded that peace is maintained in the prisons because of the voluntary compliance of the inmates who outnumber the guards.[63] Cooperation from the inmate's perspective is contingent on officers not displaying openly authoritarian demands.[64] I would agree with Vinter and Janowitz that, within this context, "the necessity for adequate custody poses a major dilemma in achieving desirable staff-client relations, since it appears to dictate procedures which limit the base for co-operation. Furthermore, maintenance of consistency and infusion of co-operation into all areas of staff-client relations may be especially problematical for larger institutions."[65]

It is in the interests of both offenders and officers to establish a cooperative working relationship. In this respect, prison organizations are no different from other social organizations; they operate as human relations enterprises. Accordingly, even a cursory familiarity with officers reveals that many of them enter the prison with a human service attitude and are oriented to and engage in service exchanges based on a human relations perspective.[66] Officers provide goods and services for inmates, act as referral agents or advocates, and help with inmate institutional adjustment problems. The emphasis is on the constructive side of their jobs away from just turning keys at best or passively observing inmate behavior at worst. As Johnson underscores:

> These officers discover that in the process of helping inmates and thereby giving them more autonomy, security, and emotional support, they gain the same benefits: more control of their environment, more security in their daily interactions with prisoners, and a sense of community, however inchoate or ill-defined, with some of the men under their care. In solving inmate adjustment problems, in other words, staff solve their own problems as well.[67]

To be sure, most offender-officer interactions are not of a therapeutic nature but are based on the day-to-day needs of the inmates and officers. The ecological dimensions of prison environments (that is, whether inmates are in a maximum-, medium-, or minimum-security facility) shape much of the behavior and attitudes of inmates and staff. Officer-offender relationships are conditioned by the ecological factors, overlaid, in my view, by the prevailing ideology.[68]

On the one hand, officer-offender relationships may lean toward informal interaction and discretionary decision making rather than formalistic and bureaucratic interaction. Within this context, social distance and differences may be reduced, thus creating the opportunity for a greater sense of self-esteem and empathy between officers and offenders.

Tangentially, whether such informality also creates an opportunity for the relationship to be unethical and corrupting is debatable.[69] From the point of view of absolute integrity, it is, as Anechiarico and Jacobs have suggested, impossible for organizational relationships to be completely corruption free.[70] They suggest that this is because the relationships involve human beings relating to one another. Logic and reasonableness, then, dictate that corruption should be viewed in relative terms. From this perspective, drug, sex, or money exchanges between officers and inmates should be considered as high-level corruption requiring criminal or administrative action or both. But exchanges such as bringing in newspapers or facilitating other relatively innocuous exchanges should be viewed as low-level or noncorrupting behavior.

On the other hand, it is my sense that, given the current dominance of retributive ideology, officer-offender relationships have become more formalistic and bureaucratic, especially in maximum- and medium-security facilities.[71] Much of this change in practices has undoubtedly resulted from overcrowding, along with attempts to address this rapidly by building new prisons.[72] Given the need to manage large numbers of offenders, staff have fallen back on formal rules and regulations.[73] Lombardo, for example, traced how one maximum-security facility changed its modus operandi from one of informality to one of formality.[74] He observed that, in the 1970s, corrections officers exercised a great deal of discretion in determining the shape of the task that was required by specific job assignments (by fitting the job to the man), whereas the 1980s were characterized by formal accountability (by fitting the man to the job). At the same time, the human services role was reduced to one of impersonal controlling and monitoring. Ironically, the resort to centralization, universal training, and unionization has generated the idea that officers are interchangeable and equally able to do any task.

Offender Change via Staff

Institutional Corrections Programs and Staff

Helping offenders survive institutional corrections, exemplified by officers oriented to human services, is not the same as helping them to avoid recidivism through exposure to academic, vocational, and, perhaps most importantly, therapeutic counseling programs.[75] I refer to counseling staff specifically because they are formally designated as treatment staff and must officially attempt to change offenders. We need, then, to examine program offerings in relationship to the program staff and the relationship of both to the custodial structure and staff. In this connection, I agree with Dilulio that "programs facilitate good inmate-staff and intrastaff relations and communications. The administration of programs routinizes personal interaction among and between inmates and staff."[76]

It is not, however, programs per se that facilitate good inmate-staff and intrastaff relations, but programs that are perceived by the inmates to be effective .[77] Whether inmates appreciate the value of program participation is, of course, problematic and partly a function of their belief in the credibility of staff, program offerings, and feedback.[78] Though inmates may believe that they are getting good training and education while incarcerated, they may discover, upon release, that they are unable to get a job related to their training. This in turn may feed back negatively to those inmates who had been contemplating program involvement but may now reconsider. There is a true dilemma here. On the one hand, the in-prison training may actually be state of the art but cannot be transferred to the community because of the ex-offender's stigmatized status. On the other hand, the in-prison training may be poorly suited to the contemporary labor market. In my view, either situation underscores a lack of true coordination and feedback communication between correctional staff and parole. Better coordination and communication would provide a quality-control mechanism for the programs that should be offered.

Staff competence and commitment also varies with beliefs about offenders. Although program staff, like others in corrections, are conditioned by the prevailing ideology and the type of facility, they are likely to have one of four beliefs about offenders. These are that offenders are basically hedonistic, dependent and require coercive controls; they are basically self-directed, requiring little if no intervention by the worker; offenders cannot change and therefore intervention makes little sense (here the worker is usually alienated from the client as well as the organization); offenders can be changed (here is where there will be maximum effort expended by both the client and worker to change).[79]

Like officers, most treatment staff enter corrections optimistic that they will be able to positively influence offender change within a correctional environment. Such optimism was not difficult to sustain during the era of rehabilitation when there was considerable governmental and financial support for that effort. Case loads were manageable due to a lower population. If a counselor chose, he or she could have conducted individual or group therapy sessions in addition to doing the service unit work (establishing visiting, mailing list, or transfers to other facilities, and so forth) required for their case loads. Many counselors, however, chose for a variety of reasons not to be as responsive to offender change as they could have been. One significant factor, as the population changed and grew, was the growing disparity between themselves and the offenders.[80] Another important factor was the inherent conflict between custody and restoration as objectives of the correctional environment. Counselors had to resolve this conflict by becoming either more custodially oriented or alienated from the organization. Like officers, counselors differed in their responses and commitment depending upon the type of facility in which they worked. Many counselors in maximum- and medium-security facilities became pessimistic about offender change in such environments or adopted a custodial orientation that aligned them with custodial staff and against the offenders. Administrators expect that counselors will resolve dilemmas involving the divulging of inmate confidences in favor of facility security.[81]

Community Corrections and Staff

To this point we have been considering staff-offender relationships at the institutional corrections level. Do differences exist in community corrections, where treatment is considered a dominant objective? When offenders are on probation and have not had an incarcerative experience? When offenders are released from prison to parole? Most importantly: Is community corrections a more effective offender change mechanism than institutional corrections? The simple answer is yes, because of the historically shared expectations of both external interest groups and internal members of correctional organizations. Institutions have always had an artificiality about them and perhaps this is the prime reason that the just deserts movement has been successful in arguing that rehabilitation cannot take place in a prison.[82] Prison environments differ from those of community corrections. Because they are, the attempt to prepare offenders for their eventual return to society without the actual experience of freedom may be an unattainable objective. In this respect, I share with Hall and his co-authors a sense of the difficulty of creating a real-world experience: "Ultimately, the change agent would hope to create the conditions under which the changee can begin to assess reality and its implications for himself. To do so, however, requires that the changee have an opportunity not only to reevaluate his situation as it relates to the situation of the rest society, but an opportunity to practice and experiment with new behavioral patterns as well. It is only in this way that the changee will be able to generalize from the experiences he has during change to his workday world."[83]

Those conditions can be created only via community corrections.[84] To paraphrase Duffee and McGarrell, community corrections is innovative and, by inference, more flexible than institutional corrections; it reduces crime by providing corrective resources in the community; it is intended to change the relationship between offenders and the community; it requires the development of a local constituency for corrections. Community corrections also avoids the use of institutions and provides us with greater diversity in correctional options. In addition, they assert that the most recent development is the compatibility of community corrections with the demand for retribution and restitution.[85] Although Duffee and McGarrell argue that despite the positive expectations for punishment in the community, there is little or no evidence to show that community corrections is any more effective than institutional corrections,[86] I would claim that community corrections can never be as ineffective as institutional corrections. In addition, we now know what minimally needs to be done for offenders in the community: They need viable employment, family support or at least interaction, avoidance of negative peer group contacts, and the cessation of drinking or drugging.

Community and Institutional Corrections:
Staff-Offender Relationships

Duffee's Model of Correctional Policies, which emphasizes both the offender and the community,[87] seems to suggest that minimum-security facilities that are community based are in the best position to put into practice an effective policy of reintegration. In facilities of this type, offenders have a better opportunity to demonstrate whether they have a high degree of self-control and staff have the best opportunity to seek out community-based resources to assist the inmate in his or her adjustment. More than that, offender-staff belief systems are highly conditioned by whether you are in a maximum- or minimum-security facility.

In at least two respects, Grusky's study of prison camps[88] is analogous to the work-release facilities that I have operated. Both usually operate as minimum-security facilities, and both have mission objectives in which treatment is dominant. In both settings, then, custodial staff need to have or develop a treatment orientation that maximizes their interaction with inmates. This requires that staff trust inmates, and in some cases creates an uncomfortable dilemma for those custodial staff who have transferred from maximum-security facilities where there was little trust and where keeping a social distance between themselves and the inmate was emphasized.

Grusky hypothesized that role conflict was created because the facility's organizational leadership emphasized treatment over custody and the facility was directed by a centralized system that mandated that both custody and treatment goals had to be achieved. This created ambiguity for the custodial staff because departmental-wide custodial rules were often not expected to be enforced. Officers adapted to this either by fully embracing the treatment goals and acting cordially with both treatment staff and offenders or by becoming alienated.[89] Those who became treatment oriented experienced job gratification. Those who did not became overtly custodial and were often abrasive. Additional findings from the study included the effects of administrative succession. This underscored the importance of replacing administrators with others who had treatment experience because nontreatment experienced administrators tended to formalize relationships between the staff and inmates and emphasized "closer supervision and stronger security."[90] The effect was to resolve role ambiguity for custodial staff but to increase it for treatment staff. They also found that the size of the organization made a difference—the smaller the organization the less likely were rules and interactions to be formalized and the more likely was help to be extended to inmates.

Grusky's prison-camp findings show similarities to and differences from those of work-release facilities. A major difference is that prison camps tend to be in rural areas whereas work-release facilities are usually urban based.

As a result, offenders in work-release facilities experience more frequent community and family interaction than those in rural-based prison camps. There is no doubt that offender-staff relationships are closer to the real world than those in prison-camp settings. Offenders in work-release settings tend to be insistent that their relationship with staff, both custodial and treatment, should be based on mutual respect. The appointment of an administrator who is not treatment oriented or the transfer-in of custodially oriented officers has had an insignificant impact on the reintegrative cultural process that characterizes a facility based in the community. Even centralization, as hypothesized by Grusky, does not diminish offender control while they are in the community. Custodial concern develops only as an exception to the normal rather than as a normal state of affairs. Recognizing the constraints on custodial staff, offenders will attempt not to give custodial staff any justification for expelling them from the program. Offender failure rates in work-release programs are therefore relatively low.[91] The reason for this is largely due to offender self-direction rather than staff intervention. Because staff intervention tends to be reactive, offenders shy away from interactions with staff that may force negatively viewed disclosures. Such disclosures have often resulted in additional restrictions and/or removal from the program. Staff-offender relationships, then, are cursory and of short duration. Predictably, treatment staff do not explore root causes for the offenders' criminality or develop comprehensive intervention plans to forestall a return to criminal behavior. Although some of the lack of meaningful intervention relates simply to the amount of time available, the offender case load–staff ratio is also a factor. The presumption is that the higher the case load the less time will be available for staff intervention. Other possible scenarios can be seen in the following table.

It does not follow axiomatically that staff will rise above or fall below expectations when the ideal or the worst-case scenarios present themselves. Treatment staff in work-release facilities, like staff at any security level, vary in their responses—depending upon their ideology and commitment, they are proactive or reactive. I have observed that their management of time and case loads depends very significantly on their personal styles.[92] Indeed, the normal response of treatment staff in the situation in which there is much

Table 5.1 Factors Affecting Meaningful Intervention

		Case Load	
		Low	High
Time Available for Intervention	More	Best	Better
	Less	Good	Worst

available time and case loads are high is that they are not proactive and do not rise to the occasion. Paradoxically, neither are they proactive when there is much available time and case loads are low. Whether this is only a temporary hangover from unfavorable time and case load conditions remains to be assessed.

Although it would appear that staff-offender relationships are at least minimally controlled by staff, the control is, nevertheless, significant. Discretionary decision making by both treatment and custodial staff in work-release settings can benefit both staff and offenders (a win-win situation), benefit one over the other (a win-lose or lose-win situation), or not benefit either (a lose-lose situation). In work release, such decisions range over everyday decisions to let offenders go to work and school, times for leaving and returning to the facility, work-release earnings, and urine testing to determine whether illegal drugs have been used.

On occasion, these opportunities for staff discretionary decision making have resulted in corruption, creating a situation that is ultimately non-beneficial for both staff and offenders. Staff in work-release facilities might begin or extend an illicit or romantic relationship with an offender outside the work environment. There is a low probability that such arrangements will be detected due to the ease of making them outside of the facility when staff leave work and offenders go to work. Illicit relationships rarely occur inside the facility, although arrangements may be discussed inside the facility. The understanding is: "This can wait until we're on the streets." Although contraband is hardly ever found, despite numerous searches by custodial staff and trained K-9 dogs, successful illicit exchanges between staff and offenders cannot be construed as beneficial to either staff or offenders, particularly in the long term and in relation to the objectives of the facility.

Probation/Parole Staff and Offender Relationships

To this point we have viewed staff-offender relationships from the inside out and now need to view staff-offender relationships from the outside in, seeing how this affects the inside. Are they relationships of mutual conflict or cooperation? How genuine are they?

Meyerson claims that relationships between offenders and probation practitioners may range from their being pseudo allies to their being natural allies. In the former case, although the relationships give the impression of being helping ones, they are not; in the latter case, the relationships are mutual and genuinely helpful. Duffee distinguished four types of parole officers:

1. officers who look for reasons to revoke, based on their perception that the parolee is not to be trusted;

2. officers who spend most of their time in their offices recording the parolee's behavior;
3. officers who are primarily paternalistic, tending "to coach the client rather than actively intervene, and to stress attitude and adjustment rather than specific behaviors"; and
4. officers who act as brokers for services needed by the parolee.[93]

It appears that, as with their counterparts in probation, parole officers spend most time in their offices and are least likely to serve in a broker role. The typical relationship is conditioned by what I have observed as a lack of familiarity with the community in which the offenders reside. Jester, for example, found a positive correlation between parole officers who were oriented toward law enforcement (that is, retribution, deterrence, and incapacitation) or social work (that is, rehabilitation) and the geographical areas in which they worked.[94] Her study indicated that there was a correlation between location in a rural or urban area and the way and manner in which parole officers performed their jobs. In rural areas there was a sense of pride and prestige associated with being a parole officer, and this was reinforced by community support. In urban areas, by contrast, parole officers were alienated from the community.

Duffee suggests "that community reentry programs of the reintegration type would benefit from their attachment to the restraint-oriented sentencing guidelines and prison disciplinary code." By this he means that staff-offender relationships should involve only minimum intervention and only for clearly defined rule violations with certainty of punishments for transgressions. He goes on to say: "In terms of actual behavior of the offenders in the community programs, much of the conflict between staff and offenders revolves around similar issues. Offenders frequently feel that staff should let them alone unless they seek assistance or advice, and they feel that their behavior should be self-determined unless they break laws or center rules about conduct."[95]

Empirically, however, due to the fact that community corrections has begun to serve as an overcrowding release valve for correctional institutions, this approach may have contributed to a higher than expected failure rate. This has been exacerbated by what Andrew Scull is reported as asserting— the "dumping of offenders and other deviants into certain communities that serve as the new walless institutions for the waste products of the political economic system that we value."[96] Duffee concludes that the reintegration movement "may simply be integrating offenders into the already large segment of the American populace that is economically and politically segregated from the mainstream of American life."[97]

Summary and Conclusion

Offender-staff relationships cannot be effective unless practitioners are willing to serve in both broker and advocacy roles. The current emphasis on punitiveness, at both the institutional and community correctional levels, makes it difficult for practitioners to assume an advocacy stance, even if they desire to do so. Like welfare reform, correctional reform has shifted in the direction of attributing to offenders complete individual responsibility for their plight, regardless of their circumstances. Therefore, as Cullen and Gilbert have astutely noted, it has fostered the view that the "state not only has no right but also no obligation to do anything about the condition or needs of an offender."[98] It appears to me that the state's position is reinforced by popular culture, which stresses the unredeemability of a correctional population that is disproportionately minority.[99] This popular stereotype feeds the view that the current correctional population is, to quote Sloop, "unqualified rhetorically for rehabilitation programs and alternatives to incarceration, alternatives that require trustworthiness and rationality."[100] It is hardly coincidental that the decline in rehabilitation and the increase of retribution have paralleled changes in the racial composition of the correctional population.[101]

Practitioners who are true professionals must embrace the notion that rehabilitative and reintegrative efforts are win-win strategies for everyone—society, the community, practitioners, and the offender. There needs to be a willingness on the part of practitioners, from the executive to line levels, to establish or reinforce ties between the offenders and the community.[102] But equally, offenders who are released from institutions must be more tolerant of practitioners who are guided by the desire to help them stay straight. Such help must extend beyond states "providing jobs and job training in lower-end economic enterprise"[103] to include a comprehensive restorative justice approach that involves practitioners, the community, and the offender.

Notes

1. Jess Maghan notes that well-meaning attempts to improve prisons have backfired and made them worse. He suggests that one reason for this can be found in the periodic ideological battles between rehabilitation and retribution, and contends that this battle could end if we replaced ideology with practical knowledge, that is, those practices that have been shown to work. See Jess Maghan, "The Dilemmas of Corrections and the Legacy of David Fogel," *International Journal of Offender Therapy and Comparative Criminology* 41, no. 2 (1997): 113–15. Another inquiry of interest, suggested by Randall L. Atlas and Roger G. Dunham, is how prison architectural changes have reflected changes in correctional philosophy.

While I believe that prison physical designs can enhance or detract from the prevailing correctional ideology, it is my contention that ideology will be more influential than the design of the physical plants. See Atlas and Dunham, "Changes in Prison Facilities as a Function of Correctional Philosophy," in _Are Prisons Any Better?: Twenty Years of Correctional Reform,_ ed. John W. Murphy and Jack E. Dison (London: Sage Publications, 1990), 43–60.

2. On this point, see J.Thorsten Sellin, _Slavery and the Penal System_ (New York: Elsevier, 1976), 145–62, where he describes how the penal system was developed primarily to control the emancipated slaves. Their incarceration was, of course, justified by the prevailing mythology that ex-slaves, like slaves, were inferior and too dangerous to be mingling with whites, particularly middle- and upper-class whites, in a free society.

3. Todd R. Clear, _Harm in American Penology: Offenders, Victims, and their Communities_ (Albany: State University of New York Press, 1994), 78–87.

4. Claude Faugeron, "The Changing Functions of Imprisonment," in _Prisons 2000: An International Perspective on the Current State and Future of Imprisonment,_ ed. Roger Mathews and Peter Francis (New York: St. Martin's Press, 1996), 126–28.

5. On the inmate's psychological adjustment to prison life John Galtung's assessment is consistent with Toch's (_Living in Prison_) and Johnson's (_Hard Time_) in his enumeration of the various escape mechanisms in which many inmates indulge. They include: (1) "escape into the prison community," in which prisoners accommodate to staff and other inmates while doing their time; (2) "escape into the prisoner's community," in which prisoners adopt the inmate code and identify with an inmate primary group; (3) "escape into isolation," in which the inmate has minimum interaction with both staff and inmates and attempts to maximize contacts externally with family members and friends; (4) "escape into his own case," in which the inmate resolves to prove his innocence largely through the appeal process; (5) "escape into expiation," in which the inmate concedes his guilt and willingly accepts punishment that fits his or her crime; (6) "escape into violation of the prison regulations," in which there is usually a display of aggressive behaviors against staff and other inmates as well as against the prison administrators; and (7) "escape into illness," in which there are frequent health-related complaints, both real and imagined. "The Social Function of the Prison," in _Prison within Society,_ ed. Lawrence E. Hazelrigg (Garden City, N.Y.: Doubleday, 1968), 27–49.

6. Faugeron, "The Changing Functions of Imprisonment," 127.

7. John M. Sloop, _The Cultural Prison: Discourse, Prisoners, and Punishment_ (Tuscaloosa: University of Alabama Press, 1996). See, especially, chapters 3–5.

8. Bert Useem and Peter Kimball, _States of Siege: U.S. Prison Riots 1971–1986_ (New York: Oxford University Press, 1991), 218–31.

9. Robert Martinson, "What Works? Questions and Answers about Prison Reform," _Public Interest_ 35 (1974): 22–54.

10. As an observer within corrections, I agree with John DiIulio's assessment of the status of rehabilitation over the years. He indicates that there were three stages: (1) from 1940 to 1975, a belief that "everything works," with Karl Menninger as its primary proponent; (2) the period from 1975 to 1985, a belief that "nothing works," with Robert Martinson as its primary proponent; and (3) the period from 1985 to 1990, a belief that "something works," with Paul Gendreau as its primary proponent. See John J. DiIulio, Jr., _No Escape: The Future of American Corrections_ (New York: Basic Books, 1991), chapter 3.

11. See Clear, *Harm in American Penology*, 1–37.

12. See Francis T. Cullen, Patricia Van Voorhis, and Jody L. Sundt, "Prisons in Crisis: The American Experience," in *Prisons 2000*, 21–52.

13. See Elliot Currie, *Crime and Punishment in America: Why the Solutions to America's Most Stubborn Social Crises Have Not Worked—and What Will* (New York: Metropolitan Books, 1998), chapters 1–2.

14. See Pernille Baadsager, Barbara Sims, Justin Baer, and William J. Chambliss, "The Overrepresentation of Minorities in America's Imprisonment Binge," *Corrections Management Quarterly* 4, no. 1 (Winter 2000): 1–7.

15. Zimring and Hawkins make some impressive points on the link between public opinion and imprisonment in their chapter "Politics and Public Opinion." See Franklin E. Zimring and Gordon Hawkins, *The Scale of Imprisonment* (Chicago: University of Chicago Press, 1991), 125–30. David Garland expands on this point by noting that the professional middle classes who had been supportive of "penal welfarism" are now more "supportive of punitive responses to crime," due in part to their perceived lack of social distance from criminal victimization. See David Garland, "The Culture of High Crime Societies: The Social Preconditions of the New Politics of Crime Control" (paper presented at a conference on "Crime, Neo-Liberalism and the Risk Society," New York, April 1999), 22.

16. Garland, "The Culture of High Crime Societies," 13.

17. Clear, *Harm in American Penology*, 43–47.

18. Zimring and Hawkins, *The Scale of Imprisonment*, 117–222.

19. See Michael Tonry, "Racial Disproportion in the Criminal Justice System," in *Malign Neglect: Race, Crime, and Punishment in America* (New York: Oxford University Press, 1995), 49–80. A prime reason for this (at least in the U.S.) appears to be the differential prosecution of blacks, who have a preference for crack cocaine, and whites, who prefer powder cocaine. Drug offenders comprise more than 50 percent of the growth of the prison population. Tonry, *Malign Neglect*, 81–123.

As I indicated earlier, the disproportionate incarceration of minorities is not a recent phenomenon but has consistently been the case for the past 150 years. See Sellin, *Slavery and the Penal System*; also Baadsager, Sims, Baer, and Chambliss, "The Overrepresentation of Minorities in America's Imprisonment Binge." In the latter article, the authors definitively establish that racism is the underlying reason why there is a disproportionate number of minorities under some form of correctional supervision.

20. Others under sentence of death included Native American Indians (twenty-nine), Asians (eighteen), and other races (thirteen). Also included were forty-eight women and 314 Hispanics. See Bureau of Justice Statistics, *Capital Punishment 1998* (Washington, D.C.: U.S. Department of Justice, December 1998). As Dennis R. Longmire indicates, where minorities have been convicted of killing whites, the so-called race of victim effect is a salient factor in the death penalty sanction. "Race, Ethnicity, and the Penalty of Death: The American Experience," *Corrections Management Quarterly* 4, no. 1 (2000): 36–43.

21. The punitiveness means not only that offenders are given extended sentences but also that they do not get "country-club" treatment while in prison. Richard Sparks has illustrated this by means of the concept of "less eligibility," namely, that "the level of prison conditions should always compare unfavorably to the material living standards of the laboring poor." See Richard Sparks, "Penal 'Austerity': The Doctrine of Less Eligibility Reborn?" in *Prisons 2000*, 74.

22. As Cullen et al. rightly note, the "intermediate sanctions" movement is neither cost efficient, necessarily effective, nor successful in solving the problem of prison overcrowding. "Prisons in Crisis," 21–52.

23. See Jonathan Simon's chapter, "Dangerous Classes, Laboring Classes, Underclasses," in *Poor Discipline: Parole and the Social Control of the Underclass, 1890–1990* (Chicago: University of Chicago Press, 1993), 250–67. Simon discusses such theories as "containment" and "waste management" but does not consider the possibility that execution might also be used as a social control mechanism.

24. On this point Joan Petersilia has noted that we should make a clear distinction between probationers who are misdemeanants and those who have felony status. Misdemeanant offenders on probation are successful at a ratio of three to one while felony offenders on probation are failing at a ratio of three to one. "Probation in the United States: Practices and Challenges," *National Institute of Justice Journal*, no. 233 (September 1997): 4.

25. See Peggy B. Burke, "Issues in Parole Decision Making," in *Correctional Theory and Practice*, ed. Clayton A. Hartjen and Edward E. Rhine (Chicago: Nelson-Hall, 1992), 213–34.

26. Francis A. Allen, *The Decline of the Rehabilitative Ideal* (New Haven, Conn.: Yale University Press, 1981), 88.

27. On this point, Feeley and Simon elaborate on the "new penology" by indicating that there is also a "new discourse" that accommodates it. "A central feature of the new discourse is the replacement of a moral or clinical description of the individual with the actuarial language of probabilistic calculations and statistical distributions applied to populations. . . . The task is managerial not transformative." Malcolm M. Feeley and Jonathan Simon, "The New Penology: Notes on the Emerging Strategy of Corrections and its Implications," *Criminology* 30, no. 4 (1992): 452.

28. See Peter Benekos, "Beyond Reintegration: Community Corrections in a Retributive Era," *Federal Probation* 54 (March 1990): 52–56.

29. See Simon, *Poor Discipline*, chapter 6.

30. Feeley and Simon, "The New Penology," 449–74.

31. See J. Irwin and J. Austin, *It's About Time: America's Prison Binge* (Belmont, Calif.: Wadsworth, 1994), chapter 5.

32. On this point, the so-called Intensive Supervision Programs (ISPs) have effectively become a means of "netwidening." They have become a means of maintaining control over low-risk offenders instead of assisting them in obtaining viable treatment and/or a job. See Joan Petersilia, "A Decade of Experimenting with Intermediate Sanctions: What Have We Learned?" in National Institute of Justice, *Perspectives on Crime and Justice, 1997–1998* Lecture Series (November 1998), vol. II: 79–106.

33. To quote George H. Grosser: "The term caste is more appropriate here, however, since there is no possibility of vertical mobility across caste lines in the prison." "External Setting and Internal Relations of the Prison," in *Prison within Society: A Reader in Penology*, ed. Lawrence E. Hazelrigg (Garden City, N.Y.: Doubleday, 1968), 10.

34. In 1968, Grosser remarkably and prophetically wondered "whether the mere fact of imprisonment itself, even under the most enlightened and humane conditions, always will produce an in-group that constitutes a reference group

hostile to the society and its representatives in the prison administration." "External Setting and Internal Relations of the Prison," 15.

35. See Stanton Wheeler, "Socialization in Correctional Communities," in *Prison in Society*, 150–79.

36. Wheeler, "Socialization in Correctional Communities," 151.

37. Donald Cressey, "The Nature and Effectiveness of Correctional Techniques," in *Prison in Society*, 349–73.

38. It is also David Duffee's view that in order for offender change to take place correctional managers must accept change in the normal relationships of power, prestige, and status in corrections specifically and in society generally. See Duffee, *Correctional Management: Change and Control in Correctional Organizations* (Englewood Cliffs, N.J.: Prentice-Hall, 1980), chapter 10.

39. See Harold Garfinkel, "Conditions of Successful Degradation Ceremonies," in *Prison within Society*, 68–77.

40. See Michael Welch, *Corrections: A Critical Approach* (New York: Penguin Books, 1996), 136–46.

41. Welch, *Corrections*, 145–46. Unfortunately, professional development by officers is unlikely to occur, given its contradictory relationship to paramilitary structures. Indeed, Welch concludes that both unionism and professionalism may achieve pyrrhic victories because neither is likely to result in more control for the officers and less control for management and inmates.

42. See Dean J. Champion, *Probation, Parole and Community Corrections* (Upper Saddle River, N.J.: Prentice-Hall, 1996), 52–64.

43. It is estimated that probation officers "spend as much as 70 percent of their time filling out paperwork associated with presentence reports." Champion, *Probation, Parole and Community Corrections*, 63.

44. See Garfinkel, "Conditions of Successful Degradation Ceremonies," 71–75.

45. Wheeler, "Socialization in Correctional Communities," 173. Owing to their need to survive in the prison culture, many inmates leave prison unprepared for reintegration into their communities. Wheeler suggests that "[t]his interpretation may help account for the profound states of anxiety and lack of confidence in themselves which even seemingly 'tough' inmates frequently display prior to release." He goes on to say that this is why "sociological research should be as concerned with the process of re-entry into the community as it has been historically with the problem of assimilation in prison."

46. Charles Stastny and Gabrielle Tyrnauer, *Who Rules the Joint? The Changing Political Culture of Maximum-Security Prisons in America* (Lexington, Mass.: Lexington Books, 1982).

47. See the category New York State Prisons in the *New York Times Index* 1976, especially the strike of August 23, 1976, which occurred five years after the Attica prison riot/rebellion.

48. Erving Goffman, *Asylums: Essays on the Social Situations of Mental Patients and Other Inmates* (Garden City, N.Y.: Anchor, 1961).

49. See Duffee, *Correctional Management*, 95.

50. See Ron Classen, "Restorative Justice: Fundamental Principles" (paper presented at the NCPCR, 1995); Howard Zehr, "Restorative Justice: The Concept," *Corrections Today* 59, no. 7 (December 1997): 68–70.

51. Restorative justice may be viewed as one step beyond reintegration because the victim is seen as an integral part of the crime solution in a community. By the same token, reintegration may be viewed as one step beyond rehabilitation because it includes the community in a similar way. As Duffee has noted, the focus of rehabilitation has been exclusively on the offender. *Correctional Management*, 91.

52. Champion discusses traditional probation/parole, also known as community corrections, and nontraditional community corrections, defined as "any community-based corrections program designed to supervise convicted offenders in lieu of incarceration, . . . that provides various services to client-offenders, that monitors and furthers client/offender behaviors related to sentencing conditions, that heightens client/offender responsibility, . . . and that provides for a continuation of punishment through more controlled supervision and greater accountability." *Probation, Parole and Community Corrections*, 277.

53. See Petersilia, "Probation in the United States," 2–8.

54. "Given an estimated 50,000 probation employees in 1994, and given that 23 percent of them (11,500 officers) were supervising about 2.9 million adult probationers, the average case load that year was 258 adult offenders per line officer. This contrasts with what many believe to be the ideal case load of 30 adult probationers per line officer." Petersilia, "Probation in the United States," 3.

55. Petersilia claims that high recidivism rates (65 percent) appear to be the norm rather than the exception in "When Probation Becomes More Dreaded Than Prison," *Federal Probation* 54 (March 1990): 23–27.

56. "In 1994, State prisons held 88,100 sex offenders. . . . Most will return to the community. . . . In addition, many . . . of those convicted of sexual assault felonies are sentenced to probation or to other forms of community supervision." Kim English, Suzanne Pullen, and Linda Jones, "Managing Adult Sex Offenders in the Community: A Containment Approach," *NIJ Research in Brief*, January 1997, 1.

57. See Michael Foucault, *Discipline and Punish: The Birth of the Prison* (New York: Vintage Books, 1979), 293–308.

58. John R. Hepburn and Clesta Albonetti, "Role Conflict in Correctional Institutions: An Empirical Examination of the Treatment-Custody Dilemma among Correctional Staff," *Criminology* 17, no. 4 (February 1980): 445–59. Barbara Meyerson suggests that role conflict may be a conceptual fiction derived from academics rather than a pragmatic amalgamation of two roles by practitioners; see her "Role Definition for the Practitioner of Correctional Supervision," in *Correctional Theory and Practice*, 86. Furthermore, though it is recognized that role exchanges do take place, in which corrections officers at times act as counselors and vice versa, it is still my contention that there is no confusion about which is the dominant role.

59. Meyerson, "Role Definition," 89.

60. Meyerson, "Role Definition," 90.

61. It is recognized that community control is quite problematic given that in practice offenders are largely unsupervised. Nevertheless, offender control, whether in prison or in the community, is an overriding concern of practitioners. Zimring and Hawkins draw the distinction between control in the community and control in prison via a distinction between monitoring and control. See Zimring and Hawkins, *The Scale of Imprisonment*, 160. In their view, community control is nothing more than the capacity to control as opposed to actual control (e.g., custody). Control in prison, however, is incapacitating—the offender does not have the op-

portunity to commit new crimes.

62. Duffee asserts that it is a fundamental tendency of organizations or groups to elaborate modes of cooperation. The latter he defines as "the ability of two or more groups to negotiate a state of interaction in which each unit can achieve objectives satisfactory to itself." *Correctional Management*, 5. With regard to inmates and staff, he postulates—I think correctly—that the inmate's highest objective is freedom from correctional supervision and staff; in contrast, the staff's highest objective is complete conformity of offenders. Given these two seemingly contradictory positions, correction managers may be organizing their facilities for failure —as Duffee suggests—by their pursuit of certain controlling policies and their cultural understanding of the offender (10).

63. See Lynn E. Zimmer, *Women Guarding Men* (Chicago: University of Chicago Press, 1986). She makes the point that "the ability of the officers to physically coerce compliance is illusory due to the fact that the inmates outnumber the guards" (22). On the one hand, the danger of interacting with inmates is that they may withdraw their voluntary compliance. On the other hand, the more that officers interact with inmates the more they will foster an accommodating relationship with them. See also Kelsey Kauffman's discussion, "Power in a Prison," in *Prison Officers and Their World* (Ann Arbor: University Microfilms International, 1985), 143–229.

64. See Michael Braswell, Tyler Fletcher, and Larry Miller, *Human Relations and Corrections* (Prospect Heights, Ill.: Waveland Press, 1998), 94–95; Kauffman, *Prison Officers and Their World*, 367–73; Zimmer, *Women Guarding Men*, 21–22.

65. Robert Vinter and Morris Janowitz, "Effective Institutions for Juvenile Delinquents: A Research Statement," in *Prison within Society*, 190.

66. See Braswell, Fletcher, and Miller, *Human Relations and Corrections*, 94–95; Robert Johnson, "To Protect and to Serve: The Prison Officer's Private (Correctional) Agenda," in *Hard Time: Understanding and Reforming the Prison* (Monterey, Calif.: Brooks/Cole, 1987), 137–56; and Lucian Lombardo, *Guards Imprisoned: Correctional Officers at Work* (New York: Elsevier, 1981), 59–72.

67. Johnson, *Hard Time*, 154.

68. Johnson, *Hard Time*, 163–65, and Lombardo, *Guards Imprisoned*, 159–71.

69. Lombardo, *Guards Imprisoned*, 98–110.

70. Frank Anechiarico and James B. Jacobs, *The Pursuit of Absolute Integrity: How Corruption Control Makes Government Ineffective* (Chicago: University of Chicago Press, 1996), 3–17.

71. Braswell, Fletcher, and Miller have noted that "in recent years, a competing view of criminal behavior, based upon utilitarian principles that hold the individual responsible for criminal acts, has increased the use of correctional officers as advocates for punishment rather than treatment." *Human Relations and Corrections*, 89.

72. Joseph V. Williams, "Prison Overcrowding" (unpublished presentation for policy analysis class at John Jay College, Spring 1994). Braswell, Fletcher, and Miller have argued that the rapid expansion of corrections has helped to set back a promising professionalism among correctional officers and, perhaps worse, has led to a de-emphasis on rehabilitating inmates. See *Human Relations and Corrections*, 89.

73. See Feeley and Simon, "The New Penology," 449–74.

74. Lombardo, *Guards Imprisoned*, 211.

75. See Jay Hall, Martha Williams, and Louis Tomaino, "The Challenge of

Correctional Change: The Interface of Conformity and Commitment," in *Prison in Society*, 309–15.

76. DiIulio, *No Escape*, 120.

77. DiIulio specifically states that a good program must have "clear statements of the program rules," an "obvious concern by program staff," "participant regard for staff members," "preparation of participants for future problems," and "utilization of community resources." *No Escape*, 110.

78. This is based on the several factors that we have previously mentioned—where, time-wise, the inmate is in his sentence, the type of facility, program staff competency, and staff commitment to serving as agents of change.

79. See Hall, Williams, and Tomaino, "The Challenge of Correctional Change," 308–28.

80. Towberman's study found that the more closely counselors matched with offenders on demographic variables and personality styles, the greater was the effectiveness of the counseling. See Donna B. Towberman, "Client-Counselor Similarity and the Client's Perception of the Treatment Environment," *Journal of Offender Rehabilitation* 18, no. 1/2 (1992): 159–72.

81. See Braswell, Fletcher, and Miller, *Human Relations and Corrections*, 126–27, and Hepburn and Albonetti, "Role Conflict in Correctional Institutions," 445–59.

82. DeLuca, Miller, and Wiedemann, colleagues of mine at both John Jay College and in the New York State Department of Correctional Services, proposed that it be conceded that prisons cannot provide a rehabilitative environment and that punishment should not extend into the community once an offender is released. They have proposed that the offender's sentence have two stages. The first stage would involve imprisonment to receive punishment commensurate with the crime committed (they see punishment in prison as including labor to maintain or support the prison), and the second stage would take the form of mandatory parole in which rehabilitation would occur. I take strong exception to their proposal. First of all, it assumes that prisons are strictly for punishment instead of—as they were originally conceived—for reform/rehabilitation/restoration. Second, it does not confront the inevitable consequence that such a prison would soon evolve into one in which hard time à la pre-Attica would once again become the norm. Overcrowding would ensure this by creating stress between inmates and staff. Third, it assumes that no permanent harm would occur to offenders who experience only punishment while in prison. Worst of all, it assumes that offenders would be receptive to rehabilitative efforts once released. Given this scenario, it is not inconceivable that released offenders would engage in their own form of retribution. See Henry R. DeLuca, Thomas J. Miller, and Carl F. Wiedemann, "Punishment vs. Rehabilitation: A Proposal for Revising Sentencing Practices," *Federal Probation* 55 (September 1991): 37–45.

83. Hall, Williams, and Tomaino, "The Challenge of Correctional Change," 323.

84. Contemporary community corrections includes community-based facilities such as work release, minimum-security camps (which may or may not be boot camps), an array of temporary release options from any security-level facility (such as furloughs for purposes of strengthening family and community ties or seeking a job or residence prior to parole release), and, of course, probation and parole services. Hahn, however, has a much more expansive understanding of

community corrections, which he links to community policing and community (restorative) justice. Together they form what he has called "three pillars for a proactive justice system." But Hahn is attempting to stimulate reform in corrections from outside in whereas I am looking at corrections from the inside out. See Paul H. Hahn, *Emerging Criminal Justice: Three Pillars for a Proactive Justice System* (Thousand Oaks, Calif.: Sage Publications, 1998), 65–157.

Further, I agree with Clear that, though "there is some evidence that effective work with drug addiction can be done in institutional settings, . . . the bulk of the evidence" is that "success will take place in the real context of the community, not in the artificial setting of the prison." *Harm in American Penology*, 167.

85. See David Duffee and Edmund McGarrell, "Community Corrections: Its Presumed Characteristics and an Argument for a New Approach," in *Community Corrections: A Community Field Approach*, ed. David Duffee and Edmund McGarrell (Cincinnati: Anderson, 1990), 3–4.

86. David Duffee and Edmund McGarrell, "The Community Field and the Future of Community Corrections," in *Community Corrections*, 299–311. See also Dan A. Lewis and Cheryl L. Darling, "The Idea of Community in Correctional Reform: How Rhetoric and Reality Join," in *Are Prisons Any Better? Twenty Years of Correctional Reform*, ed. John W. Murphy and Jack E. Dison (Thousand Oaks, Calif.: Sage Publications, 1990), 95–110.

87. Duffee, *Correctional Management*, 91.

88. Oscar Grusky, "Role Conflict in Organizations: A Study of Prison Camp Officials," in *Prisons within Society*, 455–76.

89. Adaptation of custodial staff in minimum-security environments is similar, but the converse holds for treatment staff in maximum-security environments.

90. Grusky, "Role Conflict in Organizations," 466.

91. Here, "failure" is understood as being returned to a higher level of security. A small number of violations result in automatic removal. They are, first and foremost, an arrest and subsequent conviction for a new crime; a second-time use of illegal drugs; and an abscondence that lasts over ten hours from the scheduled time of return to the facility. Any staff with firsthand knowledge of these violations must report them in order to begin the obligatory removal process.

92. Many counselors with high case loads have resorted to the *a*-rule: the first *a* is basically allowed self-direction, the second *a* get attention as they initiate or demand it, and the last *a* get an inordinate amount of counselor-initiated attention.

93. Duffee and McGarrell, *Community Corrections*, 13.

94. Jean Jester, "Technologies of Probation and Parole," in Duffee and McGarrell, *Community Corrections*, 123–63.

95. Duffee, *Correctional Management*, 375.

96. Cited in Duffee, *Correctional Management*, 377.

97. Duffee, *Correctional Management*, 377.

98. Francis T. Cullen and Karen E. Gilbert, *Reaffirming Rehabilitation* (Cincinnati: Anderson, 1982), 178. It is sad but true that, as Clear states: "This is a pretty remarkable expectation—that the government would, in its wisdom, seek to activate a marginal class of politically and economically disenfranchised poor." *Harm in American Penology*, 84.

99. Sloop indicates that in popular culture there is a dividing line between what he calls "redeemable prisoners of the 1950s," who were "ambiguously Cau-

casian and hapless," and those prisoners in the 1970s, who were perceived as an unredeemable and essentially violent criminal types and were "African-Americanized." *The Cultural Prison*, 15. This has been normalized through the media and has influenced the public, politicians, judges, and others who are external to corrections.

100. Sloop, *The Cultural Prison*, 136. See also Jim Thomas, "Racial Codes in Prison Culture: Snapshots in Black and White," in *Ethnicity, Race and Crime: Perspectives Across Time and Place*, ed. Darnell F. Hawkins (Albany: State University of New York Press, 1995).

101. See Coramae Richey Mann, "Warehousing Minorities: Corrections," in *Unequal Justice: A Question of Color* (Bloomington: Indiana University Press, 1993), 220–54; also Sloop, "Rehabilitation, Revolution, and Irrationality, 1969–1974," in *The Cultural Prison*, 90–231; Tonry, *Malign Neglect*, 49–80.

102. Musheno and his co-authors suggest that the 1967 Commission on Law Enforcement and the Administration of Justice set the stage for recognizing that the crime and delinquency problem was essentially one of social disorganization that had its origins in the community. The focus of corrections should be one of "building solid ties between offenders and the community, integrating and reintegrating the offender into the community life." See Michael Musheno, Dennis Palumbo, Steven Moody-Maynard, and James Levine, "Evaluating the Implementation of Community Corrections," in Duffee and McGarrell, *Community Corrections*, 251–68. The intent, then, in community corrections is that the field worker will broker for offender restorative services.

103. Clear, *Harm in American Penology*, 94.

Response to Chapter 5

Moral Reckoning and the Social Order of the Prison

Polly Ashton Smith

Between the lines of Joseph Williams's chapter[1] lurks a longstanding issue about the relationship between the personal ethics of decision making—the applied and professional ethics that is generally the domain of moral philosophers—and the substantive ideals of political justice adopted by states and realized through their governmental institutions—a traditional focus of social theory and political philosophy.[2] In his otherwise comprehensive discussion, Williams takes it for granted that ideals of political justice shaped in the broader society influence correction officers' ethical actions, but he does not really explain how this works. The retributive philosophy or ideology that informs current correctional practices, Williams argues, diminishes the possibility of ethically efficacious relationships between correctional staff and offenders under their supervision, which he defines as relationships characterized by mutual cooperation. And indeed the social science research reviewed by Williams generally confirms the pervasiveness of conflicted, mutually antagonistic staff-offender relationships in U.S. prisons and other correctional contexts.[3]

Like many of the researchers whose work he discusses, Williams identifies institutional goals as externally imposed on the prison community, as ideologies that reflect the dominant correctional discourse and policy making in any given era. In Williams's analysis, the control orientation of many prisons, which is derived from a broader retributive philosophy that in recent history has guided U.S. crime control policy, explains the type and tenor of ethical conflicts that correction officers encounter in their work. His major premise is: Change the values, change the structural arrangements, and the ethical quality of relationships will follow. A degree of sociological determinism, the assumption that structure is antecedent to and in significant ways shapes the kind and character of choices people make, may be found in Williams's chapter and in the scholarship he reviews.

The sociological literature on the prison reflects the general social science debate about human agency and social structure. Researchers employ competing theoretical perspectives that model differently the interplay of individual norms and values and social context and structure to argue about the dynamics of social order in correctional institutions. In general, prison staff and inmates are portrayed as either defined by their roles within the social institution[4] or as autonomous individual decision makers. The latter account is represented in applied and professional ethics. The former, represented in Williams's chapter, typically criticizes applied ethics as one variation on the "rotten apple" approach to corruption, an approach that emphasizes individual responsibility while ignoring the broader social and organizational contexts in which corruption germinates.

By assuming that external goals, dictated by the values and ideals defined by various correctional ideologies, are the locus of the problem of ethical decision making and interaction within the prison, Williams overlooks an important and difficult question, one that represents a persistent but somewhat subliminal theme in correctional scholarship[5]: Is a correctional ethic a real possibility, or does this phrase obscure a foundational immorality at the very core of the prison enterprise?[6] For if some a priori substantive injustice inheres in the very nature of prison society, as Brookes argues,[7] then no ideals of justice or morality imposed by well-meaning policy makers, no degree of vigilance in the upholding of prisoner and staff human and constitutional rights, and no amount of training and education of staff and administrators in ethical standards and principles will lead to prison organizations that can establish longstanding, ethically efficacious relationships between correctional staff and their charges. Instead, staff-offender relationships will be continually shaped by and infused with this primary immorality or injustice.

The point of view I sketch here, in response to Williams, addresses this question directly, and, with some qualifications, concludes that correctional ethics cannot overcome a foundational problem of injustice within the prison enterprise. My argument is based on an analysis of the interconnections among trust, the legitimization of authority, and the possibilities for practical-moral reasoning within the prison social order. In general terms, I understand the prison as a uniquely modern institution, one that operates with a particular set of political and social-structural conditions that both constrain and enable the ongoing kind and quality of social action within the institution's specific organizational contexts. The account of social action I outline here, however, differs significantly from that of other prison researchers. The social structural conditions combined with the bases for social action, both of which I outline below, best explain, I believe, the incontestable historical reality of virtually all prison systems: perennial disorder, disruption, and inter- and intragroup conflict,[8] punctuated by brief intermissions of relative stability and harmony.

Sociological research on the social order of the prison has failed to account for a most important factor that influences ongoing social interaction and prison managers' ability to carry out their objectives: the microlevel accountings that staff and inmates provide of organizational conflict, or, in other words, participants' own justifications for social action that violates moral-ethical dictates that they themselves recognize as binding.[9] As I will explain, staff and inmates are not, as they are often implicitly portrayed, atypically undeveloped or inferior moral reasoners; they are typically average moral reasoners who live and work in an atypical social order that continually puts them in decision-making contexts that make action consistent with their moral integrity extremely difficult. In a real and important sense, the prison social order illuminates more clearly than in free society the close relationship between individual ethics, institutionalized practices, and social justice. In the terms of contemporary sociological theory, the relationship I am seeking to explain is that between human agency, social interaction, and social structure. The moral point of view is by no means absent in prison societies, but there it meets one of its most anguishing challenges.

The Prison: Modernity Turned Inside Out

The prison as we know it—a generic edifice embodying the idea of physical incarceration as criminal punishment—came into being along with the other fundamental institutions of modernity: capitalist economies and their complex divisions of labor, representational and parliamentary democratic governments, and the organizations created from public and private funds for the sole purpose of providing those universally required goods and services that free markets cannot sustain in ways affordable and accessible to all citizens, including the services provided by agencies responsible for public safety. The Enlightenment ideal of individual liberty was the philosophical and political linchpin of the new world order. The free individual of modernity is created by a set of political arrangements that establish government's coercive power over him on the basis of his political franchise and his implicit but contingent consent. He makes his own fortunes in life through self-motivated economic transactions involving his labor and his property; and his statuses, roles, and social prestige are a matter of choice and responsibility, as are his possible downfalls through poor judgment and vice.

By inverting or turning inside out these essential conditions of modernity, the prison casts its members into a kind of quasi premodern society, into a world the broader society now reviles and rejects. Like the serf in feudal society, the convict assumes only one important status in the prison, that of the prisoner, and that status, once the doors close, is ascribed, not achieved. Hence, although an individual may have achieved a broader social status of criminal or wrongdoer, his organizational status, prisoner, is better described as ascribed because it involves a universal set of roles that within the prison society permanently define the prisoner's core identity vis-à-vis all non-prisoners. The prisoner has no political franchise and he has no role in developing and maintaining the formalized set of protocols that govern his activities and social relations inside. He has no formal economic status at all in this society. Whatever labor he might engage in is at the will of his keepers and serves no important purpose in the ongoing, larger economy of the prison, and he has only a minimal right to property and no right to contract in any business activity related to it. Regardless of any humanitarian laws or rules derived from rights imported from the outside that may protect him from the worst depredations of his keepers, in the most significant social, political, and economic terms of modernity, he is a nonperson.[10]

Unlike his premodern counterparts, however, the modern denizens of prison society do not participate in a Great Chain of Being, a chain that provides explanation of why society is so ordered, legitimation for the chain of command of feudal authorities, and redemptive hope for relief from these earthly conditions. Here, in the prison, are the conditions of premodern, feudal society without the scaffolding of belief that gave meaning and purpose to those conditions, if not actual comfort to the great mass of its humblest inhabitants. And the lack of that scaffolding makes it a very bleak social landscape.

Trust and Confidence

Social relations in prison society, that is, relations between inmates and staff and between the members of each group, are not, indeed cannot, be characterized by trust. As recent scholars have argued,[11] trust is an essential and historically unique attribute of (free) social life in modern societies. Adam B. Seligman, whose recent book on this subject provides the most comprehensive and nuanced analysis of this topic, maintains that "[t]rust is something that enters into social relations when there is role negotiability, in what may be termed the 'open spaces' of roles and role expectations. Another way of saying this is that trust enters into social interaction in the interstices of system, or at system limit, when for one reason or another systematically defined role expectations are no longer viable."[12]

Since "modern social relations are characterized by: a. fewer status positions encompassed by any one role, b. more roles, c. more complex and differentiated role sets within any one status position, [and] d. greater numbers of reference group members,"[13] the individual is likely to experience conflict and contradiction between the expectations of his own roles and an ambiguity in his role expectations (obligations and commitments) of others. The degree of "lability" or "indeterminacy" inherent in all roles produces a greater degree of negotiability of role expectation in social relations. To confirm this insight, we have only to recall current public discourse on what it means to be a parent or an employee or a citizen, and what each of these role sets requires of us morally and practically.

Consequently, as Seligman argues, the conditions that characterize modern social relations produce the possibility for mistrust and confusion, and hence the necessity and possibility for trust. The modern individual's identity is not circumscribed by relatively few and relatively fixed sets of statuses and concomitant roles assigned to these statuses. It is rather defined by the surplus or extra identity that spills over the many statuses and role sets that are combined in the life of one person.

Trust, on this account, is something extended to and between persons who are not simply the incumbents of particular statuses. It makes possible the concerted social action between persons that otherwise would be very difficult to achieve given the complexity, unpredictability, and obscurity of their perceived role expectations. Trust is both personal, extended to the "I" who is beyond my statuses and roles, and abstract, because this "I" is the moral agent, who is the universal subject of modern democratic societies.[14]

The reasons for my claim that trust does not, and cannot, define social relations and interaction in the prison should now be obvious. As mentioned earlier, prisoners' social identities are clearly circumscribed by their one overriding status and the relatively simple and straightforward role expectations that follow.[15] This also holds true, more or less, for custodial staff. Once at work inside, their relations to inmates and to each other follow closely from their status as keeper and its role expectations, with some predictable variations based on the rank of the particular staff.

The distinction between trust and confidence is crucial for understanding the social order of the prison. As Williams and many correctional scholars have reiterated, the normatively prescribed patterns of behavior in prison societies are determined in significant ways by the personal predilections and managerial styles of correctional authorities and vary, in part, according to prevailing correctional philosophies (or ideologies) that influence the publicly articulated policies and purposes of the penal organization. The systemic absence of trust does not translate into disorder and conflict in the prison because it is not a society premised on the conditions that make trust necessary and significant. On the contrary, if confidence is high in both tacit and explicit normatively defined patterns of behavior, stability and relative harmony within and between staff and prisoner groups will follow. Confidence is external to relationships: it is defined as the predictability of a particular system, whether its resources will be distributed in pre-established, prescribed ways. For example, the building tender or trustee system described by researchers in the 1950s and 1960s was characterized by high levels of confidence. In other words, in settings in which "confidence in the fulfillment of role expectations and the various forms of social control and sanctioning mechanisms that ensure such performance"[16] pervades social interaction, the prison will be relatively free of the extreme symptoms of instability (for example, riots) so often seen in the past thirty-five years.

Two caveats, however, must be entered. First, as the building tender system and its famous abuses illustrate,[17] high confidence and relative stability in prison society have virtually no implications for the ethical efficacy of its social relations. In such mechanical societies, members coordinate their actions to achieve normatively defined goals, but they do not cooperate in the sense of producing mutually defined goals and social relations that promote and maintain the moral agency of all the participants.

The second and related caveat will be obvious to anyone who has worked in or studied any system or method of correctional control. The fact that social action in the prison might stem from confidence in relatively simple, fixed sets of role expectations does not mean that members do not negotiate various accountings of their behavior and justifications for the desired outcome of their situation.

Confidence-based prison administration limits the danger for all members from revolutionary chaos between the keepers and the kept, but rather than the risk that pervades trust-based societies, danger is the correlate of confidence-based societies.[18] Unlike risk, danger implicates members' self-preservation, one of Thomas Hobbes's primary natural rights that sovereign authorities must respect. Danger comes in the form of the threat of physical harm, if one's peers decide for various reasons not to offer protection (this applies to both staff and inmates), or in the related threat of social isolation, which can be a kind of identity extinction in such societies, or, in the case of correctional staff, in the threat of actual job loss or demotion in rank.

The Problem of Legitimacy

If the prison authority's own ability to ensure compliance is threatened, then confidence will suffer. In his now-classic study, *The Society of Captives*, Gresham Sykes first analyzed the issue of nonconsensual authority in the prison and its implication for social order and social relations. In Sykes's analysis, prison societies are fragile combinations of inmates' two possible responses to what I am calling their premodern, confidence-based social structure.[19]

Not surprisingly, Sykes's "two poles" of inmate response to the deprivations of prison society represent the two dominant models of social action in post–World War II sociological and social psychological theory: rational choice and social learning theory. Both poles have correlates in typical policies of correctional control. In the first, rational choice or instrumental model, deterrence of both inmate disruption and staff corruption is emphasized.[20] This explanation of the sources of social order and disorder assumes that social actors always act to maximize their personal utility. Prison authorities achieve deterrence through the skillful manipulation of both positive and negative incentives, which serve to direct individual members' utility calculations toward conforming behaviors (behaviors desired by the authority).

The second explanatory perspective, which, because of its history within the discipline of sociology, predominates in correctional scholarship, focuses on socialization processes in the prison and the formation of staff and inmate subcultures. These subcultures are often at odds with the formal policies and practices of prison authority. Researchers employing this perspective have argued, or at least implied, that the return to order in an unstable prison could be accomplished only with the establishment of some form of working normative consensus within, minimally, a dominant inmate group or in some cases a dominant staff group or subculture.[21] The salient issue, as these scholars understood it, was how much control prison management would be able to exert over the content of the new (post-organizational crisis) normative consensus.[22] The normative model, which incorporated the basic social-psychological assumptions of social learning theory to explain social action, is often applied in a deterministic way to analyze specific social phenomena. This model seems to imply, as one of its early critics argued, that "the individual is to himself what his place in an organization defines him to be,"[23] and, for the purposes of analysis, he appears to be in the harsher terms of another famous critic, a "judgmental dope."[24]

As I hope is obvious from this very brief summary, both these dominant explanations of how compliance in the prison is or is not achieved ignore a third possible perspective, one that is based in the concept of legitimacy and that assumes that members (inmates and staff) may take a moral point of view that cannot be reduced to either individual self-interest or unreflective normative consensus with one's affiliation group. Legitimacy is a major theme of modern political philosophy and expresses the idea, explicitly raised by Hobbes at modernity's inception, that the presence of authority and the recognized obligation to comply with its demands do not necessarily coincide.

Compared to other historical systems of government, democracy is "inherently self-legitimating."[25] This is because, based on assumptions about the moral autonomy of its citizens, democratic ideals require that authorities (and authority in general) produce public justifications for their decisions to act, especially when those actions involve coercive force against citizens. If, as the theory goes, government authority cannot provide adequate justifications for its decisions (policies and so forth) to the public most concerned and/or affected by them, then they cannot proceed.

Clearly, as my earlier discussion about its premodern character suggests, the prison has an inherent "legitimacy deficit" relative to free society.[26] Prisoners, even if they admit blame for their criminal acts, do not consent to their captivity, which in practice means a sustained condition of both extreme vulnerability and deprivation. Inmates typically exist with omnipresent threats to their psychological and physical survival, making some kind of adaptive process both necessary and extremely difficult in terms of achieving an easy deference to the powers that maintain them in this condition. Accordingly, as suggested earlier, the maintenance of a relatively stable social order that is based on some degree of compliance with custodial objectives always involves ongoing negotiation between authority and those over whom authority is exercised. The basic questions to be answered, both empirically and normatively, are: On what basis does authority negotiate with its citizens/captives? and, by direct implication, Does this basis achieve legitimacy for them, thus obligating their obedience?

What are the conditions necessary for the legitimatization of authority? This question received its most famous and sustained treatment from one of sociology's founding fathers, Max Weber, who maintained that people's belief in an authority's legitimacy implies their consent to the authority's dictates.[27] Even though Weber recognized the important analytic distinctions between law, convention (that is, custom), and ethics, he argued that "the relations [between these] do not constitute a problem for sociology,"[28] essentially because he believed that the basis of both law and ethics is conventionally established beliefs in the ultimate values expressed by ethical standards and legal systems. Political philosopher David Beetham[29] has identified Weber's failure to distinguish expressed belief from reflective justification of belief. Beetham argues that a "given power relationship is not legitimate because people believe in its legitimacy, but because it can be justified in terms of their beliefs."[30] By inference, one reason for this is that beliefs in support of or against an authority can be reported (as in an opinion poll) within ideological or popular frames of reference that have little to do with the actual standards, principles, and values that those same people might wish the authority to uphold in practice.

> Contributing to legitimacy . . . are . . . a number of different factors operating at different levels. There is the legal validity of the acquisition of power; there is the justifiability of the rules governing a power relationship in terms of the beliefs and values current in the given society; there is the evidence of consent from actions expressive of it . . . . Together these criteria provide grounds, not for a "belief in legiti-

macy," but for those subject to power to support and cooperate with its holders; grounds, that is to say, not for belief, but for obligation.[31]

Power can be said to be legitimate to the extent that:
i) it conforms to established rules
ii) the rules can be justified by reference to beliefs shared by both dominant and subordinate, and
iii) there is evidence of consent by the subordinate to the particular power relation.[32]

Beetham's argument is distinctly modern and democratic in its basic premises because legitimacy, understood as the obligation to obey authority, depends on whether authority and its dictates have been established by methods and conform to rules of procedure to which all rational-moral individuals would give their assent. This assumption, which is at the heart of both modern institutions and modern identities, has two components. The first reiterates the point just made, that there are standards and principles that transcend the partisan and expedient interests of particular groups of which society is composed. The second is that, by virtue of their transcendent nature, these standards and principles can be used by both dominant and subordinate groups in a given power relation to adjudicate conflicts of partisan interests that may be expressive of different values and goals.

Moral Reckoning and the Social Order of the Prison

Significant for our discussion of the prison social order, if members of the dominant group deny their subordinates' reference to these standards and principles, they are, in essence, denying the subordinates' personhood and imposing their will in a way that does not obligate obedience. Returning to the earlier discussion of trust, in free society each subordinate individual, just like his or her dominant counterpart, is assumed to be able to detach him or herself from the given set of institutional statuses that he or she occupies, with these statuses' concomitant contextualized and particularized values and goals. Individual identity is based on the sense that I am not merely the sum total of my parts (the statuses I occupy and roles that I play). Rather, my identity inheres in the space of my detachment, in the self that reflectively deliberates between these parts. Not honor, an attribute that attaches to premodern identities,[33] but integrity is the defining characteristic of a self that is able to maintain this reflective detachment. Doing the right thing and maintaining one's moral integrity means that the individual displays the capacity to avoid being subsumed by the partisan interests and values of his or her designated institutional statuses and role expectations.[34]

In sum, the process of negotiating the legitimacy of authority in modern societies brings to bear a third basis of decision making in prison contexts, the moral point of view.[35] Sociological and social-psychological accounts of the prison social order have by and large excluded this perspective, thereby ignoring some of the most salient grounds for explaining passive and active dissent toward authority by inmates and custodial employees.[36]

Both inmates and staff enter prison with the cultural assumptions of modern identity intact. Yet the institutional contexts in which they live and work demand that they continually make decisions that have moral implications—that is, decisions involving the treatment of others in terms of fairness and mutual well-being—from the standpoint of their ascribed statuses rather than from the standpoint of their individual integrity. Any possible basis for the legitimacy of specific prison authority and/or his policies and rules is continually threatened by the volatile conditions of prison organization,[37] including a high turnover in management and staff, regular revision of basic operating policies and procedures, and contentious public discourse on prisoner and employee rights. Confidence (as we defined it earlier) in the prison authority's ability to maintain basic order is therefore continually eroded.

Custodial staff and inmates typically find themselves forced into a series of moral reckonings that have serious consequences for their self identities: to choose between doing the right thing (in correctional argot: acting "righteous") and preserving their own individual integrity or doing the expedient thing, that is, protecting themselves from imminent psychological and physical danger. In the long run, most average individuals faced with constant threats to the very core of their sense of self-worth and -esteem succumb and disintegrate into Sykes's two poles: either becoming individuals at war with each and every other (the bully inmate or the rogue correction officer), with no basis for social solidarity, or by allowing their selves to be subsumed in premodern terms to the mechanical normative dictates of social action pregiven by their ascribed status in the organization. I do not mean to imply that exceptional people do not emerge within the prison society. They do. These are people, inmates and staff, who find within themselves a means to act morally (with integrity, in the terms culturally inculcated and affirmed by the broader society) in spite of and perhaps in a deeper sense because of the dangers involved in doing so.

The important point here, however, is that the organization of which they are "members"—the prison—by its very nature cannot support these exceptional individuals, at least for very long. As in the broader society, acting morally and acting legally do not always coincide. In the prison society, when an individual staff member or inmate chooses to act morally (in the terms that most people would accept) in spite of and against stated legal and rule prescriptions or informal group norms applicable to the context of his decisions, he faces grave danger. Not only might he face formal sanction from prison authorities, but he may also be subject to censure or expulsion from the familial group that protects him and provides direction and meaning to his everyday activities. Hence, in prison society, morally courageous individuals may be socially extirpated, but even if they are not, they cannot become models or leaders for the average inmate or staff member in any real, practical way.

Though laudable goals, neither a change in the correctional philosophy that informs prison management policies nor a concerted attempt to educate prison staff (or offenders) in ethical decision making can address the fundamental problem of legitimacy that is at the heart of the prison. The problem of legitimacy was not an intended problem—incarceration as a primary form of criminal punishment was originally conceived as a reform of more brutal practices that offered no hope to convicted offenders. Yet an important lesson we can learn from our experience with prisons is that societies produce their own working conceptions of human identity and moral selfhood, and these conceptions are embedded in significant ways within their social institutions. The prison is a fundamentally flawed institution because it interferes with its members' abilities to interact socially in ways that foster moral learning and individual integrity, within the definitions that our society has historically given to those terms. In any given prison, the social order will include individuals who act morally, but it will never be a moral social order.

Notes

1. Joseph V. Williams, "Ideology into Practice/Practice into Ideology: Staff-Offender Relationships in Institutional and Community Corrections in an Era of Retribution," in this volume, 149–78.

2. In fact, a tacit question about this relationship seemed to inform much of the discussion between the conference participants: Is there some inherent or intrinsic problem with the modern institution of the prison, a fundamental injustice that militates against the very possibility of ongoing, ethically inspired social action and prevents the prison social order from being a moral order?

3. See also Audrey J. Bomse, "Prison Abuse: Prisoner-Staff Relations," in this volume, 79–104, and Amnesty International, "Rights for All—Campaign on the USA," Report, chapter 4, "Violations in Prisons and Jails," October 1998–May 1999. <www. rightsforall-usa.org/> (8/21/00).

4. The classic statement of this perspective was made by Donald Cressey: "[The] many traits exhibited by individual staff members and inmates are properties of the organization, not the person in question. . . . [Hence] if the traits are to be changed the organization, not the person, must be the object of modification." *The Prison: Studies in Institutional Organization and Change* (New York: Holt, Rinehart, and Winston, 1961), 8.

5. For example, in the first American sociological study of the prison (1940), Donald Clemmer concluded that, in prison, "[t]here is no consensus for a common goal. The inmates' conflict with officialdom and opposition to society is only slightly greater in degree than conflict with themselves. . . . It is a world of 'I,' 'me,' 'mine,' rather than 'ours,' 'theirs,' or 'his.'. . . In a sense the prison culture reflects American culture, for it is a culture within it." *The Prison Community* (New York: Holt, Rinehart,

and Winston, 1958), 154. Many pessimistic statements, which, like Clemmer's, often took the form of an aside or an afterthought, can be found in the classic prison studies of the 1950s, 1960s, and 1970s. Most researchers did not explicitly embrace a "nothing works" view since their analyses and explanations of prison disorder and corruption generally had direct implications, at least in theory, for the solutions. But they were not typically optimistic that political or organizational resources would in the long run be up to the task of creating and maintaining stable, relatively corruption- and violence-free organizations.

6. The terms "corrections" and "prison" are used somewhat interchangeably in this and several other chapters. Of course, corrections includes institutions such as parole and probation and alternative or intermediary programs that are nonincarcerative. But nonincarcerative corrections, I believe, is historically and practically dependent on the prison as the centerpiece of criminal punishment. The prison is the system's default position; nonincarcerative options are defined and justified strictly in terms of what they offer in lieu of carceral punishment, which is always available in the event of offender and/or program failure. My chapter is specifically focused on the social/moral order of the prison and assumes that nonincarcerative programs and practices are generated and directed by the penal corrections of modern, Western societies.

7. Derek R. Brookes, "The Possibility of a Correctional Ethic," in this volume, 39–68.

8. See Richard Sparks, Anthony Bottoms, and Will Hays, *Prisons and the Problem of Order* (New York: Oxford University Press, 1996), on the perennial problem of order in prisons.

9. American and British scholarship on the prison includes notable examples of the sociology of social action, or microsociology, based on ethnomethodological, phenomenological, and symbolic interactionist perspectives, which stress social actors' ongoing construction of meaning and the processual aspects of local social orders. But even these studies have failed to elucidate the moral point of view as a normative basis for social action that is distinct from other, conventional normative bases formed by and within societies and groups. (See also note 35, page 192.)

10. I am employing the term "status" sociologically, to mean a position that one occupies in a society or organization, such as father, student, vice president, etc., and not in the popular sense as a synonym for "prestige." Moreover, for the sake of the argument I develop, it is important to understand that I am providing a generalized description of the prisoner status, not a description of individual prisoner/offender characteristics, nor, much less, a normative prescription. Individual prisoners can retain their human dignity even under extremely degrading conditions, just as can serfs, slaves, and all "lower-caste" people.

11. For example, Adam B. Seligman, *The Problem of Trust* (Princeton, N.J.: Princeton University Press, 1997); Francis Fukuyama, *Trust* (New York: The Free Press, 1995); Diego Gambetta (ed.), *Trust: Making and Breaking of Cooperative Relations* (Oxford, U.K.: Basil Blackwell, 1988); Niklas Luhmann, *Trust and Power* (New York: Wiley, 1979); Anthony Giddens, *Central Problems in Social Theory* (Berkeley: University of California Press, 1979).

12. Seligman, *The Problem of Trust*, 24–25.

13. Seligman, *The Problem of Trust*, 39.

14. "Trust . . . is a recognition of alter's agency, an agency which . . . only

appears when the 'fit' between the person and the role is loose, when the role does not—indeed cannot—circumscribe all of alter's possible behavior." Seligman, *The Problem of Trust*, 62.

"When most aspects of alter's behavior can be convincingly explained (and planned for) in terms their role incumbency, trust is not called for, confidence in systematically defined normative patterns is sufficient." Seligman, *The Problem of Trust*, 63.

15. See, for example, sociologist Erving Goffman's famous discussion of the "moral careers" of prison inmates and mental patients whose sense of autonomous selfhood is "colonized" by staff's imputation of all behavior as manifestations of the inmate's/patient's role as an "official" deviant, in *Asylums* (New York: Anchor Books, 1961), and "(1) On the Characteristics of Total Institutions: The Inmate World" and "(2) On the Characteristics of Total Institutions: Staff-Inmate Relations," in *The Prison: Studies in Institutional Organization and Change*, ed. D. R. Cressey (New York: Holt, Rinehart, and Winston, 1961), 15–106.

16. As Williams expressed it in his conference presentation, 25.

17. The building tender system is famous for supporting serious corruption (e.g., underground economies; collusion between staff and inmates in "punishing" inmate dissenters or whistle-blowers; coercive, nonconsensual sexual relations between inmates and inmates and staff), which is why prisoners' rights advocates have been so vocally critical of it.

18. See Seligman, *The Problem of Trust*, 172–75 for a discussion of how risk is associated with trust-based societies and danger is associated with confidence-based societies.

19. "On the one hand, the prisoner can engage in a highly individualistic war of all against all against which he seeks to mitigate his own plight at the expense of his fellow prisoners; on the other hand, the prisoner can attempt to form a close alliance with his fellow captives and to present a unified front against the custodians. It is the changing mixture of these antithetical behavior patterns and their underlying values which makes up the social system we label so grossly, so overly simply [sic], as the prison community." Gresham M. Sykes, *The Society of Captives* (Princeton, N.J.: Princeton University Press, 1958), 131.

20. See Sparks, Bottoms, and Hays, *Prisons and the Problem of Order*, for a description and analysis of the "incentives as means to order system."

21. Now classic examples of the normative model can be found in Richard Cloward, Donald R. Cressey, George H. Grosser, Richard McCleery, Lloyd E. Ohlin, Gresham M. Sykes, and Sheldon L. Messinger (eds.), *Theoretical Studies in the Social Organization of the Prison* (New York: Social Science Research Council, 1960); and Cressey (ed.), *The Prison*.

22. See, for example, James B. Jacobs, *Stateville* (Chicago: University of Chicago Press, 1977).

23. Goffman, *Asylums*, 320.

24. Harold Garfinkel, *Studies in Ethnomethodology* (Cambridge, U.K.: Polity Press, 1967), 68.

25. Sparks, Bottoms, and Hays, *Prisons and the Problem of Order*, 86.

26. Sparks, Bottoms, and Hays, *Prisons and the Problem of Order*, 85.

27. Max Weber, *The Theory of Social and Economic Organization* (New York: The Free Press, 1964), 130–31.

28. Weber, *The Theory of Social and Economic Organization*, 129.

29. Sparks, Bottoms, and Hays, whose analysis I cite several times, also note Beetham's critique of Weber as an important contribution to their argument about the importance of legitimacy for analyzing problems of prison social order. I do not, however, cite their analysis, including their use of Beetham's critique, as the source of my own views. This is because I independently developed and incorporated Beetham's critique into my own analysis of legitimacy (Polly A. Smith, "A Reconstructed Approach to the Sociology of Morals Illustrated with a Study of Conflict in a Large Urban Jail System," unpublished dissertation, City University of New York, 1997) before Sparks, Bottoms, and Hays, *Prisons and the Problem of Order*, became available in the United States. Happily, however, Sparks, Bottoms, and Hays's analysis and research, which is one of the best recent discussions of the issue of the perennial problem of prison order, generally confirms my own.

30. David Beetham, *The Legitimation of Power* (Atlantic Highlands, N.J.: Humanities Press, 1991), 11.

31. Beetham, *The Legitimation of Power*, 12–13.

32. Beetham, *The Legitimation of Power*, 16–17.

33. See Frank Henderson Stewart, *Honor* (Chicago: University of Chicago Press, 1994).

34. It should be clear that this description of modern identity is a sociological and historical observation that relates to the specific conditions of Western societies, rather than a psychological or normative philosophical claim about any putatively objective characteristics of selfhood. A large body of literature from numerous disciplines supports my description. See, for example, V. Lee Hamilton and Joseph Sanders, *Everyday Justice: Responsibility and the Individual in Japan and the United States* (New Haven, Conn.: Yale University Press, 1992); Richard A. Shweder, *Thinking Through Cultures: Expeditions in Cultural Psychology* (Cambridge, Mass.: Harvard University Press, 1991); Charles Taylor, *Sources of the Self: The Making of Modern Identity* (Cambridge, Mass.: Harvard University Press, 1989).

35. The moral point of view is typically described as including certain characteristics that appear in the language we (as members of modern, Western societies) use to account for decision making that is grounded in morally justifiable terms, for example, the reasoning involved is impartial and objective; it is oriented towards consequences that would benefit all concerned; it will lessen harm and pain; it is grounded in principles or rules to which all rational people would give their consent; it takes account of the special needs of vulnerable persons, etc. These terms are amply documented in research conducted by moral psychologists, although not all of these researchers qualify their findings historically and culturally. See, for example, A. Colby, Lawrence Kohlberg, and collaborators, *The Measurement of Moral Judgment*, 2 vols. (Cambridge, U.K.: Cambridge University Press, 1987); J. Haidt, S. H. Koller, and M. G. Dias, "Affect, Culture, and Morality, or Is It Wrong to Eat Your Dog?" *Journal of Personality and Social Psychology* 65, no. 4 (1993): 613–28; Eliot Turiel, *The Development of Social Knowledge: Morality and Convention* (Cambridge, U.K.: Cambridge University Press, 1985).

36. For a supporting account of the role of legitimacy in obligating social members to obey authority, see Tom R. Tyler, *Why People Obey the Law* (New Haven, Conn.: Yale University Press, 1992).

37. See, for example, John DiIulio, Jr., *Governing Prisons* (New York: The Free Press, 1987); and Sparks, Bottoms, and Hays, *Prisons and the Problem of Order*.

Response to Chapter 5

The Path of Least Resistance: Sexual Exploitation of Female Offenders as an Unethical Corollary to Retributive Ideology and Correctional Practice

Zelma Weston Henriques

Joseph Williams examines a number of critical correctional issues from a historical perspective to demonstrate that in the United States there are forces that both shape and continually transform staff-offender relationships in the field of corrections.[1] He discusses, for example, the post-Attica structural/organizational changes that resulted in titular alterations in both agency and staff identities. Although those changes were designed to address the internal balance of power, he believes they failed because of the deep-rooted nature of our custodial legacy. The alleged transformation was instead part of a cyclical pattern of greater and lesser offender control exercised directly or indirectly and legitimately or illegitimately by correctional personnel.

Referring to Martinson,[2] Williams notes the demise of the rehabilitative ideal upon an alleged empirical showing that nothing works. The Martinson research influenced a shift from a correctional mission of rehabilitation or therapeutic assistance as the path to offender change back to the notion of deserved punishment as the single or primary function of both institutional and community-based corrections,[3] making the physical confinement of more offenders in locked facilities easily justifiable. Community corrections became a sentence deserved only by low-level offenders and then only under conditions of heightened control. Hence electronic monitoring and other forms of technological incarceration were born and proceeded to flourish.

As Williams observes, the ideological shift from viewing offenders as persons worthy and capable of change via assistance to ones in which they are seen as fallen persons requiring penance or deserving punishment affects the way in which correctional personnel view inmates both collectively and individually. In the former case, correctional staff, hired in either a custodial or treatment role, may be more likely to interact with inmates or individuals under community supervision in ways that indicate that they are deserving of humane treatment. Under a retributive ideology, however, correctional staff may come to view their role as representing the larger society that has been wronged by the offender. The role of corrections may thus be viewed by its personnel as intended either to exact some measure of payment for the wrong done or, more simply, to treat the offender as the least-deserving person that he or she has proved to be. Under Rousseau's formulation, once having broken the social contract, the offender is seen as undeserving of its benefits. This view of the offender, coupled with the almost absolute control that correctional personnel have over inmates confined to institutions and to a lesser degree over inmates under community supervision, raises serious ethical questions about staff-offender relations.

My response to Williams has two parts. The first is meant to provide an evaluation of his argument by highlighting its strengths and weaknesses. And then, using the sexual abuse of female offenders as an example, the second part argues that a correctional practice that operates with retribution as its dominant ideology creates and sustains an atmosphere in which the rights[4] of inmates are easily violated, standards of ethical and professional conduct are easily ignored, and the operation of a humane corrections system becomes nearly impossible, despite outward appearances to the contrary.

Correction through Retribution: The Easy Way Out

According to historians, houses of "correction" existed in England as early as the late 1500s.[5] What has been difficult to pin down over time is the exact meaning of the term "correction." Although Williams's talk of correction's "failure"[6] conjures up unanswered and perhaps unanswerable questions as to the meaning of correction's success, in modern times, recidivism or the lack thereof has come to be regarded by most as the singular indicator of correction's success. The quality of life enjoyed by ex-offenders is given little thought unless they return to the rolls of the arrested and/or convicted.

In his chapter, Williams separates his analysis of corrections into ideology, which he defines as "beliefs held by members of interest groups in the larger society,"[7] and correctional functions or practices that, though influenced by ideological beliefs, amount to the way in which systems and personnel dubbed as "correctional" operate on a daily basis. Given that the predecessors to houses of corrections were almshouses and poorhouses, it seems that the tension between rehabilitative and retributive aims of corrections has always existed and carries with it a certain value judgment about those in need of correcting. A definitive answer to the question of when an individual is sufficiently corrected remains unresolved, especially within the context of the current hyperdynamic modern (and some would claim postmodern) life.

Williams notes that reform ideology involves the "belief that through reflection, repentance, and hard work within prison an offender will be forced to change."[8] The definition leaves open the question of what exactly the offender is expected to change into. Surely no one among us, the non-incarcerated, can honestly say that he or she has lived a totally crime-free life. And though only touched upon at various points throughout the chapter, the determination of who falls within the official offender category is heavily laden with socio-political influences and implications. Who sits in judgment as to whether the appropriate reform has taken place? And, except in clearly extreme cases such as murder, rape, and serious assaults, what are the appropriate criteria for making such a judgment?

As Williams notes, rehabilitation, considered by some a corollary of reform, encompasses the belief that offenders can be cured of deviancy through intensive treatment. But as he also notes, determining the appropriate treatment for massive numbers of individuals within a closed and highly restrictive environment with limited resources is an enormous task. And the transferability of any such treatment effects into the outside world is questionable.

On the other hand, reintegration, or the idea that recidivism can be reduced by preparing offenders for release into a community in which some things are certain (for example, the availability of drugs, guns, and criminal associates) and other things are not (for example, legitimate means of employment, adequate housing, and health benefits), presupposes that correctional personnel can and will have a competent understanding of each offender's needs, his or her relationships, and the social milieu of the community to which he or she will return. Given the social distance between most correctional personnel and the majority of the correctional population that they oversee, it is unlikely that such a comprehensive level of competency can or will be achieved in the near future.

Alternatively, retribution, the idea "that offenders should be imprisoned for punishment,"[9] is attractive because of its simplicity and the perceived ease with which it can be executed in correctional practice. In the United States, governed as it is by a constitution that contains specific language about the legal parameters of punishment, arguably the only challenge is to determine and observe appropriate limits on such punishment. Consequentially, the custodial, control, and maintenance functions that Williams identifies, even in the absence of any sinister reactionary motive, appear most practicable. Although the demarcation between custody and control is not made clear and may not be significant, the custodial, control, and maintenance functions require little or no scientific knowledge and involve little or no guess work. This explains their attractiveness.

On the other hand, the restorative function, which is never clearly explained in Williams's chapter, appears to have no real role in retributive corrections. Unless the case is made that the punishment of offenders restores the larger society's faith in social order, it appears that, given the dismal socioeconomic background shared by a majority of offenders, restoration (to their earlier lives) is hardly appropriate to their leading law-abiding lives. However, Williams's statement, "Without at least some tangible evidence to inmates that rehabilitation could and does take place the management of prison systems would become nearly impossible," needs clarification.[10] What evidence do we have that inmates have ever seen prison confinement as rehabilitative?

At one point, Williams appropriately chastises correctional program staff for their failure to document that certain inmates showed clear evidence of positive (that is, law-abiding) change associated with their participation in certain prison programs, thus leaving the experiment with rehabilitation as the dominant correctional ideology open to the criticism that nothing works.[11] In the absence of concrete (that is, social scientific) evidence that large-scale offender change was taking place, based on inmates' involvement in nonpunitive therapeutic prison programs, it was easy for politicians and others to cater to public fears. However, Williams's brief reference to the failure of program staff to fight for the right type of programs and/ or to do the right thing with reference to such programs oversimplifies the processes of evaluation, problem identification, and service provision required to address effectively the needs of a large and diverse correctional population. Although the bulk of the population under correctional supervision may share certain characteristics, it is still the case that individual factors may require special attention (for example, physical environment, employment history, family relations and responsibilities, mental and/or physical health problems). Correctional caseloads, whether within institutions or within the community, make inattention to these individual factors likely. Despite the best efforts of those involved, mass-produced rehabilitative initiatives have proved ineffective for certain offenders. The determination of the "right" thing cannot be made with scientific certainty. In the absence of such certainty, the primal reliance on coercive authority and punitive control provides psychological comfort to the general public.

The promise of controlling and incapacitating offenders, even temporarily, has always appealed to the masses. Political campaigns that court public fear and encourage this appeal, along with criminological theories that unabashedly attribute crime to individual maladies such as lack of self-control,[12] increase rather than decrease the likelihood that a retributive ideology will remain the dominant influence on correctional practice. In addition to its public appeal, punishment as the primary goal of corrections lends itself to a system that can be administered with relative philosophical and operational ease. The fact that correctional populations overwhelmingly comprise individuals already thought of as the undeserving (that is, the poor and undereducated, and members of minority groups) influences correctional practices to an even greater extent than Williams acknowledges. As issues of gender, race, ethnicity, class, and culture continue to separate the keepers from the kept, the corrections environment has been and will continue to be vulnerable to the perception that those who end up there are somehow flawed and therefore undeserving of social benefits and deserving of punitive treatment. The longevity of this perception and the ease with which correctional practice consistent with it (that is, punishment and control) can be carried out accounts for its attraction as a recurrent default position even in the absence of scientific proof of its effectiveness (in reducing recidivism) because of the psychological comfort that it provides to the masses. Punitive measures give the impression that something is being done about crime. However, both pre- and post-Attica, the idea that offenders are part of an undeserving group, to a greater or lesser degree, has haunted correctional practice with its strong potential for fostering exploitative and abusive relationships between officers and offenders.

Whether within institutions or as part of community supervision, the focus on punishment and control in the name of public safety has meant that those under correctional supervision are subject to the will of correctional personnel. While I do not suggest that there are no correctional staff members who carry out their duties with dignity and in a humane fashion, when the prevailing atmosphere is overwhelmingly focused on custody rather than care it seems fair to say that only a courageous few actually muster the energy to serve willingly in the role of broker or advocate for inmates/offenders.

In addition, as Williams notes, the custodial legacy sets the stage for one of the worst kinds of corruption, namely, sexual contact between corrections staff and inmates/offenders.

Retributivism as a License for Exploitation

I now describe how the retributive ideology creates and contributes to a correctional context in which women, in particular, become extremely vulnerable to abuse. Although Williams notes that some have suggested that the informality and discretionary decision making associated with a rehabilitative model of corrections reduces social distance between correctional staff and inmates, creating opportunities for unethical and corrupting relationships between the two,[13] I suggest that such relationships are more likely to occur under a retributive model and that women offenders are most vulnerable to demands/requests for sexual exchanges, one form of what Williams identifies as "high-level corruption."[14]

As noted previously, under the retributive ideology, persons confined in institutions or otherwise under correctional supervision are viewed as deserving of punishment. As a corollary, such persons are often also seen as undeserving of the benefits and protections afforded free people. Evidence that women, in particular, are vulnerable to developing an undeserving self-concept, based on their confinement, is reflected by the following comment from a female inmate engaged in a sexual relationship with a member of the correctional staff: "In their eyes I was the criminal, so why not go with the officer."[15] When females under correctional supervision (institutional or community-based) come to view themselves as tainted and undeserving of decent treatment, this reduces the likelihood that they will vigorously resist efforts by others to exploit them, particularly when such efforts come from males who have control over their lives. Richie notes that many women who end up in the criminal justice system have already acquiesced to a lifetime of male influence, domination, and control.[16]

Even with the advent of greater numbers of female correctional personnel, the vulnerability of women under correctional supervision is particularly acute given the masculine nature of custodial models.[17] Rafter notes that the structure and functioning of women's prisons were derived from that of men's prisons, including, in particular, its retributive purpose and male-dominated authority structure.[18] As a consequence, female offenders are likely to find themselves under the care, custody, and control of male correctional staff. Given the relational nature of women's socialization,[19] Rafter notes that incarcerated women are "probably lonelier [than are men]."[20] When these factors—loneliness, relational socialization, and feelings of undeservedness—come together in a male-dominated custodial setting, women are especially vulnerable to sexual exploitation, whether by coercion or consent. Even if sex in prison is consensual, based on emotion or the belief that it will earn various privileges or rewards, is it ethical for a corrections officer who is in a position of power and control to initiate or acquiesce in such relationships? Whether consensual or coerced, such conduct undermines the correctional function because of the manipulation and abuse it involves. It blurs the line between "just" punishment and over-reaching and unethical control. It violates the integrity of the correctional process, whatever its actual goal, by creating a power dynamic unacceptable and unjustifiable to those involved in the conduct, to those who are aware of the conduct, or to both.

In addition, since female offenders are among the group considered undeserving, many cases of sexual abuse go unreported. The reasons given by female inmates for failing to report sexual contact with staff include both fear of reprisal and fear that their accounts will not be believed. Similar to the English common law notion that convicted felons could not be credible witnesses, in cases of alleged sexual abuse, the jailer is considered more believable than a woman locked up for committing a crime.[21] This lack of reporting increases the likelihood of incidents. In order to increase the likelihood of being believed, confined women have had to resort to the degrading practice of saving physical evidence such as semen and used condoms.[22] Or, as in the case of convicted child killer, Susan Smith, such liaisons come to light only when the female victim contracts a sexually transmitted disease.[23] Hence even successful prosecutions may act as sexual exploitation of a different type. The revelations necessary for a conviction may degrade and belittle the well-being and self-esteem of the confined female victim, potentially increasing the possibility of future victimization.

Given the closed nature of correctional institutions and the barriers to reporting sexual abuse, the exact numbers of male or female prisoners sexually assaulted while in correctional custody are unknown. Statistics for 1995 estimate that approximately 135,000 rapes of female inmates occur nationwide for a female prison population of 69,028.[24] Although the American Jail Association and the American Correctional Association, along with many local corrections departments and jails, have codes of ethics, it appears that such codes have not worked sufficiently to prevent sexual contact between female inmates and male correctional staff. Criminal justice policy decisions, such as the war on drugs, have brought more women into secure correctional settings, but there are indications that even when the sexual exploitation of female inmates comes to light, few members of prison staff who engage in sexual relations with female prisoners ever face disciplinary or prosecutorial action.[25] Although the Federal Bureau of Prisons amended its policy statement on sexual assault in 1997 to include instances of staff-on-inmate sexual abuse or assault, the policy does not specify the action(s) to be taken when the sexual aggressor is a member of the correctional staff. This failure of clear and specific guidelines for action against offending staff leaves correctional administrators free to do nothing and/or to deny the existence of a problem. Henriques and Gilbert argue that when women are imprisoned for punishment, their exploitation by male custodial officers is an additional degradation of imprisonment.[26] They note in addition that although imprisonment may represent just deserts for the crime committed, forced sexual assault is undeserved, unjust, and harsh punishment. With punishment and even harsh punishment as the aim of correctional practice, sexual abuse may be viewed by some staunch retributionists as the price one pays for being sent to prison.

Notes

1. Joseph V. Williams, "Ideology into Practice/Practice into Ideology: Staff-Offender Relationships in Institutional and Community Corrections in an Era of Retribution," in this volume, 149–78.

2. Robert Martinson, "What Works? Questions and Answers about Prison Reform," *Public Interest* 35 (1974): 22–54.

3. Williams, "Ideology into Practice/Practice into Ideology," 152–54.

4. Williams, "Ideology into Practice/Practice into Ideology," 154–55. See also Zelma Weston Henriques and E. Gilbert, "Sexual Abuse and Sexual Assault of Women in Prison," in *It's a Crime: Women and Justice*, 2d ed., ed. Roslyn Muraskin (Saddle River, N.J.: Prentice-Hall, 2000).

5. Harry E. Allen and Clifford E. Simonsen, *Corrections in America*, 5th ed. (New York: Macmillan, 1989), 23.

6. Williams, "Ideology into Practice/Practice into Ideology," 155.

7. Williams, "Ideology into Practice/Practice into Ideology," 150.

8. Williams, "Ideology into Practice/Practice into Ideology," 150.

9. Williams, "Ideology into Practice/Practice into Ideology," 150.

10. Williams, "Ideology into Practice/Practice into Ideology," 151.

11. Williams, "Ideology into Practice/Practice into Ideology," 152.

12. Michael Gottfredson and Travis Hirschi, *A General Theory of Crime* (Palto Alto, Calif.: Stanford University Press, 1990).

13. Williams, "Ideology into Practice/Practice into Ideology," 161, citing Lucian Lombardo, *Guards Imprisoned: Correctional Officers at Work* (New York: Elsevier, 1981), 59–72.

14. Williams, "Ideology into Practice/Practice into Ideology," 161.

15. Quote from twenty-two-year-old inmate Felita Dobbins at Bedford Hills Correctional Facility, reported in Monte Williams, "Bill Seeks to Protect Inmates from Guards Who Seek Sex," *New York Times,* April 23, 1996, A1, B4.

16. Beth Richie, *Compelled to Crime: The Gender Entrapment of Battered Black Women* (New York: Routledge, 1996).

17. N. H. Rafter, *Partial Justice: Women, Prisons and Social Control,* 2d ed. (Boston: Northeastern University Press, 1990), 21.

18. Rafter, *Partial Justice,* 21.

19. See C. Gilligan, L. Brown, and A. Rogers, "Psyche Imbedded: A Place for Body, Relationships, and Culture in Personality Theory," in *Studying Persons and Lives,* ed. A. Rabin, R. Zucker, R. Emmons, and S. Frank (New York: Springer, 1990), 86–147.

20. Rafter, *Partial Justice,* 21.

21. Human Rights Watch, *All Too Familiar: Sex Abuse of Women in Prisons* (New York: Human Rights Watch, 1996).

22. Williams, "Bill Seeks to Protect Inmates from Guards Who Seek Sex." See also S. A. Holmes, "With More Women in Prison, Sexual Abuse by Guards Becomes Greater Concern," *New York Times*, December 27, 1996, A9.

23. At least two prison guards, one a captain and thirteen-year veteran, in the South Carolina Corrections System have been formally charged with having sex with Susan Smith, a female inmate serving a life sentence for murdering her two sons. B. Hoffman, "2nd Guard in Slay-mom Tryst," *New York Post*, September 27, 2000, 28.

24. Bureau of Justice Statistics *National Crime Victimization Survey* (Washington, D.C.: U.S. Department of Justice, 1995).

25. With less frequency, women custodial staff also sexually assault female inmates.

26. Henriques and Gilbert, "Sexual Abuse and Sexual Assault of Women in Prison."

Chapter 6

Management-Staff Relations: Issues in Leadership, Ethics, and Values

Kevin N. Wright

During the late 1970s, Kelsey Kauffman studied the experiences of state corrections officers in Massachusetts. She describes the perception that officers at Walpole maximum-security prison had of their supervisors: "Overriding all else, officers saw administrators 'from the top echelons on down' as uncaring about officers and willing to betray them if necessary to purchase a transient peace. As an officer described their feelings, 'We're alone. We have only each other. The administration does not give a shit for us.'"[1]

Whether this characterization was generally true of Massachusetts's officers at the time and whether it is generalizable to prisons across the United States may be subject to debate. Nevertheless, the sentiment expressed by the Walpole employees raises an extremely important issue: what ethical consideration can prison employees expect from their supervisors? In accepting employment in a prison, does an individual give up the right to a reasonably safe work environment? Must prison employees subjugate their own judgments to those of a capricious supervisor? Does a staff member working in a prison have any right to fair and equal treatment in regard to promotion or termination of employment? What about privacy? In the name of security, can correctional administrators pry into the personal lives of prison employees?

Interestingly, the literature on prison management provides little guidance on these questions. One finds some discussion of what constitutes the ethical treatment of prisoners but virtually nothing about the ethical treatment of prison employees. Kauffman and Jacobs[2] provide some implicit consideration of ethical prison management practices. But if an administrator or scholar wished to find an explicit discussion of ethical treatment of prison employees, he or she would be disappointed.

The few books that examine good prison management are relatively silent about the ethical treatment of staff by supervisors. Neither Phillips and McConnell in *The Effective Corrections Manager*[3] nor Archambeault and Archambeault in *Correctional Supervisory Management*[4] discuss the ethical treatment of employees. John DiIulio, a recognized authority on prison administration, fails to address ethical management in either *Governing Prisons* or *No Escape*.[5] In 1993, McShane and Williams conducted a national survey of prison wardens and published their results in a volume titled, *The Management of Correctional Institutions*.[6] They addressed many aspects of supervision but did not query prison executives about their ethical obligations to employees. In 1994, I made a modest attempt to address the topic in *Effective Prison Leadership*.[7] In a section on integrity, I argued that, to be successful leaders, prison officials must be honest, consistent, and set a good example. Still, my discussion was far from comprehensive.

In 1975, the American Correctional Association adopted its Code of Ethics. It lists seventeen principles that constitute ethical practice toward prisoners, staff, and the community. Four principles apply directly to staff supervision:

- Relationships with colleagues will be of such character to promote mutual respect within the profession and improvement of its quality of service.
- Statements critical of colleagues or their service agencies will be made only as these are verifiable and constructive in purpose.
- Members will not discriminate against any client, employee or prospective employee on the basis of race, sex, creed or national origin.
- Any member who is responsible for agency personnel actions will make all appointments, promotions or dismissals only on the basis of merit and not in furtherance of partisan political interests.[8]

These are fine standards but they are limited in scope.

One might speculate about the paucity of literature concerning the ethical treatment of prison employees. Is it because prisons are closed institutions? Or is it, perhaps, that the traditional paramilitary organization of prisons precludes concern for or attention to questions of ethical practice? I happen to believe that the reason that little has been written about the ethical treatment of prison employees is that relatively little has been written about prison management generally. My purpose here is to suggest a framework for discussion of the ethical supervision of prison staff. I begin with the general question of why organizations have ethical obligations toward their employees. I introduce a set of ethical standards for employees and examine the application of these to employees working within prison settings. I conclude with a discussion of how to ensure that these principles are recognized within the prison work setting.

The Moral Status of Employees

The United States was founded on a strong belief in and commitment to individual rights and freedoms. Because these rights are recognized in the Constitution and its Bill of Rights, these freedoms have not only moral acclaim but also the force of law. Interestingly, the framers of the American Constitution were principally concerned with the harm that governments could impose on individuals through the denial of liberty, due process, and fundamental human rights. Because the criminal justice system is in the business of denying the liberty of those individuals who have harmed others or pose a threat to public safety, prisoners are afforded legal recourse for the review of the process and conditions by which their rights and freedoms are removed by government.

Prison employees, by contrast, occupy a different legal position from prisoners. As voluntary members of prison organizations who are compensated for their labor, the constitutional protections provided against government interference in one's life do not apply as directly to employees as to prisoners. Instead, a much grayer area of employment ethics must be considered. Here, the force of law generally does not apply.

A belief held by many Americans, and one that has its roots in common law, is that workers are employed at will. That is, employees have the right to choose and change their jobs at will, and employers have the right hire, direct, and fire employees at will. Defenders of this principle claim that it is necessary, for it preserves both the organizations' and the employees' freedom of choice.

Critics claim that the at-will employment principle necessarily places the employee at a disadvantage. If, as a condition of employment, the employee is expected to act responsibly, loyally, and with respect, then the principle of reciprocity demands that the organization must likewise treat the employee responsibly, loyally, and with respect.[9] Just because individuals freely join an organization, they do not relinquish their rights to such fundamental provisions as safety, equal treatment, privacy, free expression, and due process. If organizations have a moral status that affords them some degree of freedom and autonomy, then they also have concomitant moral obligations. These obligations extend to customers or clients, employees, and society.[10]

Proponents of the idea that employees have moral rights identify seven ethical principles that seem applicable to prison employees: safety, fair treatment, due process, freedom of expression, privacy, participation in decision making, and information.[11]

Safety

It is generally agreed that the most basic human right is the right to life. Without it, all other rights are superfluous and meaningless. To have life, one must have some assurance of safety and security; otherwise, life becomes perilous.

When governments threaten human life through acts of genocide, executions of political prisoners, and torture, those acts can become objects of international attention and, to stop the violence, may result in political, economic, and/or military intervention. Within the international political arena, there appears to be general agreement among people and nations that the sanctity of life overrides national sovereignty. Interestingly, the safety and health of workers in the United States has not always received the same level of concern and protection. Here, we often find an attitude that supports the inviolability of organizational freedom and autonomy even at the expense of individuals' right to safety. This position has kept courts and regulatory agencies from protecting the safety of workers. Only recently has the practice been reversed.

Clearly, jobs vary in the risks they pose to individual safety. Being a librarian is not as risky as being a laborer constructing a skyscraper or a lumberjack harvesting timber in the Northwest. However, workers have the right to understand the risks involved in a particular job and to be protected to the greatest extent possible.

Prison work is clearly more dangerous than many other forms of employment. Risks vary with the security level of the institution and job type within the facility, but the very practice of incarcerating people against their will, particularly a group of people that includes individuals who have demonstrated poor social skills and a propensity to solve interpersonal problems through violence, renders prison work risky. Staff can be assaulted by prisoners and taken hostage during a disturbance. Within such an environment, what rights to safety do prison employees have? What ethical obligations do prison officials have to assure the safety of their employees?

Just as workers employed in other hazardous settings have a right to work conditions that provide maximal safety within the parameters of what is humanly possible and economically feasible, so, too, do prison workers. This means that those responsible for administration have a positive duty to insure that the institution is as safe as possible for its security level.

The physical plant must be sound. Does this require that all facilities be brought up to the most contemporary standards of design and security technology? Probably not. Given the costs of renovation and new construction and the rapidity of technological innovation, such a requirement would be economically unfeasible. There must be balance. States and their prison systems are morally obligated to maintain the physical plant at acceptable levels. Prison structures cannot be allowed to fall into conditions of deterioration and antiquation that make them unsafe.

Beyond the physical plant, there is also a moral obligation to attend to safety practices. Policy governing security practices must be set and reviewed regularly. High expectations are the key to maintaining safe conditions and practices. Key and tool control, attention to inmate movement, and procedures for controlling high-risk prisoners must be reviewed regularly, and corrective action taken when needed. Logs must be maintained. Inmates and staff must be held accountable to standardized procedures. Provisions for emergency response must be in place. Training and retraining are essential to this process.

Prison managers have ethical obligations to inspect operations regularly to ensure compliance with security policy. When noncompliance is detected, corrective action must be taken. Important to the assurance of this right of all staff is responsiveness on the part of the institution as a whole and administrators specifically. To do otherwise is an abdication of moral responsibility.

Throughout this section, I have used the word "right" to safety and have listed a variety of actions that administrators should take if they are to act ethically toward their employees. In reality, the ability of prison managers to perform their duties ethically is constrained by organizational circumstances, budgetary limitations, and competing ethical considerations. For example, sound correctional practice suggests that administrators should do nothing that will significantly alienate the prisoner population. But when prisoners begin to view the conditions of their confinement as unreasonable and unduly harsh, they are much more likely to act out, create a disturbance, or attempt to take control of the facility. This would place staff at greater risk, thus suggesting that the administrator had been acting unethically. However, the institution's budget may be so constrained that there are insufficient funds to employ the staff needed to allow prisoners out of their cells every day. An administrator may have no choice but to lock down the institution on weekends. Such action will alienate the population and increase risk of prisoner reprisal. Administrators must constantly balance decisions that have ethical implications for staff against organizational and budgetary constraints.

Furthermore, prison administrators must struggle with competing ethical obligations. To assure the highest level of staff safety, an administrator may recognize that the facility requires a $50 million renovation. If the administrator aggressively lobbies within the state correctional system and state government for this capital improvement, knowing that if he or she is successful in securing those funds, they will be taken from public monies that would have otherwise gone to public education, is he or she acting ethically?

Fair Treatment

A second ethical principle that workers share is the right to fair treatment in the workplace. If ethical practices apply to everyone, then individuals must possess those rights equally. Individuals or groups must not possess advantages over others in the provision of and access to moral rights.

The universality of moral rights within the workplace gets expressed in terms of fair treatment. It has a number of elements. First, every person should have equal access to a job and equal consideration on the job. Organizations cannot and should not discriminate against people on the basis of their sex, race or ethnicity, economic background, or religion. Furthermore, employees should receive equal pay for equal work.

Fair treatment also requires that employees not be dismissed without cause. In other words, employees have a right to their jobs. They should be fired only for the following conditions: unsatisfactory performance of duties, criminal activity, drinking or using drugs on the job, disruption of organizational operations without a valid cause, physical or mental incapacitation, and verifiable economic reasons.

Prison staff share the right to fair treatment with other employees. In fact, as public employees, this right is guaranteed legally by the Civil Rights Acts. However, there is a positive moral duty on the part of the organization and its managers to assure that this right is secured. The moral obligation goes beyond a legal one. As with the duty to maintain security, active attention is necessary. Policy that directs hiring, firing, and promotion practices must be firmly established and reviewed.

Within prisons, the right to fair treatment also carries with it an added moral obligation. As law enforcement officers, prison personnel must be prohibited from illegal activities, inappropriate behavior, corruption, and abuses of power. If all employees are to be treated fairly, the organization must be vigilant in detecting staff who engage in prohibited behaviors, and their behavior must be penalized. Not to do so is to treat law-abiding and ethical staff unfairly.

Here, too, ethical decision making and practice are bound by organizational constraints. Fair treatment is frequently influenced by civil service laws and regulations and by union contracts. Fair treatment of employees would dictate that an individual who is particularly derelict or inept in the performance of his or her duties should be removed from service. It is not fair to other conscientious employees that this individual be permitted to shirk responsibility. Such failure could pose a security threat and place other employees at risk of harm. In some systems, the protections of employees provided within the civil service system or through the union contract make it virtually impossible for supervisors to fire employees. Prison managers may be constrained under these circumstances from performing their supervisory functions ethically.

Due Process

For fair treatment to be sustained in the workplace, checks and balances are required on the capricious exercise of power by supervisors. Otherwise, employees may have a moral right to fair treatment but no guarantee to it since bosses can hire and fire at will. Due process is the method by which rights are protected, either from governmental or organizational intrusion. Before an employee can be fired, demoted, or punished, he or she has the right to peer review and a hearing.

The provision of this right within the justice system takes on added meaning. At the core of the criminal justice system is the right to due process. For government to take away an individual's right to freedom, there must be due process. To provide criminal offenders due process but to deny staff the same right makes a mockery of the very foundation of the system of justice, to say nothing about the impact on employee morale. Surely, staff members have the same moral rights as prisoners. Therefore, for a prison employee to be demoted, sanctioned, or fired, the right to a fair hearing is essential.

As with the two previous ethical principles discussed here, the provision of due process appears to be incontrovertible, but may be limited by the structure and climate of prison. An employee caught bringing drugs into the facility must be suspended immediately. The need to maintain security and to uphold legal behavior outweigh the provision of due process in the moment. A hearing to establish guilt must wait.

In an ideal world, politics would not influence the provision of fair treatment and due process. In reality, however, who gets disciplined is influenced by the politics of various constituencies within an institution. Strong unions can protect some employees. In this circumstance, no matter how correct an administrator believes an action may be, his or her ability to carry it out may be constrained.

Freedom of Expression

Like due process, freedom of expression serves to balance the distribution of power within organizations and to protect other ethical principles bearing on the treatment of individuals. Employees must have the right to protest, without reprisal, acts of the organization that may be illegal or immoral. The expression of this freedom can take the form of speech, conscientious objection, or whistle-blowing.

The provision and operationalization of this ethical principle for employees working in prisons is troublesome and controversial. Control and predictability are essential in prisons. The prevention of escapes and violence requires a degree of authoritarianism within both the organization and its administration. Traditionally, prisons have been structured as paramilitary hierarchies with clearly differentiated lines of authority and limited discretion for line staff. Recent research has shown that fragmentation within the organizational structure is associated with greater likelihood of riots.[12]

Permitting freedom of expression for staff would appear to be antithetical to the need to maintain control and predictability. Dissension among the staff could threaten the stability of the institution. Again, balance is necessary. Prison staff cannot have unbridled freedom to criticize the administration. Nevertheless, like all employees, prison workers must have the right to protest, without reprisal, against acts of the organization that may be illegal or immoral.

If it is widely recognized that some staff administer their own disciplinary action against aggressive inmates in the form of beatings that take place outside the range of surveillance cameras and, moreover, that prison officials do not take corrective action, then a staff member should be able to report such actions without fear of reprisal. It would be unethical for an administrator to take action against the reporting individual. But what about a prison employee who decides that physical restraints, shackles used while transporting prisoners, are barbaric? Does that individual have the right to go to the press with this belief and to publicly criticize the institution for its use of such devices? Who gets to define "immoral"?

Privacy

Humans have a moral right to be left alone, to have personal lives, and to be self-directed. For this to happen, they need privacy. Individuals must be able to control what information about themselves is known and disseminated. Werhane explains the necessity of this provision as follows: "Unless their privacy is respected persons lose a sense of self-identity, because what separates one from another, what identifies her to herself, becomes indistinguishable from what others know about her. Without privacy one's personal freedom is, at best, restricted, since the source of free choice, one's autonomy, is not safeguarded."[13]

Within the workplace, privacy involves the separation of personal and work lives. Clearly, employers must have access to certain kinds of personal information, but that access should be limited to work-related information, such as educational background. The personal lives of employees after work hours, provided they are legal, are generally not subjects about which employers have a right to know.

This, too, proves to be a testy issue in prison administration, and one that calls for balance. Two aspects of prison employment impact on the parameters of this right. As law enforcement agencies, prisons are obliged to uphold the highest standards of law-abiding behavior. Prison employees must adhere to this standard, and their institutions have an obligation to assure that this requirement is met. The need to prevent corruption requires some scrutiny into the personal lives of employees.

Illegal behavior among employees can jeopardize security. And prison staff who use drugs or abuse alcohol outside of the workplace may not exercise sound judgment on the job. In this regard, therefore, prison administrators have the right and obligation to maintain surveillance of employees' outside behavior. This may include drug testing.

If, furthermore, prisoners learn of illegal or inappropriate behavior on the part of staff, they may be able to use such information to extort special treatment from staff. Here, too, the organizational need to maintain security and standards of law-abiding behavior demand some restriction and surveillance of employee behavior outside the workplace.

In the examples presented so far, the need of the organization to pry into the personal lives of employees regarding illegal behavior is sufficiently compelling to justify such action. Other instances requiring a balance between personal freedom and organizational needs are not so clear cut. Prison employees who abuse sick leave force their institutions to require other employees to work increased overtime, an expedient that adds to security risks. Does the organization have a right to determine whether the employee is truly sick? Establishing a balance that does not pose undue or overzealous scrutiny and respects the individual autonomy of employees at the same time as protecting organizational needs for security and stability creates a significant challenge for management.

Participation in Decision Making

Few people would take issue with the notion that individuals have a moral right to freedom of choice and self-determination. These are fundamental elements of individual freedom. Individuals must have autonomy, independence, and the opportunity for self-development.

In accepting employment, do individuals give up the right to freedom of choice and self-determination? Does the organization's autonomy and that of its managers outweigh the autonomy of individual employees? Or are workers left only with the right to leave their employment if they are dissatisfied with the conditions of their jobs or if they find their work experience unfulfilling? It would appear that participation in workplace decision making fulfills the promise of purposeful and meaningful work and contributes to employees' self-development. Establishing a balance between the rights of the organization and its managers and the rights of the employees assures freedom of choice and self-control for all members of the organization, not just those in positions of authority and power.

The counterargument to this provision is that such an arrangement infringes unduly upon the right of managers to control the organization. As Werhane points out, participation does not imply the restriction of managers' control but limits their right to control everything.[14] Well-orchestrated participation has been demonstrated to enhance both morale and performance within the organization, thus enhancing the well-being of all with the organization.[15]

As with the preceding ethical issues, providing prison employees with the right to participate in decision making is a challenge for correctional supervisors. The need for control and predictability requires that prison operations be highly structured and that individual discretion be limited and specified. During times of crisis, decision making must be autocratic. However, in the course of day-to-day operations, prison staff should have a right to participate in decision making and to exercise autonomy in job performance within the parameters of policy specification. Not only does this provision allow employees to engage in their own personal development, but it also provides for enhanced correctional outcomes. In previously published empirical research, my collaborators and I demonstrated that participation in decision making resulted in improved employee performance and greater commitment to the organization.[16]

Still, allowing prison staff to participate in decision making and to have job autonomy must necessarily be constrained. What if the employee is a member of the Aryan Nation and expresses racist sentiments or advocates for differential treatment of white and black prisoners? Clearly, such dialogue is inappropriate and the employee's right to participate in decision making is limited. But what if the employee is a member of Amnesty International, an organization that frequently takes the position that practices found in many American prisons are inhumane? Can supervisors restrict this employee's criticisms and his or her promotion of alternative incarceration practices? Who gets to decide the limitations that managers can impose on the provision of this and other ethical principles while remaining ethical in their treatment of employees?

Information

The final ethical principle to be considered is the right to be informed. All other employee rights hinge upon this right. Since managers control information, employees can exercise other rights only if they know and understand what is going on within the organization and how it impacts on them. For example, employees can know about the risks they face in their jobs only if they are informed about those risks. If their right to safety is to be secured, they need information about the hazards associated with their jobs. Do the materials they work with pose environmental health risks? If employees are knowingly kept in the dark about risks, they do not know that they are in danger and cannot exercise their right to health and safety.

A similar situation exists regarding the right to fair treatment. If information about criteria and decision making associated with hiring and promotions is hidden, then employees have no basis for exercising their right to fair treatment.

The right to be informed can be problematic within the prison organization. With information comes power. Prisoners can use information to gain tactical advantage over staff. Information about such things as prison routines and operation of the control system can be used in planning escapes and prison takeovers. Knowledge about snitches and prisoners' crimes can lead to assaults. Information about movement of prisoners can lead to resistance and disturbances. For these reasons, secrecy and control of information is vital to prison security.

Still, within the parameters of the other six rights, prison employees have a right to know. They should be informed about the safety risks they face. When tension is mounting within the facility, staff have a right to be informed about what is occurring and what precautions are being taken. Staff have a right to know about decisions regarding promotions and other personnel decisions. They have a right to know about policy and changes in policy. Prison administrators have a positive duty to keep staff informed. Acknowledgment is not enough—active communication is required.

Practices to Assure Ethical Compliance

I have argued that prison employees have seven major ethical rights. However, in considering the application of these rights to prison settings, it became clear that the ability of prison managers to see that these ethical considerations are recognized and respected is constrained by organizational circumstances, budgetary limitations, and competing ethical considerations. It is one thing to claim that employees have the right to as safe a work place as possible and yet another to operationalize that belief in practice. How then should a prison manager proceed to supervise staff in a way that respects the claims of staff?

Larry May, an existentialist philosopher who studies professionalism, proposes the following model of moral responsibility for harm:

A person is morally responsible for a given harm or character defect
if:
(a) the person's conduct played a significant causal role in that
harm or defect; and
(b) the person's conduct was blameworthy or it was morally
faulty in some other way.[17]

Compliance with the first of these is generally straightforward. If prison
organizations and their administrators act in ways that clearly deny an
employee's rights, they have committed a moral harm. If, for example, an
employer discriminated against an employee in a promotion decision because of that employee's race, that individual is harmed. It is a morally
reprehensible act of commission.

Condition (b) adds a further dimension to moral responsibility for prison
organizations and their administrators. If the organization and those who
administer it act in a manner that is morally faulty, this, too, can cause blameworthy harm. Prison administrators have a moral responsibility not only to
recognize employee rights but to assure them. Acts of omission, the failure to
attend to and assure employee rights, is also egregious. Those who administer prisons must create an institutional environment that recognizes, supports, and respects the rules and principles associated with employee rights;
otherwise, they will be lost within the bureaucracy and day-to-day operations of the facility.

This second condition shows us how to proceed ethically when decisions are constrained by organizational circumstances, budgetary limitations, and competing ethical considerations. This is important, for May argues that the very nature of bureaucracies works against the recognition and
protection of individual rights:

> [I]nstitutional socialization in bureaucracies transforms individuals
> into cogs; that is, these individuals come to think of themselves as
> anonymous. As anonymous cogs, they lack the face-to-face confron-
> tation with one another, and with the consequences of their actions,
> that is necessary for a developed sense of responsibility. Lacking this
> personal dimension in their institutional lives, they are likely to lose
> their sense of responsibility in institutional settings as well.[18]

The loss of identity and sense of responsibility afflicts all members of an
organization, worker and manager alike. Nevertheless, the culture of an
organization is not fixed. Support and socialization enhance recognition of
any organizational value, whether it be quality control, integrity, or ethical
behavior. Managers have the authority and responsibility to shape the organizational culture.

To take an example: by its nature, incarceration creates an environment
that encourages the abuse of prisoners. Some of those who end up in prisons

have demonstrated a proclivity for using violence and disrespecting the rights of others. Incarceration enhances this tendency, and many prisoners therefore resist their keepers. Some lie and manipulate, verbally and physically attack staff, disobey the rules, insult, and even throw feces at staff. In response to the strain posed by such behavior, staff can easily drift into the abuse of their power and disrespect of prisoners. To counter this, those who administer the prison must actively promote a culture that treats prisoners humanely, respectfully, and without brutality.

The prison and its administrators can also promote a culture that recognizes the rights of staff and counteracts organizational pressures to act otherwise. If this is to come about, several factors must be in place. There must be a statement of ethical principles for the treatment of staff. Ideally, it will be part of the organizational mission statement. But to be effective, such principles must not be buried in an institutional document that is seldom visited but be part of a living document that becomes a guiding instrument for institutional culture and operations.

New employees and new managers must be socialized to believe in, adhere to, and attend to these principles. They must be discussed, reinforced, and supported within the day-to-day managerial routine. Both training and regular retraining are essential.

The Federal Bureau of Prisons makes a valuable contribution to the discussion. As part of its mission statement, the Bureau outlines a set of cultural anchors or core values, five of which relate to the treatment of employees:

1. *Bureau Family* The Bureau of Prisons recognizes that staff are the most valuable resource in accomplishing its mission, and is committed to the personal welfare and professional development of each employee. A concept of "family" is encouraged through healthy, supportive relationships among staff, and organization responsiveness to staff needs. The active participation of staff at all levels is essential to the development and accomplishment of organizational objectives.

2. *Correctional Workers First* All Bureau of Prisons staff share a common role as correctional workers, which requires a mutual responsibility for maintaining safe and secure institutions and for modeling society's mainstream values and norms.

3. *Promotion of Integrity* The Bureau of Prisons firmly adheres to a set of values that promotes honesty and integrity in the professional efforts of its staff to ensure public confidence in the Bureau's prudent use of its allocated resources.

4. *Career Service Orientation* The Bureau of Prisons is a career-oriented service, which has enjoyed a consistent management philoso-

phy and a continuity of leadership, enabling it to evolve as a stable, professional leader in the field of corrections.

5. High Standards　The Bureau of Prisons requires high standards of safety, security, sanitation, and discipline, which promote a physically and emotionally sound environment for both staff and inmates.[19]

These values are frequently published in Bureau documents. They are used in the training of new staff and new managers. They serve as guiding principles in the day-to-day management of institutions and are part of the socialization of personnel into the Bureau culture.

It is important that there is an organizational culture that supports the analysis of ethical considerations. The ways in which ethical principles get bounded and limited, and who gets to determine these restrictions, must be an arena for active discourse. There is a positive duty to attempt to act ethically, and this requires active consideration, discussion, and analysis of ethical challenges.

Integrity

A discussion of employee rights and their realization within the organization would be incomplete without some mention of integrity. Several studies have been conducted to determine the characteristics that employees most admire in their leaders. Consistently, employees have desired honest leaders. They want the people who direct, guide, and make important decisions regarding their work lives to be trustworthy, ethical, and principled.[20]

Officials who fail to follow through with agreements or make false promises to, deceive, and undermine staff will lose the allegiance, loyalty, and trust of their people. If the organization states that employee rights are important, it must support and protect those values. Hypocrisy is the quickest way to lose trust. Leaders must model the way; they must set the standard for moral and ethical practice.

Integrity rests on consistency. When staff know what their leaders stand for, they do not have to wrestle with uncertainty and try to negotiate some hidden agenda or political game. Knowing the values of the leader avoids confusion, indecision, and conflict. When rules are uniformly applied and no one is able to act with impunity, integrity avoids inequity. Integrity instills within the organization an elemental commitment to inviolable human values.

If the institution makes claim to recognizing and supporting the employees' right to safety, then officials must attend to the business of creating a safe environment. If the institution indicates that employees will be treated fairly, then that provision must be uniformly and consistently applied. Because the need for control and predictability to maintain security impinges on the prison employees' freedom of expression, privacy, and participation in decision making, balance must be sought. The substance of that balance ought to be clearly and openly defined. Employees must know what the rules of the game are and expect that they will be consistently applied.

For prison employees to have basic rights, it all boils down to prison officials acting as moral agents in the task of realizing and assuring them. To act with integrity, prison officials must attend to ethical practice. It has to be part of their vocabulary and managerial practice.

Notes

1. Kelsey Kauffman, *Prison Officers and Their World* (Cambridge, Mass.: Harvard University Press, 1988), 35.

2. James B. Jacobs, *Stateville: The Penitentiary in Mass Society* (Chicago: University of Chicago Press, 1977).

3. Richard L. Phillips and Charles R. McConnell, *The Effective Corrections Manager: Maximizing Staff Performance in Demanding Times* (Gaithersburg, Md.: Aspen Publications, 1996).

4. William G. Archambeault and Betty J. Archambeault, *Correctional Supervisory Management: Principles of Organization, Policy, and Law* (Englewood Cliffs, N.J.: Prentice-Hall, 1982).

5. John J. DiIulio, Jr., *Governing Prisons: A Comparative Study of Correctional Management* (New York: Free Press, 1987), and *No Escape: The Future of American Corrections* (New York: Basic Books, 1991).

6. Marilyn D. McShane and Frank P. Williams III, *The Management of Correctional Institutions* (New York: Garland Publishing, 1993).

7. Kevin N. Wright, *Effective Prison Leadership* (Binghamton, N.Y.: William Neil Publishing, 1994).

8. Listed in Archambeault and Archambeault, *Correctional Supervisory Management*, 253.

9. Patricia H. Werhane, *Persons, Rights, and Corporations* (Englewood Cliffs, N.J.: Prentice-Hall, 1985), 81–93.

10. Roger Folger, "Fairness as a Moral Virtue," in *Managerial Ethics: Morally Managing People and Processes*, ed. Marshall Schminke (Mahwah, N.J.: Lawrence Erlbaum, 1998), 13–34, 26.

11. These seven principles, along with several others that are not discussed here, are introduced in Werhane, *Persons, Rights, and Corporations*, 81–93.

12. Bert Useem and Peter Kimball, *States of Siege: U.S. Prison Riots, 1971–1986* (New York: Oxford University Press, 1989).

13. Werhane, *Persons, Rights, and Corporations*, 119.

14. Werhane, *Persons, Rights, and Corporations*, 138.

15. For a review of research on the benefits of worker participation in decision making, see Kevin N. Wright, Scott Camp, Evan Gilman, and William G. Saylor, "Job Control and Occupational Outcomes among Prison Workers," *Justice Quar-*

terly 14 (1997): 601–25.

16. Wright, Camp, Gilman, and Saylor, "Job Control and Occupational Outcomes among Prison Workers."

17. Larry May, *Sharing Responsibility* (Chicago: University of Chicago Press, 1992), 15.

18. Larry May, *The Socially Responsive Self: Social Theory and Professional Ethics* (Chicago: University of Chicago Press, 1996), 71.

19. Federal Bureau of Prisons, "Cultural Anchors/Core Values," *Federal Prisons Journal* 3 (Spring 1992): inside front cover.

20. See James M. Kouzes and Barry Posner, *The Leadership Challenge: How to Get Extraordinary Things Done in Organizations* (San Francisco: Jossey-Bass, 1998), 16–19.

Response to Chapter 6

The Ethical Dilemmas of Corrections Managers: Confronting Practical and Political Complexity

Michael Jacobson

In calling for the ethical treatment of correctional staff by correctional administrators, criminologist Kevin Wright acknowledges a difficult and seldom discussed subject.[1] In a total institution that is managed through the threat and use of force, how is the ethical treatment of staff possible? Wright focuses on the ethical obligations of prison administrators to their workers as he attempts to answer, or partly answer, this question. In detailing the ethical obligations of correction administrators toward their staff, he rightly lists among these obligations the provision of safety, fair treatment, due process, freedom of expression, privacy, participation in decision making, and information regarding work-related matters. Yet though these workers rights are eminently fair and reasonable, they raise a host of other thorny issues that are barely addressed in Wright's chapter.

Indeed, precisely because prisons exemplify what Erving Goffman has referred to as "total institutions,"[2] they involve interactions among multiple parties who include, but are not limited to, corrections officers. Discussing ethical issues about corrections as though they exist in a vacuum omits some of the more complex problems and obligations that correctional administra-

219

tors face. These more complex problems, which include the correctional administrator's ethical obligations to prisoners and their families, to the public, and to furthering rationally conceived correctional policy, all greatly complicate the relationship between administrators and their staffs. Once the correctional administrator's obligations to all these groups, interests, and principles are taken into account, the assessment of what constitutes ethical behavior becomes far more intricate.

Using Wright's discussion as a point of departure, my purpose is to argue for the importance of taking these multiple considerations into account in order to accommodate, rather than oversimplify, the complexity of correctional ethics. First, I address two of Wright's specific policy suggestions; specifically, I suggest that policies beneficial to corrections officers are sometimes at odds with other essential services that government must also provide. Second, I consider ethical obligations that correctional administrators may have not only toward correction officers but also to the larger society of which the prison system is part. And finally, I discuss the way in which the growing privatization of corrections and the influence of private capital have complicated and obscured the effectuation of ethical behavior by corrections administrators. Only the first section responds directly to Wright's own observations. It is because of Wright's tendency to envision correctional ethics rather narrowly that the second and third sections leave his comments behind and place the current problems of corrections managers within a broader social and historical framework.

What Constitutes the Ethical Treatment of Corrections Officers?

It is hardly controversial to contend, as Wright does, that corrections officers ought to be treated ethically by their supervisors. For corrections officers have one of the most difficult jobs in the criminal justice system. They work inside institutions that are dangerous, and often they must use force to maintain order. On a daily basis, they encounter a wide range of humanity that may include violent prisoners as well as people who are drug addicted and mentally or physically ill. More often than not, these officers are outnumbered by the prisoners they supervise; it is not uncommon for housing officers to supervise as many as 50 to 150 inmates at any time. But even with this intensive workload they are expected to maintain control and order among this captive and frequently hostile population without having to resort to force. Like police, corrections officers must frequently work rotating shifts, but unlike police officers, many work in prisons far from their homes and families. Not surprisingly, the divorce and alcoholism rates among corrections officers are high. The occupation is difficult and stressful for both mind and body.

The people who perform these jobs are certainly entitled to fair and ethical treatment by correctional administrators. But matters are complicated by the fact that prisoners are also constitutionally entitled to fair and humane treatment. This tension—between treating both prisoners and staff fairly—can result in situations in which the assessment of what constitutes ethical treatment of correction officers can become extremely challenging.

Wright says that a crucial ethical obligation of prison officials is to provide due process in cases in which it becomes necessary to discipline correction officers.[3] Who would object to the proposition that any progressive correctional system should provide due process and an appeal mechanism for correction officers who must undergo disciplinary proceedings? But, given the extraordinary power that corrections officers possess to control every aspect of prisoners' lives, some traditional notions of due process have a limited relevance. Let me develop what I mean by this seemingly controversial contention.

Abuses of power wielded by correctional administrators and staff are well-documented facts. In the last several years alone, high-profile stories have highlighted the systematic beating of prisoners at a New Jersey detention center for illegal immigrants; the participation of the Georgia prison commissioner in the beating of prisoners; and the fatal beating of an inmate in a Long Island jail after he complained about not receiving his methadone.[4] Because of such ever-present potential for abuse, the most important characteristic of a humane and well-run correctional facility is that it quickly and severely punishes the unjustifiable use of force by correction officers. By this criterion—also an ethical one—the best run prisons are characterized by the least use of force.

But this means that there may be occasions on which making rapid symbolic points about the unacceptability of abuse in a correctional facility comes into conflict with the expectation of lengthy due process proceedings. Consider the following example. In 1997, during my tenure as New York City correction commissioner, several corrections officers and captains were indicted for participating in the beating of inmates and then covering it up. They were immediately suspended without pay. This accorded with standard practices followed by other law enforcement agencies when officers are indicted for a felony offense. However, in New York City, both city and state law mandate that the New York City Police Department (NYPD) pay its officers after thirty days if the criminal case against them has not been resolved (and most are not). Since the officers must be paid, the police department has the further option of bringing them back to work. Sometimes this has meant that even New York City police officers indicted for the most serious violent felonies are back at work—though not at patrol functions—after thirty days of suspension.

In contrast, city and state law allows New York City's correction commissioner to keep officers on unpaid suspension until their criminal case is disposed. If found guilty of a felony, the officers are immediately terminated; if found not guilty, they are entitled to return to work with their back pay reinstated. My decision in the 1997 case was to keep these indicted corrections officers and captains on unpaid suspension for the duration of their trial, though the criminal proceedings against them, from indictment to trial, lasted nearly two years.

Needless to say, my position was a controversial one. The corrections unions argued strenuously that I was punishing these staff prior to any finding of guilt and that it was un-American to do so. Additionally, the unions pointed out that whereas the police officers who fired forty-one shots in the extraordinarily publicized killing of Amadou Diallo were brought back to work and paid after a thirty-day suspension, these corrections officers, indicted for a far less serious charge (in which the victims were jail inmates), were kept on unpaid suspension indefinitely. The unions questioned how one city government could treat its different uniformed forces so unequally. Clearly, they had a point. It was bizarre that, in one case, police officers had to be paid after thirty days even after allegedly murdering an unarmed man while, in another, correction officers went unpaid for far longer for allegedly committing a less serious crime. However, I felt strongly that the crime with which these correction officers had been charged was exceptionally serious and so potentially harmful to the overriding mission and purpose of the corrections institution that I kept them on unpaid suspension. Moreover, as I knew well in this particular case, the evidence against the officers was overwhelmingly strong.

Could an argument be made that my actions toward these officers violated some due process or moral obligation on the part of administrators to correction officers? Yes. Everyone in this country is presumed innocent in a criminal proceeding prior to its disposition. Additionally, had the officers in this case been police officers accused of beating up suspects, they would have been brought back to work and paid after thirty days. Consequently, these officers were penalized simply because they were corrections officers and by a strange fluke in New York State and City law, which gave me the right to keep them suspended. But, on the other hand, where do the rights of prisoners and their families come in—let alone the right of the public to expect that correctional institutions take every possible measure to ensure a humane and violence-free environment? For practical as well as symbolic reasons, the charge of corrections officers systematically beating prisoners and then covering up this crime from law enforcement authorities should be dealt with in the strictest possible terms.

Here, then, was a situation in which several ethical considerations clashed: fair treatment of correction officers and of prisoners as well as accountability to a broader public. They were not mutually exclusive obligations; nevertheless, not all parties were likely to be pleased with any decision made by the corrections administrator. And so, in cases like the one just delineated, assessing ethical behavior can be complicated. The complications are not sufficiently incorporated into blueprints for the fair treatment of correction officers like the one proposed by Wright.

Wright also suggests other seemingly straightforward moral guidelines. On the subject of working conditions, he writes: "States and their prison systems are morally obligated to maintain the physical plant at acceptable levels. Prison structures cannot be allowed to fall into conditions of deterioration and antiquation that make them unsafe."[5] As before, this seems a patently unobjectionable point: correctional administrators have a basic obligation to provide their staff with a safe working environment. It is a particularly salient responsibility because many corrections officers work in facilities that are quite old. Later in the same section, however, Wright raises a point that introduces a further complexity:

> Furthermore, prison administrators must struggle with competing ethical obligations. To assure the highest level of staff safety, an administrator may recognize that the facility requires a $50 million renovation. If the administrator aggressively lobbies within the state correctional system and government for this capital improvement, knowing that if he or she is successful in securing these funds, they will be taken from public monies that would have otherwise gone to public education, is he or she acting ethically?[6]

This is an insightful and thoughtful question. Unfortunately, Wright does not then proceed to explore its ramifications.

Despite the relatively recent fiscal health[7] of most states' economies, most state budgeting is premised on a zero-sum game. That is, since most governors and state legislatures are likely to cut rather than increase taxes (as occurred in the 1980s and 1990s), budget officials are restricted by finding that there are no more tax levy funds available from the tax proceeds of new years' budgets. Consequently, government agencies must compete for scarce and relatively fixed funds. If, for instance, a state decides to increase the size of its transportation department, this is likely to be achieved at the expense of some other governmental function. In this zero-sum situation, substantial new funding for one governmental function usually creates problems for other governmental agencies. And, of course, the dilemma applies to states' experiences with the relationship between corrections and education budgets. According to the National Association of State Budget Officers (NASBO), the only two governmental functions to increase as a percentage of total state spending from 1987 to 1999 have been Medicaid and corrections. Every other area of state government declined as a percentage of state spending, including primary and secondary education, public assistance, transportation, and environmental protection.[8] Thus, it is no accident that as expenditures on corrections have increased over the last decade, other governmental expenditures—and services—have declined proportionately.

Given this historical trend and current budget practice, the action of a correctional administrator who lobbies aggressively for massive new funding is likely to bring real world consequences for the delivery of other social services. To take a hypothetical though by no means unusual example, a correctional manager who succeeds in obtaining an additional $50 million for needed prison renovation may have also succeeded at preventing the construction of a needed school building in a poor neighborhood. This problem is likely to be especially acute in municipalities in which total budgets are much smaller than those of a huge city such as New York.

Under such circumstances, what is the ethical obligation of the correctional administrator? Is it to let someone else worry about these tradeoffs? After all, it is the correctional administrator's job to be concerned about corrections. One could argue further, moreover, that it is the job of governors and state legislatures to base their resource allocation decisions on the articulated needs of government agency heads. Let the corrections commissioner make her case, the education superintendent make his case, and elected officials can afterward sort it all out. The correctional administrator may adopt this rationale to justify the aggressive pursuit of capital improvements that would benefit both corrections staff and prisoners. In the world of Realpolitik, however, the sophisticated corrections manager knows well that lawmakers will pay much more attention to budget requests from law enforcement agencies that are strongly supported by powerful unions, as is frequently the case with corrections. It is the height of naïveté to believe that these kinds of resource decisions are made by coldly rational policy makers simply on their case-by-case merits.

Thus, the corrections manager cannot so easily get off the hook by projecting such difficult decisions onto other governmental managers. And, consequently, the question remains unanswered as to what ought be done in situations in which, though a newly renovated correctional facility would benefit staff and workers, a new school might provide even greater societal benefit to tens of thousands of school children and teachers. One possibility is that, after weighing the moral costs and benefits involved, the corrections administrator decides not to pursue funding for a correctional facility. Or the administrator might decide not to have her or his actions determined by politically charged budget constraints and call publicly for increased taxes to meet all the legitimate demands for governmental services. Should this last tack be taken, though, the administrator would almost surely lose her or his job. The other possibility is that the corrections administrator decides just "to do my job and let others in government grapple with larger concerns." This is the most pragmatic response and understandably the one most frequently adopted by corrections administrators. Yet even though this is arguably the least ethical of all the responses to securing governmental funds for correctional agencies, it may also be the one that most closely conforms to Wright's criteria for corrections administrators fulfilling moral obligations to their staffs.

Am I saying, then, that all corrections and police administrators should act on the basis of the impact that they believe their actions will have on other parts of government as well as their own? Perhaps not. But I am saying that the dilemma posed by current zero-sum politics is not one that can be blithely ignored. Moreover, it is particularly salient at present when corrections administrators are part of a two-decades-long trend that has witnessed the number of people incarcerated in the United States rising from five hundred thousand to two million and total correctional expenditures now over $41 billion.[9] In this context, corrections administrators do have an ethical obligation to consider how their actions will affect other functions of government. And in some cases this may lead to the conclusion that moral obligations to staff are sometimes outweighed by other, more significant, moral obligations to society.

In practice, no doubt, this is a difficult challenge to operationalize. It would require that correctional administrators be well-informed about the relative health of their local or state budgets as well as about pressing needs elsewhere in government. It would require that these same administrators use this knowledge in the budget process to help guide the size and timing of at least some of their budget requests. Other budget requests would still automatically be made; for example, new staff or space based on increased population should always be funded to ensure the safety of staff and prisoners. Yet there is a subset of all budget requests—new programs, replacement or renovated space, or enhancements to current programs—that probably should be subject to additional examination and critique by correctional administrators in terms of other pressing social needs.

Are There Greater Moral Obligations for Correctional Administrations to Act Upon?

Thus far, using Wright as a point of departure, I have addressed specific obligations that correctional administrators may have toward prisoners as well as officers and toward society as well as their own agencies. But Wright does not go further to reflect on the overall social and political environment in which corrections managers have had to operate in the 1980s and 1990s. At this point, then, I leave Wright behind and turn to the contemporary character of punishment.

For there are even larger and more fundamental ethical issues that correctional administrators face in the context of increased use of incarceration, eliminated education and rehabilitation programs, harsher sentencing of juveniles as adults, and striking racial disparities in prison populations.[10]

Over the last thirty years, policy making in the field of corrections has witnessed a diminished role for the criminal justice or corrections expert and the increased prominence of state legislatures and governors in making correctional policy. It is elected officials who now largely determine what prisons look like in terms of educational, recreational, and work programs. They are the ones who are usually responsible for increasing lengths of stay driven by the diminished role of parole and mandatory sentencing and for the increasing numbers of ever younger offenders entering adult institutions. In New York, for instance, one of Governor Pataki's first acts upon taking office was to eliminate all college-level education courses in prisons. This was not a particularly surprising decision because other states have also eliminated a variety of education programs in recent years. In 1994, Congress eliminated all Pell grants for prisoners; these grants had helped to pay for higher education classes in prison. Additionally, in the last several years fourteen states have completely eliminated parole,[11] and many other states have reduced historical parole release rates.

Although there are certainly some correction administrators who believe that these recent trends in corrections were long overdue, others—and probably more—feel that they fly in the face of good correctional practice. In fact, even the American Correctional Association (ACA) proclaims that in its legislative priorities for the year 2000 it:

- supports (re)habilitation and prevention programs and services;
- supports management practices that reduce crowding and the deterioration of conditions of confinement in adult or juvenile systems and that provide effective management of community supervision caseloads; and
- supports correctional industry programs.[12]

That the largest professional correctional association in the country supports rehabilitation and industry programs, as well as resources for community supervision, suggests that a large group of corrections professionals disagree with current retributive policies. What, then, is the moral responsibility of corrections administrators when their state governors and/or legislatures make policy that they feel to be antithetical to solid correctional practice? Would the reasoning outlined above again apply—that is, we should do nothing since others (namely, lawmakers) have the constitutional right to enact criminal justice policies restricting prison programs and the use of community corrections and parole? After all, state directors of corrections work for governors. Is it not their job simply to carry out the policy directions set by elected officials? Moreover, being a state corrections director is a prestigious and high-paying government job. As a corrections director, one is in charge of a huge staff, large numbers of prisoners, and significant budgets. It is also a job that entails a good deal of stress as well as a variety of managerial and organizational challenges. These positions are difficult to obtain.

Once one becomes a corrections director, the specter of riots, escapes, or other high-profile events constantly reminds the director that his job security may well be fleeting. In addition to the difficulty of becoming a corrections director and the simultaneous rewards and stresses inherent in the job, do these directors also have a moral obligation to take a public stance against policy and legislation they believe to be harmful to prisoners, staff, and good corrections practice?

The easy answer to this question is yes. After all, if corrections administrators do not protest bad correctional policy, it will be left to advocacy groups and public defenders, and they are easily marginalized and ignored. On the other hand, the political weight on prison system administrators publicly speaking out about the abolition of parole (for instance) would be substantial. There are many corrections administrators who believe that eliminating discretionary parole release and significantly increasing prison length of stays is terrible public policy. The potential harm to staff who manage prisoners who are not rewarded for good behavior, let alone the damage done to prisoners themselves, is very real; the hope of attaining early release has been important in managing correctional facilities. Therefore, were a number of prison administrators, law enforcement officials who are hardly viewed as soft on crime, to criticize this policy publicly, it might change the tenor of public debate.

Why does this not happen? One reason—mentioned above—concerns the problem that corrections administrators would face were they to deplore the zero-sum game of corrections-or-social-service funding: analogously, were corrections directors to speak out against eliminated parole in a state in which the governor supported this policy, they would probably be fired. One of the rules of the game in running a government agency is that you work for the governor, and thus you are expected to support the governor's positions in the public arena. You might express your opposition internally and discreetly, but once a policy decision has been made you must be publicly supportive of it. This is a truism of almost all levels of government. If a disagreement is too strong, the agency head has the option to resign. Thus, the corrections director is faced with some very unpleasant options. He must publicly support, and in some cases must aggressively lobby for, policies that he feels are wrong and unethical. Or he can resign. But resignation means not only the loss of a prestigious and challenging position and of the income and (relative) security that come with it but also being labeled as a troublemaker, a characterization that will greatly limit future employment possibilities with other governors. Neither one of these Hobsonian choices is particularly attractive.

Not all law enforcement officials face such stark choices. District attorneys in cities and counties are usually elected officials. Although they are overwhelmingly conservative on law and order issues (because this is what the voting public generally expects of prosecutors), many prosecutors publicly take surprisingly liberal positions on criminal justice issues. This is possible both because they can make their own decisions on what policies to support or criticize and because they politically calculate that taking some traditionally liberal positions will not hurt them with voters. To take an example, Charles Hynes, the elected district attorney in Kings County, is known nationally for developing alternatives to incarceration programs for drug dealers who would otherwise be sent to prison for long sentences. Ronnie Earle in Austin (Texas) and Michael McCann in Milwaukee County (Wisconsin) have also been known to take public positions on issues such as alternatives to incarceration and the death penalty that are very unusual for prosecutors. The fact that some prosecutors publicly support nontraditional forms of punishment sends a powerful message simply because of who they are. But the structural and political position of prosecutors is quite different from that of correctional directors; it is the latter who, ultimately, have their overall policy set by other elected officials. Although a group of correctional directors taking public positions against the current retributive tide in American corrections would be as influential as these prosecutors taking unpopular positions on law enforcement issues, it is far less likely—and more difficult—for them to do so.

In circumstances such as these, most corrections directors choose some version of the first option. That is, they argue on the inside against policies—such as three-strikes laws, eliminating recreation/weightlifting programs, eliminating or greatly restricting the use of parole—that are considered to be poor correctional practice. Once the internal battle has been lost, a public stance of passive or low-profile support can allow the corrections director to save face and not completely support policies he may find offensive. The rationale for this course of action is fairly clear. Most progressive corrections directors believe it preferable that they be in charge of the prisons system (even if they must tacitly support regressive public policy) than that they be in the hands of the true believers in retributive policies who would be likely to replace them should they be fired on principle. By means of this rationale, corrections administrators can not only keep their jobs but also exert some influence on correctional policy in an otherwise unfriendly, retributive environment.

I return then to this section's basic question: What ethical obligation do corrections administrators who operate in "hostile" environments have to speak out or not speak out? Should they resign over principle or work inside the system for changes that may mitigate perceived harm through managerial control of day-to-day prison operations? Ultimately, I have no simple solution to this complex ethical and personal dilemma. Fighting within the system for change is an admirable pursuit, but it may not result in the public being presented with alternative correctional policies to those that are presently dominant. Speaking out against policies promulgated by one's employer may be politically effective; this may raise issues, at least temporarily, that would otherwise not be aired. Taking positions through professional associations such as the ACA or the Association of State Correctional Administrators (ASCA) may also be useful though probably too low profile to change current public policy and discourse about punishment and corrections. Corrections administrators must make their own decisions or find their own voices in terms of how best to deal with policies with which they disagree. However, it is important for officials to struggle with these issues so that they do not get entirely lost in the day-to-day details and bureaucracy inherent in running large complex organizations. There is meaning simply in wrestling with these larger ethical concerns and in thinking about which kinds of policies exceed one's ability to provide even passive support. Finally, being prepared to speak out when or if the situation arises is important in how correctional administrators live their professional lives as well as for the evolution of corrections.

What Are the Implications of Privatization for Correctional Ethics?

Private correctional facilities have grown at an astounding rate over the last two decades. From 1989 to 1997 the number of private beds in adult correctional facilities has grown from 15,000 to 64,086.[13] In addition to the growth of privatization in the United States, private correctional firms have been awarded substantial new contracts in Great Britain, Australia, and South Africa. Although the substantial growth of the private prison industry is well documented, the debate about whether private prisons are cheaper or more effective than similar public prisons is still unsettled. There are vocal proponents of increased correctional privatization[14] as well as of its phasing out.[15] Arguments for and against privatization usually tend to make the case that one or the other is more effective and cheaper to operate. However, according to the authors of the latest and most reliable research on the topic: "Our conclusion regarding costs and savings is that the few existing studies and other available data do not provide strong evidence of any general pattern."[16] With regard to effectiveness, this study also found that "given the shortcomings and the paucity of systematic comparisons, one cannot conclude whether the performance of privately managed prisons is different from or similar to that of publicly operated ones."[17]

   With a paucity of reliable empirical data to support or oppose private prisons on efficiency grounds, the arguments on both sides of the issue tend to be more ideological. A key pro argument is that the private sector is the epicenter for innovation and creativity, especially in relation to government. It is also claimed that private companies are not encumbered by the same nightmarish bureaucracy, civil service and union rules, and procurement policies as government. Private prisons are therefore a priori likely to be more efficient and effective. The competition between public and private sectors will, moreover, improve the performance of all prisons. On the con side, it is typically argued that corrections constitutes a core governmental function and that only government has the moral right to punish and use force against other citizens. Since private prisons are motivated solely by profits, they will inevitably skimp on training, services, and security, thus resulting in poorly run facilities.

Caught in this debate are correctional administrators who must deal with the practical and ethical aspects of a new phenomenon that is, for the most part, out of their control. Practically speaking, correctional privatization has both advantages and disadvantages for public sector corrections administrators. Private prisons can provide fast relief from overcrowded public prisons and thus help to alleviate one of their most pressing problems. On the other hand, private prisons can fail miserably and thus be the cause of huge political problems for correctional directors who contract with a private prison; this is what recently happened in Louisiana.[18]

However, corrections managers may also experience personal and professional benefits in the growth of private prisons. That is, private prisons have greatly extended the career path and longevity of public prison administrators. Despite the rhetoric that the private sector is the place where innovation and creativity blossoms, an overwhelming number of private prison wardens have come from the public sector. It is not uncommon for a warden of a state or federal prison to retire and then become a warden at a private facility. Not surprisingly, wardens who have had successful careers at managing prisons are very attractive prospects for private firms seeking qualified corrections administrators to run their facilities. This allows the public prison warden not only to collect her or his government pension but also to earn a substantial salary as a private correction administrator. For senior corrections administrators, it is financially a very attractive career.

Thus, corrections directors may find themselves on each side of this issue. But whichever side they are on, complex moral dilemmas are sure to arise. Most correctional administrators are likely to have strong opinions on privatization. To air them publicly may have the same effect as opining on other aspects of correctional policy set by lawmakers in their state: unemployment. Thus, coming out against privatization in a state that, because its legislature and governor both support it, has committed itself to operating private prisons, will certainly put one's career in jeopardy. It will, moreover, likely end the potentially lucrative prospect of becoming an executive in a private correctional firm.

For those correctional administrators who work in private prisons, there is an additional layer of complexity that obscures the determination of ethical behavior. Beyond the multiple parties whose needs must be accommodated in public prisons—guards and their unions, other staff, prisoners, and families of prisoners—there is a further powerful group, namely, investors. The addition of investors into the total institution of prisons compounds the notion of assessing ethical behavior by administrators. Do the interests of staff supersede the financial interests of investors? What may be good for staff (more training) may also be good for prisoners but bad for investors (training costs money). Given this complication, how heavily does the private corrections administrator weigh ethical considerations toward staff? Throwing the interests of private capital into the mix makes it extremely difficult for private correctional administrators to think and act ethically.

Conclusion

It is not to be doubted that correctional administrators have moral and ethical obligations to their staffs. Nevertheless, prisons are highly complex institutions in which the interests of various parties may conflict. Consequently, assessing what, in particular situations, constitutes ethical behavior becomes an extraordinarily complicated task. The calculus of correctional ethics must take into account not only parties inside but also those outside prisons. A decision that is ethical for one group (for example, bettering the working conditions of correctional staff) may well have a detrimental impact on another (for example, inner-city school children awaiting new school buildings).

Adding further layers of complexity are questions related to whether correctional administrators have an obligation to speak out when correctional practice and policy made by legislators conflict with their own moral and political judgment. Most recent among these areas of disagreement is the issue of private prisons, which, because of the introduction of private capital and its interests, vastly complicates the ethical situation. For public correctional administrators, criticizing privatization may lead not only to their firing from public service, but also to eliminating a career path in the private prison sector. Presumably, a public corrections administrator speaking critically about the entire concept of privatization would not want to become a private correctional administrator. However, an administrator who is critical not of privatization itself but of how privatization is used strategically by the state, or who is critical of specific private prison managements, may also find that his potential for future private prison employment is greatly limited. Corporate CEOs are no more accepting of criticism, no matter how muted, than are governors. For private correctional administrators, on the other hand, weighing the interests of staff and prisoners may put their decisions at odds with the concerns of investors and corporations who are paying their salaries.

There is, therefore, no easy ethical typology by which correction administrators may live. What is clear is that correction administrators have ethical obligations to a variety of groups and interests both inside and outside the prison. For these administrators, it is both a personally and intellectually difficult task to determine what comprises ethical behavior in their institutional role. However, to acknowledge and struggle with this complexity, rather than to pretend that it does not exist, may itself constitute ethical thought and practice. And the struggle has the potential to improve the lives both of those who work and live in prisons and of the communities that surround them.

Notes

1. Kevin N. Wright, "Management-Staff Relations: Issues in Leadership, Ethics, and Values, " in this volume, 203–18.

2. Erving Goffman, *Asylums: Essays on the Social Situation of Mental Patients and Other Inmates* (Garden City, N.Y.: Anchor Doubleday, 1961).

3. Wright, "Management-Staff Relations," 205.

4. Somini Sengupta, "Immigrants Settle Lawsuit over Jail Beatings for $1.5 Million," *New York Times*, September 21, 1998, B2; Rick Bragg, "Prison Chief Encouraged Brutality, Witnesses Report," *New York Times*, July 1, 1997, A12; David Halbfinger, "Abused Behind Bars: A Special Report," *New York Times*, February 1, 1999, A1.

5. Wright, "Management-Staff Relations," 207.

6. Wright, "Management-Staff Relations," 207–08.

7. In the past several years, state budgets have benefited from the strong national economy. This has allowed some states to spend additional funds without having to commensurably reduce other expenditures as states collect greater amounts of personal income and sales tax from their residents. Despite this recent burst of fiscal health, state budget offices usually try to keep year-to-year expenditures the same (but for inflation and workload increases) with new funds going only toward governors' or legislatures' highest political priorities.

8. National Association of State Budget Officers, *State Expenditure Report* (Washington, D.C., 1999), 9.

9. Bureau of Justice Statistics, *Justice Employment and Statistics Abstracts, 1982–1996* (Washington, D.C., 1999), Table 1.

10. In 1997, the number of whites sentenced to prison per 100,000 was 386 with the corresponding number for African Americans being 3,209. See Ann L. Pastore and Kathleen Maguire (eds.), *Sourcebook of Criminal Justice Statistics*, Table 6.31, <http://www.albany.edu/sourcebook> (November 2000).

11. Paula Ditton and Doris Wilson, *Truth in Sentencing in State Prisons* (Washington, D.C.: U.S. Department of Justice, Bureau of Justice Statistics, 1999).

12. "ACA Legislative Priorities for the Year 2000" at <www.corrections.com/aca/legisl/priorities.html> (11/02/00).

13. Douglas McDonald, Elizabeth Fournier, Malcolm Russell-Einhorn, and Stephan Crawford, *Private Prisons in the United States: An Assessment of Current Practice* (Cambridge, Mass.: Abt Associates, 1998).

14. Charles H. Logan, "Objections and Refutations," in *Privatizing Correctional Services*, ed. Stephen T. Easton (Vancouver, B.C.: The Fraser Institute), 127–38; Charles W. Thomas, "Testimony Regarding Correctional Privatization," testimony before the Subcommittee on Crime of the House Committee on the Judiciary, Washington, D.C., June 8, 1995.

15. Judith Greene, "Prison Privatization: Recent Developments in the United States," paper presented at the International Conference On Penal Abolition, Toronto, Canada, May 2000).

16. McDonald, Fournier, Russell-Einhorn, and Crawford, *Private Prisons in the United States*, v.

17. McDonald, Fournier, Russell-Einhorn, and Crawford, *Private Prisons in the United States*, v.

18. A federal judge in Louisiana found that Wackenhut Corporation ran a juvenile justice facility that routinely brutalized the children in its care. The company agreed to vacate the facility and the state's correction commissioner called the private prison (for whose oversight he was responsible) a failure. See Fox Butterfield, "Settling Suit, Louisiana Abandons Private Youth Prisons," *New York Times*, September 8, 2000, A14.

Additional Resources

The field of correctional ethics has developed unevenly. Certain topics, such as the philosophy of punishment and responsibility, have been staples of formal ethical inquiry and debate for as long as people have pondered ethical questions. Other issues—particularly those concerning a professional ethic for corrections officers or the privatization of prisons—have entered into the ethical debate much more recently and have been subjected to relatively unsystematic scrutiny.

What follows is not so much a bibliography of materials that deal with the various facets of correctional ethics as a guide to contemporary resources—places that will assist the reader who wishes to pursue these issues further.

One obvious starting point is provided by the endnotes to the various chapters in this collection— materials on which the authors drew or to which they responded in developing their discussions of different facets of correctional ethics.

A further useful resource can be found in an annotated and topical bibliography in *Teaching Criminal Justice Ethics*, ed. John Kleinig and Margaret Leland Smith (Cincinnati: Anderson, 1997, but now available from the Institute for Criminal Justice Ethics, John Jay College of Criminal Justice, 555 West 57th Street, New York, NY 10019). Texts on—and other general discussions of—criminal justice ethics frequently give some of their attention to questions of correctional ethics. But the bibliography also includes a section devoted specifically to materials in correctional ethics. Additional materials can be found in Frank Schmalleger and John Smykla, *Corrections in the 21st Century* (Woodland Hills, Calif.: Glencoe/McGraw-Hill, 2001), a text that focuses on professionalism in corrections but which also has associated with it a large arrange of on-line resources: <http://www.glencoe.com/ps/corrections/>. Frank Schmalleger's site also contains links to correctional institutions, organizations, and other resources: http://talkjustice.com/links.asp?453053900.

The Institute for Criminal Justice Ethics also sponsors a web site to which it has linked on an ongoing basis many web-based resources on correctional ethics: <www.lib.jjay.cuny.edu/cje/html/correctional.html>. This site organizes its links so that researchers may access other web sites having a substantial focus on issues in correctional ethics, ethically oriented reports into correctional institutions, articles on correctional ethics, correctional codes of ethics from around the world, and syllabi in correctional ethics that have been posted on the web. The site also provides links to many groups and organizations that are currently seeking to institute practices of restorative justice within the correctional domain.

Another valuable resource on correctional ethics can be found in various judicial decisions relating to correctional institutions, for they help to provide something of a reality check on the theory of correctional ethics—whether what is proclaimed as the "philosophy of corrections" is or is not capable of being implemented by the institutions currently devoted to correctional purposes. Many of the major cases are referred to in the endnotes to the chapters in this volume.

Index of Names

Albonetti, Clesta, 174, 176
Alexander, Elizabeth, 33
Allen, Francis A., 172
Allen, Harry E., 200
Anechiarico, Frank, 161, 175
Anno, B. Jaye, 124
Archambeault, Betty J., 204, 217
Archambeault, William G., 204, 217
Atlas, Randall L., 169–70
Austin, J., 155

Baadsager, Pernille, 171
Baer, Justin, 171
Barr, Heather, viii, xiv, 148
Barrier, Gary, 15
Barrington, Bob, 9
Becker, R., 146
Bedau, Hugo, 124
Benekos, Peter, 172
Benson, Bruce L., 37
Beetham, David, 186–87, 192
Bomse, Audrey, viii, xiv, 27, 33, 36,
    105–111, 145, 148, 189
Bonnie, Richard, 146
Bottoms, Anthony, 190, 191, 192
Bragg, Rick, 100, 232
Braithwaite, John, 64, 67
Braswell, Michael, 175, 176

Breard, Angel Francisco, 26
Brennan, Justice, 80
Brenner, Elsa, 37
Breyer, Stephen, 29
Brookes, Derek, viii, xiv, 13, 69–73,
    75–77, 180, 190
Brown, John, 71, 77
Brown, L., 200
Buchanan, Robert, 31
Burke, Peggy B., 172
Butterfield, Fox, 139, 233

Camp, Scott, 217, 218
Carroll, Leo, 145
Chambliss, William J., 171
Champion, Dean J., 173, 174
Chandler, D. C., 138
Chavkin, Samuel, 147
Christie, Nils, 64
Chung, Susanna Y., 36
Classen, Ron, 173
Clear, Todd, xv, 31, 170, 171, 177, 178
Clemmer, Donald, 189–90
Clinton, William Jefferson, 81
Cloward, Richard, 191
Colby, A., 192
Conover, Ted, 11, 14–15, 148
Covington, Mark, 146

Crawford, Stephan, 232, 233
Cressey, Donald, 173, 189, 191
Cullen, Francis T., 169, 171, 172, 177
Curran, Nadine, 32
Currie, Elliot, 171
Curtis, J., 146

Darling, Cheryl, L., 177
Davis, Angela, 31, 75–76, 77–78
Decaire, Michael, 14, 146
DeLuca, Henry R., 176
Demleitner, Nora V., 31
Diallo, Amadou, 222
Dias, M. G., 192
Dickens, Charles, 95, 103
DiIulio, John J., Jr., 152, 170, 176, 192,
    204, 217
Ditton, Paula M., 31, 32, 137, 232
Dobbins, Felita, 200
Douglass, Frederick, 71
Dubler, Nancy, 124
DuBois, W. E., 72, 77
Duffee, David, 164–65, 167–68, 173,
    174, 175, 177
Dunham, G., 169–70
Dwyer, Jim, 146

Earle, Ronnie, 228
Eisenhower, Dwight, 77
English, Kim, 174
Erez, Edna, 146

Fallon, Richard H., Jr., 35
Faugeron, Claude, 170
Feeley, Malcolm, 23–24, 33, 34, 172, 175
Feinberg, Joel, 62, 68, 114, 124
Fletcher, Tyler, 175, 176
Folger, Roger, 205
Foucault, Michel, 13, 174
Fournier, Elizabeth, 232, 233
Freire, Paulo, 68
Fukuyama, Francis, 190

Gallie, W. B., 70, 77
Galtung, John, 170
Gambetta, Diego, 190
Gangi, Robert, 30
Garfinkel, Harold, 173, 191
Garland, David, 171

Garner, Wayne, 100
Geer, Martin, 36
Gendreau, Paul, 170
Giddens, Anthony, 190
Gilbert, Karen E., 169, 177, 199, 201
Gilligan, C., 200
Gilman, Evan, 217, 218
Ginger, Ann Fagan, 36
Gizzi, Lisa, 146
Goffman, Erving, 173, 191, 219, 232
Goldberg, David, 75, 76, 77
Golove, David M., 35
Gottfredson, Michael, 200
Greenberg, Jack, 32
Greene, Judith, 37, 233
Grosser, George H., 172, 191
Grusky, Oscar, 165–66, 177

Hahn, Paul H., 176–77
Haidt, Jonathan, 192
Halbfinger, David, 232
Hall, Jay, 164, 175, 176
Hamilton, V. Lee, 192
Hampton, Jean, 65, 68
Hawkins, Gordon, 33, 171, 174
Hays, Will, 190, 191, 192
Heffernan, William C., viii, xiv, 99, 102,
    103, 112
Helms, Jesse, 36
Hemmens, Craig, 11
Henderson, Thelton, 83
Henriques, Zelma, viii, xiv, 199, 201
Hepburn, John R., 174, 176
Hills, Holly A., 138
Hirschi, Travis, 200
Hirschman, Albert O., 14
Hitler, Adolph, 71
Hobbes, Thomas, 184–85
Hoffman, B., 201
Holman, Charles, 102
Holmes, S. A., 201
Howard, John, 21
Hynes, Charles, 228

Irwin, J., 172

Jacobs, James B., 175, 191, 204, 217
Jacobson, Michael, x, xiv
Janowitz, Morris, 160, 175

Jester, Jean, 168, 177
Johnson, Robert, 161, 170, 175
Jones, Linda, 174
Justice, William Wayne, 24

Kauffman, Kelsey, 10, 14, 31, 175, 203, 217
Keliher, Leo, 65
Kellar, Mark, 33
Kent, David, 146
Kimball, Peter, 170, 217
Kincade, Patrick T., 146
Kipnis, Kenneth, ix, xiv, 125–27, 131, 133, 137, 139, 141–43, 145, 147
Kleinig, John, ix, xiv, 13, 14, 17–21, 30, 31, 65, 235
Kohlberg, Lawrence, 192
Koller, S. H., 192
Koson, Dennis F., 37
Kouzes, James M., 216
Kubweza, Bomani, 34

Leone, Matthew, 146
Levine, James, 178
Lewis, C. S., 61, 67
Lewis, Dan A., 177
Lincoln, Abraham, 71
Locke, John, 5–6, 13
Logan, Charles H., 233
Lombardo, Lucian, 162, 175
Longmire, Dennis R., 171
Luban, David, 10, 14
Luhmann, Niklas, 190
Lynch, Arthur, 137

Maahs, Jeff, 37
Macallair, Dan, 30
Maddow, Rachel, 37
Maghan, Jess, 169
Maguire, Kathleen, 232
Mann, Coramae Richey, 178
Marsh, Robert, 15
Marshall, Tony F., 68
Martell, David A., 137
Martinson, Robert, 152, 170, 193–94, 200
Mason, C., 146
Mathiesen, Thomas, 60, 63, 66, 67, 68

Mavrodes, George, 66
May, Larry, 213–14, 218
McCann, Michael, 228
McCleery, Richard, 191
McConnell, Charles R., 204, 217
McDonald, Douglas, 37, 232, 233
McGarrell, Edmund, 164, 168, 177
McMath, Tracy, 12
McNair, James, 37
McQuiston, John T., 34
McShane, Marilyn D., 204, 217
McWhorter, Ray, 100
Mead, Dean M., 139
Mendoza, Martha, 100, 101
Menninger, Karl, 170
Merry, Sally, 68
Messinger, Sheldon L., 191
Meyerson, Barbara, 160, 167, 174
Michaels, David, 137
Michalos, C., 146
Miller, Thomas J., 175, 176
Moody-Maynard, Steven, 178
Moore, David B., 68
Moore, Michael, 67
Moretti, Diane, 34
Morris, Herbert, 68
Mueser, Kim T., 138
Murphy, Jeffrie, 65, 66
Musheno, Michael, 178

Najavits, Lisa M., 138
Napoleon, John, 89, 102
Neoral, Lubor, 146
Nunn, William Stanley, 34

Ohlin, Lloyd E., 191

Palumbo, Dennis, 178
Pastore, Ann L., 232
Pataki, George, 136, 226
Peters, Roger H., 138
Petersilia, Joan, 172, 174
Phillips, Richard L., 204, 217
Pittman, John, xi, xiv
Pizzuto, Thomas, 83
Posner, Barry, 218
Pratt, Travis C., 37
Pullen, Suzanne, 174
Puisis, Michael, 17, 146

Rafter, N. H., 200
Rawls, John, 114, 124
Rehnquist, William, 81
Reiman, Jeffrey, 74, 77
Rein, Andrew, 139
Richie, Beth, 200
Roberts, Clifford "Dhoruba," 34
Rockefeller, Nelson, 100
Rogers, A., 200
Rousseau, Jean-Jacques, 194
Rubin, Edward L., 24, 33, 34
Ruiz, David, 24
Russell-Einhorn, Malcolm, 232, 233

Sadurski, Wojciech, 67
Saint Paul, 47
Sanders, Joseph, 192
Saylor, William G., 217–18
Savas, E. S., 37
Scalia, Antonin, 26, 35
Schiraldi, Vincent, 30
Schlanger, Margo, 34
Schlosser, Eric, 77
Schmalleger, Frank, 235–36
Schneider, Gertrude, 52
Scull, Andrew, 168
Segal, Lydia, 12
Seligman, Adam B., 182–83, 190, 191
Sellin, J. Thorsten, 170, 171
Senghor, Taharka, 34
Sengupta, Somini, 232
Shaw, G. B., 39, 63
Shields, Wesley P., 146
Shweder, Richard A., 192
Silove, D., 146
Simon, Jonathan, 172, 175
Simonsen, Clifford E., 200
Sims, Barbara, 171
Skolnick, Andrew A., 146
Sloop, John M., 169, 170, 177, 178
Smith, Margaret Leland, x, xiv, xv, 148, 235
Smith, Polly Ashton, ix, xiv, 192
Smith, Susan, 199, 201
Smykla, John, 235
Snyder, Jean Maclean, 35
Sparks, Richard, 171, 191, 192
Sreenivasan, Shoba, 146

Stastny, Charles, 158, 173
Stern, Vivien, 64, 67
Stewart, Frank Henderson, 192
Stohr, Mary K., 15
Strang, H., 64
Stroup, Timothy, 112
Sullivan, John, 99
Sundt, Jody L., 171
Sykes, Gresham, 58–61, 64, 65, 67–68, 184–85, 188, 191

Taqi-Eddin, Khaled, 30
Taylor, Charles, 192
Teplin, Linda A., 138
Thomas, Charles, 29, 37, 233
Thomas, Clarence, 26, 35
Thomas, Jim, 33, 178
Thompson, Anne, 34
Thurmond, Strom, 32
Toch, Hans, 67, 170
Tomaino, Louis, 175, 176
Tonry, Michael, 171, 178
Torrey, E. Fuller, 138
Towberman, Donna B., 176
Tunick, Mark, 70, 77
Turiel, Eliot, 192
Tyler, Tom R., 192
Tyrnauer, Gabrielle, 158, 173

Umbreit, Mark, 66
Unger, Cindie A., 31
Useem, Bert, 170, 217

Vinter, Robert, 160, 175
von Hirsch, Andrew, 64, 66, 68
Voorhis, Patricia Van, 171

Warren, Earl, 22, 80, 97
Weber, Max, 191, 192
Weinberger, Linda E., 146
Weiser, Benjamin, 34
Weiss, Roger D., 138
Welch, Michael, 173
Werhane, Patricia, 210, 212, 217
Wheeler, Stanton, 156, 173
Whitelow, Karen, 31
Wiedemann, Carl F., 176
Williams, Frank P., 204, 217

Williams, Joseph V., x, xiv, 14, 175, 179–80, 183, 189, 191, 193–99, 200–201
Williams, Martha, 175, 176
Williams, Monte, 200
Wilson, Basil, xv
Wilson, Doris James, 31, 232
Winerip, Michael, 139
Wright, Kevin N., ix, xiv, 95, 104, 204, 217–18, 219–21, 223, 225, 232
Wynn, Jennifer, 139

Zehr, Howard, 173
Zhang, Yurong, 13
Ziedenberg, Jason, 30
Zimmer, Lynn E., 175
Zimring, Franklin, 33, 171, 174

Index of Subjects

AAUP (American Association of University Professors), 123

abolition of prisons, 3–4, 69–78

abuse in prisons: administrative solutions, 107–11; excessive use of force, 83–85; failure to protect, 87–88, 93; injunctive relief from, 80, 107; negligence, 89–90; punishment of, 221–22; purposeful, 83–88; sexual, 85–86, 193–200; social Darwinism, 99n32; systemic nature of, 91–95; torture of prisoners, 26; and trustee system, 98n13; types of, 82–83

abuse of drugs, 126–31, 211

ACA (American Correctional Association). *See* American Correctional Association (ACA)

ACLU (American Civil Liberties Union), 97n1

ADA (Americans with Disabilities Act), 21

adaptation strategies of prison officers, 157

administrative succession, effects of, 165

administrators, prison: ASCA, 229; judicial deference to, 115; in private institutions, 230–31;

responsibilities toward employees, 213–16; as responsible for prison abuse, 82. *See also* management, prison; officers, corrections

African Americans. *See* racial issues; racism

African National Ujamaa (ANU), 94, 103n92

AI. *See* Amnesty International

AIDS/HIV, 119, 122–23, 135, 145n2

almshouses as prison predecessor, 195

American Association of University Professors (AAUP), 123

American Civil Liberties Union (ACLU), 97n1

American Correctional Association (ACA): administrative program of, 106; Attica report, 100n45; Code of Ethics, 9, 204; legislative priorities, 226; minimum standards, 27; and sexual abuse, 199

American Correctional Chaplain's Association, 9

American Correctional Health Services Association, 9

American Friends Service Committee, 97n1

American Jail Association, 199

Americans with Disabilities Act (ADA), 21

Amnesty International (AI), 26, 84, 96, 97n1

analytic ethical theory, slavery example, 71

anticipatory socialization factors, 151

ANU (African National Ujamaa), 94, 103n92

Association of State Correctional Administrators (ASCA), 229

Attica report, effects of, 100n45, 152, 155–59

at-will employment and prison employees, 205

authority: of correctional personnel, 9; legitimization of, 184–87; warden's, 158. *See also* power

Baltimore & Ohio Railroad, Chambers v., 96

basic human needs, as denied to prisoners, 42–43, 57–58, 60–63

Bayside State Prison, 84

Big Houses, pre-Attica, 158

Bill of Rights: as applied to prisoners, 79–80; First Amendment, 22–23, 34n46, 80; freedoms under, 205; and UN standards, 25. *See also* Eighth Amendment; rights, human/legal

bing, 134

black codes for crimes in antebellum South, 75

blackness of crime (racial composition of convicted criminals), 75

black-white imprisonment ratios, 153. *See also* racial issues; racism

BOP (Federal Bureau of Prisons), 86, 199–200, 215–16

brokerage, principles of, 143–45

Bureau of Justice Statistics, 31n12

Bureau of the Census, 31n12

C. F. v. Fauver, 84, 95

Camden County Jail Inmates v. Parker, 91

capitalism, privatization of prisons, 27–30

capital punishment. *See* death penalty

Casey, Lewis v., 82, 106–7

case management, as offender control method, 155

CBS (Correctional Behavioral Services), 28

CCA (Corrections Corporation of America), 29

censure, as insufficient punishment, 20

Census Bureau, 31n12

Chambers v. Baltimore & Ohio Railroad, 96

Chavis v. Holvey, 94

CHCPs (correctional health care professionals), 113–24, 142. *See also* health care

citizenship, as forfeited by prisoners, 79

civil-rights litigation, pro se, 80

civil rights of prisoners, 22–25, 29, 208

civil society and social constraints, 5–6

class action litigation, 22–23, 33n25, 84

class differences, 128, 151

CMS (Correctional Medical Services), 28, 92

codes of ethics: ACA, 9, 204; correctional, 5; development of, 14n16; police, 108; for slave-masters, 40–41, 48

coercive power, 6, 19. *See also* abuse in prisons

Commission on Law Enforcement and the Administration of Justice, 178n102

Committee against Torture, 26

community: nature of, 5; reintegration into, 150, 158, 165, 168, 195–96. *See also* rehabilitation

community corrections: Commission on Law Enforcement and the Administration of Justice, 178n102; effectiveness of, 164; elements of, 176n84; as extension of punishment, 154; as overcrowding release valve, 168; post-Attica, 157–59; pre-Attica, 155–57; role of practitioners, 160; staff-offender relationships in, 165–67; support by ACA, 226

compassion, as moral virtue, 51

conditions, prison: culpable intent standard, 91–92; deplorability of, 59; humanity of inmates under, 10; legislatively mandated, 7; over-crowding, 91–92, 153, 162, 168; standards for, 27, 80; super-maximum security facilities, 26. *See also* abuse in prisons; rights, human/legal

confidence-based societies, danger in, 184

confidence vs. trust, 183–84

conflicts of interest, 9–10, 120

conflicts of obligation in prison healthcare, 118–20

constitutional issues. *See* U.S. Constitution

containment approach to community supervision, 159

contraband in work-release programs, 167

control issue: case management as control method, 155; and em-ployee self-determination, 212; and minority social mobility, 153; and New Segregation, 76; and origins of penal system, 170n2; as primary task of corrections, 22; problematic nature of, 174n61; theories of control, 185–87

controlling function of correctional system, 151

control units and prison abuse, 94

Convention against Torture and Other Cruel, Unusual, or Degrading Treatment, 26, 36n73

convict lease system, 75

core conditions standard, 27

corporal punishment in Arkansas prisons, 97n8. *See also* abuse in prisons

correctional administrators. *See* administrators, prison

Correctional Behavioral Services (CBS), 28

correctional ethics: argument against, 41–43; and courts, 105–11; external influences on, 12; impossibility of,

39–63; prisoner-centered, 19; prospects for, 17–37; rationale for, 5–10. *See also* ethics; moral issues

correctional health care professionals (CHCPs), 113–24, 142. *See also* health care

correctional ideology, types of, 150

correctional institutions, functions of, 2, 151. *See also* prisons

Correctional Medical Services (CMS), 28, 92

correctional officers. *See* officers, corrections

Correctional Officers' Creed, 9

correctional personnel. *See* staff, corrections

correctional practices: and employee safety, 207; purpose of, vii–viii; reactive, 159. *See also* abuse in prisons

correctional structures, tridirectional, 152

Correctional Supervisory Management (Archambeault and Archambeault), 204

correctional system, as social institu-tion, 17

Corrections Corporation of America (CCA), 29

corruption, 161–62, 167, 198, 208, 211

courts: and correctional ethics, 105–11; denial of access for prisoners, 82; pretrial issues, 97n7, 129. *See also* litigation

crime: blackness (race) of, 75; and bolstering of economic elites, 74; control policies for, 76; criminals as social outcasts, 8–9; and mental health, 21; prevention as central purpose of punishment, 126; social process of, 74

criminal justice system: imperfections of, 2; retributive purpose of, 127; workers in, 25

cruel and unusual punishment: and denial of health care, 116, 147n15; due to prison conditions, 91–92; excessive use of force, 23, 29, 84,

85; under Warren court, 80. *See also* abuse in prisons; rights, human/legal

custodial institutions: failures of, 2; function of, 151; masculine nature of, 198; professional ethic for, 5–10; staff role in work-release programs, 166

Czimadia v. Fauver, 88

death penalty: condemnation by Amnesty International, 26; and criminals as social outcasts, 8–9; increased use of, 20, 23, 31n12; minority disproportionality on death row, 153

declaratory relief and prisoners' rights, 22–23

degradation ceremonies, 156

democracy: freedom in liberal, 114; self-legitimating, 185–86; social theory of liberal, 5

deprivation of liberty: and inmate code, 158; prison methods of carrying out, 60–61; purpose of, vii–viii; as sufficient punishment, 7, 13n11, 126

deterrence, as justification for incarceration, 126–27

dignity, intrinsic: of human beings, 42–43, 54–55; and moral status, 65n22; of prisoners, 18–20, 22, 24, 55–56, 58–60. *See also* rights, human/legal

disciplinary lockup and prison abuse, 94–95

discretionary power of corrections staff, 79, 154–55, 167

doctor-patient confidentiality, prisoner loss of, 134–35

drug abuse, 126–31, 211

due process: and denial of health care, 147n15; for pretrial detainees, 97n7, 129; for prison employees, 209, 221–22. *See also* rights, human/legal

Due Process Clause, rights of prisoners under, 80

economic and racial stratification in correctional ideology, 150

economy, as greater good, 51

education courses in prison, 226

Effective Corrections Manager (Phillips and McConnell), 204

Effective Prison Leadership (Wright), 204

Eighth Amendment: application to prison conditions, 26, 27; intent requirement, 98n19; and overcrowding, 91; pretrial detainees excepted, 97n7; and prison health care, 116, 143, 147n15; and strip searches, 34n46; under Warren court, 80

Emancipation Proclamation, 71

employees, corrections: due process for, 209, 221–22; ethical treatment of, 10, 203–18; private prisons, 29–30. *See also* officers, corrections; staff, corrections

employment, prison as boost to, 75

Enlightenment, ethical strategies of, 70

Equal Protection Clause and segregation of prisoners, 23

Estelle v. Gamble, 116

ethics: analytic ethical theory, 71; code for slave-masters, 40–41, 48; development of codes, 14n16; dilemmas for managers, 219–33; high-theoretical view, 70; management-staff relations, 203–18; police code, 108; retributional, vii–viii. *See also* correctional ethics; moral issues

ethnic minorities: legal protections for, 27; social mobility as controlled by incarceration, 153; unequal treatment of, 8. *See also* racial issues; racism

excessive use of force, 23, 29, 84, 85

executive branch as social structure, 6

failure to protect, negligence in, 90

fair treatment of prison employees, 208–9

Fauver, C. F. v., 84, 95

Fauver, Czimadia v., 88

Federal Bureau of Prisons (BOP), 85–86, 199, 215–16

federal funding, as denied to legal aid groups, 81

Federal Rules of Civil Procedure, 33n25

feedback communication, 163

females under correctional supervision, 29, 198–200

Fifth Amendment, rights of prisoners under, 80

financial abuse of prisoners, 93–94

First Amendment, 22–23, 34n46, 80

fixed sentences, need for, 153

force, use of excessive, 23, 29, 84, 85

Fourteenth Amendment, 34n46, 80, 91, 147n15

Fourth Amendment, 80

freedom: deprivation as punishment, vii–viii, 7, 13n11, 60–61, 126, 158; Enlightenment ideal of, 181; of expression, 22–23, 34n46, 80, 209–10; in liberal democracies, 114. *See also* Bill of Rights

freedom of choice for prison employees, 211–12

free market in correctional ethics, 18. *See also* private-sector prisons

Gamble, Estelle v., 116

goon squads and prison abuse, 84

Governing Prisons (DiIulio), 204

government role in correctional policy, 226

Great Chain of Being, 182

greater good in institutional ethic, 42, 49–53

grievance system, prison, "black hole" of, 90

group demonstrations on list of dangerous acts, 31n8

group punishments, types of, 31n7

health care: brokering of, 141–48; conflicts inherent in, 125–39; constitutional right to, 116; inadequate, 92–93; negligent denial of, 89; private contractors for, 28; role of providers, 113–24, 142; staff-prisoner relations, 87, 133–35

hierarchicalism in correctional institutions, 11

high-tech physical restraints, 84

high-theoretical view of ethics, 70, 76

HIV/AIDS, 119, 122–23, 135, 145n2

Holvery, Chavis v., 94

homelessness and increased chances of incarceration, 128–29

HRW (Human Rights Watch), 32n21, 85, 96, 97n1

Hudson v. McMillian, 83

human rights. *See* rights, human/legal

Human Rights Committee of the United Nations, 96–97

Human Rights Watch (HRW), 32n21, 85, 96, 97n1

human worth, relation to moral status, 65n22. *See also* dignity, intrinsic

illicit relationships in work-release programs, 167

imprisonment. *See* incarceration

incapacitation as primary function of imprisonment, 159

incarceration: costs of, 30n2; deterrence as justification for, 126–27; expanded use of, 23; and homelessness, 128–29; incapacitation as primary function of, 159; injustice of, 30, 42–43, 53–63; justification for, 2–3; nature of, 79; professionalizing of, 1–15; as punishment, 2–3, 4, 6–7, 13n7, 20, 114; and slavery, 27, 70–75; as solution to social problems, 153; suffering as goal of, 40; as waste of money, 136. *See also* prisons

incentives in rational choice theory, 185

indeterminate sentences, end of, 152–53

infirmaries, inadequate, 92. *See also* health care

information, prison employees' right to, 212–13

Initial Report of the United States of

America to the UN Committee on the Elimination of All Forms of Racial Discrimination, 26–27

injunctive relief, 22–23, 80, 81, 107

injustice of imprisonment, 30, 42–43, 53–63

inmate code, 156, 170n5

institutional contingency, 2–5

institutional decision, defined, 44

institutional environment, status quo of, 12

institutional ethic, defined, 41, 44

institutional reform litigation, 22

institutions: ethical constraints on, 5; purposes of, 1, 6; types of, 6, 21, 23, 26, 165. *See also* incarceration; prisons

instrumental model, 185

integrity: as defining characteristic of self, 187; and employee rights, 216–17; erosion by prison role expectations, 188–89; in prison management, 204. *See also* ethics

intensive supervision programs (ISPs), 159

interim-ethic objection, 46–49

International Convention on the Elimination of All Forms of Racial Discrimination, 26

International Court of Justice, 26

International Covenant on Civil and Political Rights, 26, 96

intrinsic dignity and worth. *See* dignity, intrinsic

involuntary servitude, as punishment for crime, 75

isolation of prisoners, 21, 23, 94

ISPs (intensive supervision programs), 159

judiciary: correctional institution oversight functions, 23, 79–96, 106–7; side effects of reform, 34n43; as social structure, 6

justice: as denied by imprisonment, 42–43, 53–63; experience of, 67n38; as greater good, 42, 53; imperfections of criminal justice system, 2,

25, 127; restorative, 151, 158, 169, 173n51. *See also* rehabilitation; retributive justice

Justice Statistics Bureau, 31n12

labor pool, prison population as, 75

Law of Nature, 5

leadership in correctional institutions, 11–12, 18, 21–22. *See also* management, prison; officers, corrections

Legal Service Corporation, 81

legal system, necessity for, 5. *See also* courts

legislation: Americans with Disabilities Act, 21; civil rights, 208; and narrowing of prisoner rights, 81; Violent Crime Control and Law Enforcement Act, 33n39, 153

legislature, as social structure, 6

legitimacy, problem of, 184–87. *See also* authority

legitimization of society, as greater good, 50

lesser evil, as insufficient justification for ethical decision, 52

Lewis v. Casey, 82, 106–7

liability insurance for correctional corporations, 29

liberty: deprivation of as punishment, vii–viii, 7, 13n11, 60–61, 126, 158; Enlightenment ideal of, 181; in liberal democracies, 114. *See also* Bill of Rights

litigation: civil-rights, 80; class action, 22–23, 33n25, 84; failure of, 24; optimal limit of, 106; PLRA, 27, 81, 86, 92, 99n23; and strip searches, 88

loss of liberty. *See* deprivation of liberty

loss of property or mail, negligent, 90

mail, negligent loss of, 90

maintenance function of correctional system, 151

malingering issue, 133, 134, 147n17

management, prison: authoritarian style of, 115; case management as offender control method, 155; circumstances of, 110; confidence-based, 184; and employee safety, 207; ethical dilemmas for, 219–33; judicial involvement in, 106. *See also* administrators, prison; officers, corrections

Management of Correctional Institutions (McShane and Williams), 204

management-staff relations, ethics of, 203–18

maximum-security prisons, deprivations in, 21

McMillian, Hudson v., 83

Medicaid, reduction in accessibility to, 129

medical care. *See* health care

medical quarantine of prisoners, 118

mental illness: and crime, 21; and deterrence, 126–27; and futility of incarceration, 127–31; and human rights of prisoners, 26; in isolation units, 95; neglect of treatment for, 89, 93; and policy to imprison mentally ill, 136–37; prisoners as targets of abuse, 84–85, 135; in prison population, 32n15; and privatization of prisons, 28; stigmatization of, 139n24

military-industrial complex, 77n9

minimum-security prisons, 165

minorities: legal protections for, 27; social mobility as controlled by incarceration, 153; unequal treatment of, 8. *See also* racial issues; racism

minors, confinement with adult prisoners, 26

"Model of Correctional Policies" (Duffee), 165

moral issues: compassion as moral virtue, 51; and greater good, 52; human worth, 65n22; justification as impossible for correctional ethic, 44–46; moral agency, 18, 184, 214; moral reckoning and prison social order, 179–92; moral view as basis of decision making, 188;

prisoners as moral subjects, 20–21; privatization of prisons, 39–40; status of prison employees, 10, 205–13; status of prisoners, vii. *See also* ethics

National Association of State Budget Officers (NASBO), 223

negligent abuse, 89–90

New Segregation, 76

No Escape (DiIulio), 204

non-traditional institutional corrections, post-Attica, 157–59

normative consensus in social learning theory, 185. *See also* moral issues

offender change via staff, 162–68

officers, corrections: adaptation strategies of, 157; educational expectations on, 8; ethical treatment of, 220–25; excessive use of force by, 23; professional conduct of, 7–8; training of, 10–11; and unions, 12

open prison, development of, 158

organizational culture and employee rights, 215–16

overcrowding, 91–92, 153, 162, 168

oversight of prisons, 23, 79–96, 106–7

Parker, Camden County Jail Inmates v., 91

parole system, 126, 157, 167–68, 226

penal system as originating in emancipated slave control, 170n2. *See also* criminal justice system; prisons

PLRA (Prison Litigation Reform Act), 27, 81, 86–87, 92, 99n23

police ethics, 108. *See also* officers, corrections

Police Ethics: Hard Choices in Law Enforcement (Heffernan), 108

policy issues: and crime control, 76; government role in corrections, 226; and imprisonment of mentally ill, 136–37

political expediency as greater good, 51

poorhouses as prison predecessor, 195

power: coercive, 6, 19; differences in
    prison, 151; discretionary uses of,
    79, 154–55, 167; excessive use of
    force, 23, 29, 84, 85; legitimization
    of, 9, 158, 186–87; in role relation-
    ships, 9–10; as substitute for
    authority, 11
prejudice, 8, 11. *See also* racial issues;
    racism
pretrial issues and due process, 97n7,
    129
prison administration. *See* administra-
    tors, prison; management, prison;
    officers, corrections
prison camps, as analogous to work
    release programs, 165–66
prison conditions. *See* conditions,
    prison
prisoners: as center of correctional
    ethic, 8, 19; inmate code, 156,
    170n5; moral standing of, vii, 7, 18,
    20–21; as nonpersons, 182, 187–89;
    responsibilities of state to, 143–44;
    as slaves of the state, 79; as
    undeserving, 197. *See also* abuse in
    prisons; rights, human/legal
prison industrial complex, 73–75
prisonization, defined, 156
Prison Litigation Reform Act (PLRA),
    27, 81, 86, 92, 99n23
prison reform. *See* reform, prison
prisons: call for abolition of, 69–78;
    central function of, 40, 72–73, 159;
    and coercive institutions, 115; and
    complex institutions, 231; func-
    tions of, 151; legitimacy deficit in,
    186; paramilitary organization of,
    11, 19, 82, 204, 210; social order of,
    179–92; structural reform of, 22–
    23; as total institutions, 219; types
    of, 6, 21, 23, 26, 165; ultimate goal
    of, 71. *See also* incarceration
privacy of prison employees, 210–11
private-sector prisons: and correctional
    ethics, 18; debate on, 27–30; impli-
    cations of, 229–31; moral justifica-
    tion for, 39–40; and prison abuse,
    83; profit motive, 64n2, 74, 230

probation, 126, 157
problem solving in correctional ethics, 19
professionalism and correctional
    ethics, 1–15, 14n16
property or mail, negligent loss of, 90
pro se litigation, 80, 88
protest, prisoner, as heavily penalized,
    19
psychological adjustment to prison life,
    170n5
public health obligations of correc-
    tional health care, 118
public policy: and crime control, 76;
    government role in corrections,
    226; and imprisonment of
    mentally ill, 136–37
public safety and incarceration, 4, 50
public service ethic, limitations of, 49
punishment: attractive simplicity of,
    196; certainty of, 153; character of,
    225–29; community corrections as
    extension of, 154; as deprivation
    of liberty, vii–viii, 7, 13n11, 60–61,
    126, 158; forms of, 30n1; group,
    31n7; as industry, 75; justifiability
    of, 109–10; as problem, 17;
    purpose of, vii–viii, 126–27; theory
    of, 67n35. *See also* cruel and
    unusual punishment; death
    penalty; incarceration; retributive
    justice

Quakers, as prison reformers, 9, 21–22
"quality of life" crime enforcement,
    128
quality of life legislation, 153
quarantine of prisoners, 118

racial issues, treatment of minorities, 8,
    27, 153
racism: and abuse of prisoners, 79, 83,
    91; as cause for abolition of
    prisons, 69–78; and correctional
    ideology, 169; institutionalization
    of, 20, 22–23, 27, 70–75; and
    isolation unit usage, 94–95; of
    prison staff, 87–88; in prosecution,
    171n19; as source of conflict, 19
rational choice theory, as basis of

control in prison society, 185

rational decision-making procedure, defined, 43

recidivism, 150, 163, 195

reform, prison: Attica report, effects of, 100n45, 152, 155–59; failure of, 30; history of, 9, 21–22; side effects of, 34n43

reformative ideology, 3, 150, 195

rehabilitation: focus on social responsibility, 7; historical phases, 170n10; ideology of, 11–12, 150; as justification for incarceration, 4, 18; of mentally ill prisoners, 21; prisons as discouraging, 164; rise and fall of, 152–54; supported by ACA, 226; through treatment/counseling, 195; treatment staff role, 162–63, 166–67; value of, 115

reintegration, 150, 158–59, 165, 168, 195–96. *See also* rehabilitation

residual rights of prisoners, 115

restorative justice, 151, 158, 169, 173n51

retributive justice: as easy way out, 194–98; ethics of, vii–viii; as greater good, 50; as humanitarian response, 61; ideology of, 150; as justification for imprisonment, 20; as license for sexual abuse, 198–201; as purpose of criminal justice system, 127; reaffirmation of, 152–54; and theory of punishment, 67n35. *See also* punishment

rights, human/legal: abuses of, viii; in correctional ethics, 18; due process, 97n7, 147n15; HRW, 32n21, 85, 96, 97n1; of prison employees, 209, 215–17, 221–22; of prisoners, 22–27, 29, 79–81, 115; Universal Declaration of Human Rights, 104n105. *See also* Bill of Rights

Rights for All, 26

riots, prison, and lack of grievance procedure, 96

role relationships: conflict in prison camps, 165; correctional officers, 9;

expectations issue, 183, 184, 187, 188–89; health care professionals, 117–18, 120–24

rule of law, 25

safety: of prison employees, 206–8; public safety and incarceration, 4, 50

security, prison: as constitutional loophole, 34n46; and health care officials, 122–23; as justification for correctional practice, 10; as obstacle to correctional ethics, 19; and punishment, 7; and reintegration, 165; restricting information for, 213; types of facilities, 21, 23, 26; warden as responsible for, 115

self-determination of prison employees, 211–12

Sensitizing Providers to the Effects of Correctional Incarceration on Treatment and Risk Management (SPECTRUM), 138n17

sentences, prison: difficulties in, 58; increases in, 20, 31n12; mandatory, 226; need for fixed, 153; two stages proposal, 176n82

sexual abuse, 29, 85, 193–201

Sixth Amendment, rights of prisoners under, 80

slavery and life in prison, 27, 40–41, 47, 48, 70–75

social class and criminal justice system experience, 128, 151

social Darwinism and prison abuse, 99n32

social institutions: contingency of, 2–5; high-theoretical basis of, 70; imperfections of, 1; prison as, 182–89

social learning theory, as basis of control in prison society, 185

social nature of humanity, 55

societal norms and custodial institutions, 6. *See also* moral issues

Society of Captives (Sykes), 58, 184

solitary confinement, 21, 23, 94

SPECTRUM (Sensitizing Providers to

the Effects of Correctional Incarceration on Treatment and Risk Management), 138n17
Spicer v. Williamson, 116
staff, corrections: abusive relations with prisoners, 29, 79–96; and Attica report effects, 155–57, 159–62; community corrections roles, 165–67; discretionary power of, 154–55; external factors in relations with prisoners, 99n32; female, 198; and health care, 87, 132–35, 143; moral issues, 9–10; obligation to law, 83; offender change via staff, 162–68; and prisoners, 131–32; private prisons, 29; racism of, 87–88; sexual misconduct of, 85; and treatment of employees, 10, 29–30, 203–18, 221–22. *See also* officers, corrections
standards, as basis of legitimacy, 187
strip searches, 7, 24, 34n44, 34n46, 88–89
subcultures in social learning theory, 185
substance abuse, 126–31, 211
suffering, human: as goal of imprisonment, 40; redemption of, 51–52; as rendering correctional ethic impossible, 41–49. *See also* punishment; rights, human/legal
super-maximum security facilities, 26, 158
supervisory techniques, changes in, 154–55. *See also* management, prison
Supreme Court, U.S., on prison practices, 21, 80–81
systemic nature of abuse, 91–95

therapeutic alliance and health care in prison, 117, 133, 135
Thirteenth Amendment, 75, 79
Tombs, riot in, 92
torture of prisoners, 26
total institutions: decline of, 158; prisons as, 219
traditional institutional corrections,

pre-Attica, 155–57
treatment staff, rehabilitative, 162–63, 166–67
trials, court. *See* courts
trust, nature of, 183
trust-based societies, risk in, 184
trustee system, 98n13, 184
truth-in-sentencing legislation, 31n11, 153

Uniform Crime Reports scheme, 31n11
unions, 12
uniqueness of prisoners. *See* dignity, intrinsic
United Nations (UN), human rights standards, 25–27
Universal Declaration of Human Rights, 104n105
U.S. Constitution: freedoms under, 205; and prison security, 34n46; standards in correctional ethics, 18; and UN standards, 25. *See also* rights, human/legal
U.S. Supreme Court, on prison practices, 21, 80–81

value conflicts in prison health care, 113–24
victim-offender mediation, 67n38, 68n39, 68n44
Vienna Convention on Consular Relations, 26
Violent Crime Control and Law Enforcement Act, 33n39, 153
visitation privileges, 93

Wackenhut Corrections Corporation, 29
warden, changing authority of, 158
war on crime as basis for prison industrial complex, 75
whistle blowing as freedom of speech, 210
Williamson, Spicer v., 116
women under correctional supervision, 29, 198–200
work-release programs, 165–66, 167

zero-sum politics and correctional ethics, 223–25

About the Contributors

Heather Barr is a staff attorney at the Urban Justice Center's Mental Health Project where she does advocacy for people with mental illness in New York's criminal justice system. Her current projects include *Brad H. v. City of New York*, a successful class action lawsuit against the City of New York for failing to provide discharge planning for mentally ill inmates being released from New York City jails. She is also the founding director of the Nathaniel Project, the nation's first alternative-to-incarceration program for seriously mentally ill felony offenders, at the Center for Alternative Sentencing and Employment Services. She is the author of forthcoming chapters on the New York Police Department's treatment of people with mental illness and the role of social workers as advocates for mentally ill offenders. She is also the author of *Prisons and Jails: Hospitals of Last Resort* (Urban Justice Center and Correctional Association of New York, 1999) and "More Like Disneyland: State Action, 42 U.S.C. §1983, and Business Improvement Districts in New York," *Columbia Human Rights Law Review* (1997).

Audrey J. Bomse is an attorney in private practice in New Jersey and co-chair of the National Lawyers' Guild—Prison Law Project. She represented the interests of the class of New Jersey prisoners from 1986 to 1993, as assistant deputy public defender, Office of Inmate Advocacy (OIA), in the New Jersey Department of the Public Advocate. When the OIA was defunded by the New Jersey legislature, she helped found the Prisoners Self Help Legal Clinic in Newark, where she is currently the legal director.

Derek R. Brookes was until recently the director of reconciliation programs (reconciliation specialist) with the Center for Justice and Reconciliation,

Prison Fellowship International. He has a Ph.D. in philosophy from the Australian National University and has been a research fellow at Yale University and the Institute for Criminal Justice Ethics at John Jay College of Criminal Justice, City University of New York. His publications include "Evaluating Restorative Justice Programs," *Humanity and Society* (April 1998).

Todd R. Clear, Distinguished Professor, John Jay College of Criminal Justice, City University of New York, is currently involved in studies of religion and crime, the criminological implications of place, and the concept of community justice. His most recent books are *The Offender in the Community* (2000), *The Community Justice Ideal* (1999), and *Harm in American Penology* (1995). He is also editor of *Crime and Justice Research*.

William C. Heffernan is professor of law at John Jay College of Criminal Justice and the Graduate Center of the City University of New York. His articles on constitutional criminal procedure have appeared in numerous law reviews. He has coedited *Police Ethics: Hard Choices in Law Enforcement* (1985) and *From Social Justice to Criminal Justice: Poverty in the Administration of Criminal Law* (2000), and is also an editor of *Criminal Justice Ethics*, a journal published by John Jay's Institute for Criminal Justice Ethics.

Zelma Weston Henriques is a professor in the Department of Law and Police Science at John Jay College of Criminal Justice, City University of New York. She gained her doctorate from Columbia University, where she was also a Rockefeller Fellow in Human Rights. She is author of *Imprisoned Mothers and Their Children: A Descriptive and Analytical Study* (1982), and her other research interests include the intersection of race, class, and gender, and crosscultural studies of crime and human rights.

Michael Jacobson is a professor of criminal justice at John Jay College of Criminal Justice and the Graduate Center of the City University of New York. Prior to becoming a professor, he was the commissioner of the New York City Department of Correction from 1995 to 1998 and the commissioner of the New York City Department of Probation from 1992 to 1996. He is currently doing research on the parole violation processes in several states.

Kenneth Kipnis is a professor in the Department of Philosophy of the University of Hawaii at Manoa. He has edited or coedited six books in legal and social philosophy and is the author of *Legal Ethics* (1986). He has written broadly on medical ethics, including pieces on the vulnerability of human research subjects, the surgical reassignment of children with ambiguous genitalia, ethicists as expert witnesses, and nontreatment decisions for severely compromised newborns. He did preliminary work for the American Correctional Health Services Association on its development of a code of ethics. Having served on the American Philosophical Association's Committee on Philosophy and Law, he was recently appointed as chair of the

APA's Committee on Philosophy and Medicine. He is currently working on the role of the ethicist.

John Kleinig is professor of philosophy in the Department of Law and Police Science, John Jay College of Criminal Justice, City University of New York, and director of the Institute for Criminal Justice Ethics. He is an editor of *Criminal Justice Ethics*. Among his publications are *Punishment and Desert* (1973), *Paternalism* (1984), *Valuing Life* (1991), *Professional Law Enforcement Codes: A Documentary Collection* (with Yurong Zhang, 1993), and *The Ethics of Policing* (1996). He is currently writing a book on loyalty.

John P. Pittman teaches philosophy and humanities courses at John Jay College of Criminal Justice, City University of New York, where he also chairs the Department of Art, Music, and Philosophy. He writes about social philosophy, race, and African American philosophy. The *Blackwell Companion to African-American Philosophy*, which he coedited with Tommy L. Lott, is forthcoming.

Margaret Leland Smith works with John Kleinig at the Institute for Criminal Justice Ethics and teaches part-time at John Jay College of Criminal Justice. As an advocate for prisoners, she helped start the Prisoners Self Help Legal Clinic in Newark, New Jersey, and edits its legal newsletter, *The Bridge*. She is a doctoral candidate (ABD) in Criminal Justice from Rutgers University, and has done research on the impact on families of the imprisonment of the father and on the process of desistance from criminal activity.

Polly Ashton Smith is assistant professor of criminal justice at Saint Anselm College in Manchester, New Hampshire. Her writing and research have focused on intergroup conflict in criminal justice organizations, sociological theory of practical and moral reasoning, moral education and legal punishment, and postmodernist theories of justice. She is currently researching the discourse characteristics of decision making among participants of reparative boards and sentencing circles in Vermont and Massachusetts. Smith earned her Ph.D. from City University of New York and holds an M.Div. from Union Theological Seminary, New York City, and a B.F.A. from New York University.

Joseph V. Williams, who has Masters degrees in criminal justice and sociology, is a New York State correctional superintendent at Lincoln Correctional Facility, New York City, a minimum-security facility that allows eligible inmates to be temporarily released to the community to attend school, to work, and/or to participate in community services. In a thirty-five-year career, he has served at all security and operational levels in the capacities of corrections officer, corrections counselor, program specialist in counseling and education, director of guidance, deputy superintendent of programs, and for the past eighteen years as a correctional superintendent. He has also taught as an adjunct professor at Dutchess Community College, Marist College, and John Jay College of Criminal Justice, City University of New York.

Kevin N. Wright is professor of criminal justice in the School of Education and Human Development at the State University of New York, Binghamton. His book, *Effective Prison Leadership*, was published by William Neil Publishing in 1994. Wright served as visiting fellow in the Office of Research at the Federal Bureau of Prison from 1989 to 1990 and from 1991 to 1992 and continues to conduct research with staff from the Bureau. His article, "The Evolution of Decision Making among Prison Executives—1975–2000," was included in the volume, *Criminal Justice 2000: Changes in Decision Making and Discretion in the Criminal Justice System* (National Institute of Justice, 2000).